Nijhoff Studies in European Union Law

Series Editors

VOLUME 25

The titles published in this series are listed at *brill.com/seul*

Assessing the Common European Asylum System

Discretionary Implementation and Street-Level Bureaucracy

By

Radu-Mihai Triculescu

BRILL | NIJHOFF

LEIDEN | BOSTON

Library of Congress Cataloging-in-Publication Data

Names: Triculescu, Radu-Mihai, 1989- author.
Title: Assessing the common European asylum system : discretionary implementation and street-level bureaucracy / Radu-Mihai Triculescu.
Identifiers: LCCN 2024039093 (print) | LCCN 2024039094 (ebook) | ISBN 9789004700819 (hardback) | ISBN 9789004700826 (ebook)
Subjects: LCSH: Asylum, Right of–Europe.
Classification: LCC KJC5202 .T75 2025 (print) | LCC KJC5202 (ebook) | DDC 342.2408/3–dc23/eng/20240823
LC record available at https://lccn.loc.gov/2024039093
LC ebook record available at https://lccn.loc.gov/2024039094

Typeface for the Latin, Greek, and Cyrillic scripts: "Brill". See and download: brill.com/brill-typeface.

ISSN 2210-9765
ISBN 978-90-04-70081-9 (hardback)
ISBN 978-90-04-70082-6 (e-book)
DOI 10.1163/9789004700826

This book is printed on acid-free paper and produced in a sustainable manner.

Contents

List of Tables IX

1 **Introduction** 1

1 Engaging with the State of the Art 5
2 The CEAS: A Long Journey to Ambiguous Complexity 7

2 **Discretionary Implementation: Ambiguity and the Work of Street-Level Bureaucrats** 16

1 Discretionary Implementation in Multilevel EU 17
2 The Breeding Ground for Ambiguity in Multilevel Governance 33
3 Role Theory and Ambiguity 36

3 **The Common European Asylum System** 42

1 Dublin Regulation 46
2 EUAA and EURODAC 48
2.1 *The European Union Agency for Asylum (EUAA)* 48
2.2 *EURODAC* 52
3 Receptions Conditions Directive 53
4 Qualifications Directive 55
4.1 *The Qualification Directive at First Glance: A Literal Analysis of Discretionary Clauses* 58
5 Procedures Directive 60
5.1 *Untangling the Procedures Directive: A Literal Analysis of Provisions* 64

4 **Interpretive Ambiguities: Case Law and Guidance** 69

1 The Union's Approach to National Implementation Post-2015 69
2 Case Law 75
3 Interpretive Ambiguities: The Work of the CJEU in Identifying and Dispelling Ambiguities 80
3.1 *General Provisions (Articles 1–3)* 85
3.2 *Assessment of Applications for International Protection (Articles 4–8)* 86
3.3 *Qualifications for Being a Refugee (Articles 9–12)* 90
3.4 *Chapter IV – Refugee Status (Articles 13–14)* 94
3.5 *Qualification for Subsidiary Protection (Articles 15–19)* 96
3.6 *Chapter VI – Subsidiary Protection Status (Articles 18–19)* 100

3.7 *Content of International Protection and Administrative Cooperation (Articles 20–37); Final Provisions* 101
4 Judicial and Legislative Analysis of the Procedures Directive 104
4.1 *Initiating the Procedures: Rules for Lodging an Application for Asylum* 106
4.2 *Procedural Guarantees* 109
4.3 *The Personal Interview* 111
4.4 *Procedural Guarantees for an Individual Assessment* 114
4.5 *Guarantees for the Examination Procedure at First Instance* 118
4.6 *Withdrawal of International Protection and Effective Remedy* 122
5 Conclusions 125

5 National Implementation of the CEAS: The Case of Romania 127
1 Constitution, Human Rights, and Good Governance 128
2 OUG 57/2019 – The Administrative Code 131
3 Managing Asylum in Romania 137
3.1 *The Structure and Role of The General Inspectorate for Immigration (IGI)* 140
3.2 *Law 122/2006 regarding Asylum in Romania and Its Norms of Implementation* 144
3.3 *Scope and Definitions in the Law* 149
3.4 *Procedural Guarantees* 150
3.5 *Street-Level Bureaucrats in Law 122* 153
3.6 *First Instance Decisions – Architecture, Rights, and Obligations* 160
4 Conclusion 166

6 National Implementation of the CEAS: The Case of the Netherlands 168
1 The Principles of Governance: The Dutch Constitution 169
2 Public Service in the Netherlands 171
2.1 *The General Administrative Law Act* 177
3 Entering the Asylum Procedure 180
3.1 *General Procedure* 184
3.2 *Conditions of Work: Implementing Provisions at the Street-Level* 189
3.3 *European Framework and Safe Countries of Origin* 192
3.4 *Institutional Capacity* 197
3.5 *Work Guidance* 200

3.6 *Credibility Assessment* 206
4 Conclusion 212

7 **Beyond Black on White: A Nuanced View of Discretion** 216
1 European Ambiguity 220
2 Building the Discretionary Space 223
3 Final Thoughts on Discretionary Implementation 231

Bibliography 235
Index 247

Tables

1 Discretionary provisions in dir. 2011/95/EU 60
2 Non-discretionary provisions in dir. 2011/95/EU 61
3 Frames of action in dir. 2011/95/EU 62
4 Discretionary provisions in dir. 2013/32/EU 66
5 Non-discretionary provisions in dir. 2013/32/EU 67
6 Attributes of the IGI in the field of asylum, according to Article 5(b)(1–12) of HG 639/2007 141
7 Main changes to asylum legislation brought about by Law 122/2006, according to the Government's Exposition of Motives 147
8 Number of appeals and number of successful appeals, 2015–2019 164
9 The 5-track system of the Dutch asylum system 181
10 Information sought during registration interview in the Netherlands 185
11 Sliding scale model for assessing risk due to indiscriminate violence 196
12 Internal and external credibility indicators 209

CHAPTER 1

Introduction

After nearly 8 years of tug-of-war, negotiations, arguments, gridlock, and stalemate, the reform of the Common European Asylum System (CEAS) is nearing an end. A process sparked by the largest migration crisis the European Union has ever faced, and punctuated by political posturing, is culminating as this book is being written. The reform package, called the Pact on Migration and Asylum, is in the process of being adopted in the first half of 2024. Much has been written already about what this reform means, and much will continue to be said in the years to come. But as others look to the future, I consider it an opportune moment to look back and understand *how the CEAS has impacted the administration of asylum policies in the more than two decades that is has been in force, and how has it been impacted by the national systems charged with implementing its provisions.*

Since its inception, the aim of the CEAS has been to harmonise the access to – and quality of – the procedure by which international protection is granted in the diverse legal and administrative contexts found across Member States of the European Union. I this book, I will embark on an exploration how discretionary implementation affects that aim. I will identify and trace the CEAS instruments relevant to first instance asylum decisions across different levels of governance and observe if and how variances emerge in the way countries translate the European asylum acquis into national procedures of bureaucratic implementation. As such, an understanding of the effect that country-specific contexts have on the establishment of a comprehensive asylum policy in the European Union emerges, providing valuable insight into the influence that street-level bureaucrats play in shaping the output of an EU level policy.

Drawing from the theoretical insights of street-level bureaucracy[1] and role-conflict,[2] discretionary implementation is defined as decisions made by policy implementers in situations of incomplete information or ambiguous policy vision and guidance. Far too often, policy analysis assumes that those working on the frontline of implementation have all the information needed to reach a decision. Yet, whether it is due to poorly drafted legislation or due to a need for

1 Michael Lipsky, *Street-Level Bureaucracy: Dilemmas of the Individual in Public Service.* (rev edn, Russel Sage Foundation 2010).

2 Robert L. Kahn, Donald M. Wolfe, Robert P. Quinn, J. Diedrick Snoek and Robert A. Rosenthal. *Organizational stress: studies in role conflict and ambiguity* (Wiley 1964).

 | DOI:10.1163/9789004700826_002

flexibility to secure support for policies, ambiguities are never absent from the documents that street-level bureaucrats turn to for implementation guidance. Discretionary implementation, then, is the decision-making context in which policy implementors must conduct their work and turn policies into practice.

This focus is valuable to our understanding of how asylum policy is implemented in the European Union. Legal scholars have created a large body of literature on how the EU's asylum acquis is interpreted, transposed, enforced, and infringed at the national level. Political scientists and sociologists have published extensively on topics related to the asymmetrical power distributions of the asylum procedure, and the tactics used by both caseworkers (as gatekeepers) and asylum seekers (as vulnerable populations) to achieve their goals. But asylum policy analysis requires a less siloed approach. Legal understanding of harmonisation is important, as is any knowledge on the interactions between those seeking protection and national authorities. However, one cannot ignore the other. Legal norms mean nothing without their implementation, and human interactions between asylum seekers and bureaucrats are strongly guided by the norms of the institution where they take place.

There is a need to bridge the gap that exists between the legal framework of Europe's asylum decision-making and the real-world context in which these decisions take place. Here, I attempt to do so by uncovering the opportunities given to street-level bureaucrats to influence the implementation of asylum policy. The core argument is that implementation is more dependent on the discretion granted to those working in national administrative structures than on the specific legislative measures. This is substantiated by a strong analysis of the legislative path, from its conception at the EU level down to bureaucratic procedures of implementation in two EU Member States, the Netherlands and Romania. By uncovering the 'capacity for judgement' given to Romanian bureaucrats, or the co-creation of norms in which Dutch public officials partake, I highlight how implementation happens in a system where discretionary and ambiguous clauses abound.

As such, the insight that we have of the effect that country-specific contexts have on defining the discretionary implementation of the Common European Asylum System is expanded. The analysis contained in these pages explains the influence that street-level bureaucrats may have on the output of a policy that starts at the EU level, but that must pass through the filters of multilevel governance. Certainly, a policy can look very different in implementation than adoption. This makes the study of what happens between the two difficult, yet crucial. Part of these difficulties arise from a treatment of policy objectives as a given: a belief that its architects both know what they want, and that what they want is communicated unambiguously. There also seems to be an assumption that policies are ambiguous because of some form of inadequacy in policy making. In fact, policies are negotiated in a way that makes the amount of ambiguity as susceptible to arbitrary choice as any other decision taken. Any talk of the concept of implementation that relies on images of consistent and clear norms simply being executed as they were envisioned ignores the fact that such consistency and clarity rarely exists. This approach creates the problems that compromise our understanding of what happens between policy adoption and implementation.

Closing the gap between adoption and implementation requires an unpacking of the discretionary implementation concept. Previous literature conceptualizes compliance as an expected response to a particular kind of request, where the target recognizes that they are expected to respond in a certain way.[3] Discretion, I argue, boils down to the options available within the 'desired way' to which the target of compliance is expected to respond. In many cases, the boundaries of the discretionary space are stretched by bureaucrats that do not strictly adhere to the role requirements of their jobs because of the ambiguity presented. This discretionary space can be represented formally, through rules and binding legal instruments, but also informally, through unwritten rules and through an established and accepted institutional culture.[4]

An ambiguous policy will likely manifest itself with a larger discretionary space for those charged with implementing said policy, because of greater degree of subjectivity and interpretation granted to bureaucrats. All levels of governance receive certain leeway in decision-making, and street-level bureaucrats are no different.[5] This allows for local realities to be considered when policies are implemented. The query, then, is to determine when discretionary space is used as it was intended by policy, and when do certain decision-making processes deviate from established policy goals.

To make this evaluation, I begin the analysis begins at the EU level, where policy is developed and enacted, then work my way down to transposing legislation at the national level, and norms of implementation at the administrative level. This will uncover the ambiguity and discretion present within these documents, deconstructing the legal basis upon which street-level bureaucrats

---

3 Robert B. Cialdini and Noah J. Goldstein, 'Social influence: compliance and conformity' (2004) 55 *Annual Review of Psychology* 591.

4 Mariglynn Edlins and Jennica Larrison, 'Street-level bureaucrats and the governance of unaccompanied migrant children' (2018) 35 *Public Policy and Administration* 403.

5 Karl Heyer, 'Keeping migrants at the margins: governing through ambiguity and the politics of discretion in the post-2015 European Migration and Border Regime' (2022) 97 *Political Geography* 102643.

must act. Several methodological tools are employed. First, frame analysis provides the framework for looking at the multilevel implementation of the CEAS.[6] Second, using the results from the frame analysis, document analysis is used to identify the ambiguities found in EU directives, national legislation, and norms of implementation. This includes ambiguities found in specific clauses, or those arising from conflicts between legislative texts and other sources of information.

Aside from an analysis of legislative acts at the EU level, a legal review of the work of the Court of Justice is also conducted. The purpose of this is to allow an observance of ambiguities that have emerged in the interpretation of legal provisions. The Court interprets ambiguity in legislation through the preliminary reference procedure and can therefore provide valuable insights into what European norms are problematic for interpretation at the national level. Policy documents of the European Commission about proposed reforms are also looked at. These give insights into the motivation behind the development of legal norms, and the ambiguities that exist in current legislation (hence, the need for reform). The two sets of auxiliary documents often interact, as the Court itself looks at the importance of motivations behind legislative initiatives (e.g., Case C-322/17, where the court relies on proposed reforms to assess the EU legislator's intentions). Intentions, then, play a crucial role in the interpretation of legislation. These can be found best in policy documents free from the technical language of legal documents.

Finally, following an analysis of the data covered, I turn my focus to differences in implementations between EU Member States with different administrative contexts and different history vis-à-vis EU institutions. The ambiguities and discretionary clauses identified in the first part of the book are tracked in legislative transposition at the national level in Romania and the Netherlands. Using the administrative legacies of the two countries as an analytical lens, the book sheds light on the ways institutional differences between Eastern and Western Member States of the EU need to be accounted for in any research dealing with EU policy implementation.

As it becomes obvious, a variety of data sources are required. EU level policy and legislative documents used include the legal texts of the mechanisms studied, explanatory memoranda and working documents of the Commission related to these mechanisms, and Council conclusions that reference the need for harmonisation of asylum policies (dating back to 1986). National level

6 Sarah Spencer and Nicola Delvino, 'Municipal activism on irregular migrants: the framing of inclusive approaches at the local level' (2019) 17 *Journal of Immigrant & Refugee Studies* 27.

policy documents, such as transposing legislation, norms of implementation (from Romania) and working instruction (from the Netherlands) supplement the EU level. Analysis also draws on over 70 preliminary ruling documents from Court of Justice of the EU, as well as relevant national court rulings. Lastly, a series of interviews were conducted with employees of the Dutch Immigration and Naturalisation Service with experience in assessing asylum applications, and a Freedom of Information Request was submitted to Romanian authorities to provide information relevant to how decisions are made by street-level bureaucrats.

1 Engaging with the State of the Art

Previous paragraphs have already highlighted some of the gaps in the scholarly state of the art that this book fills. Most importantly, it provides a new understanding of implementation centred on discretion, and therefore makes significant contributions to public administration literature, especially on street-level bureaucracy.[7] The research and analysis show that discretion in bureaucracies is not straightforward. While strict guidelines and little room for manoeuvre in implementation might point to a restricted discretionary space, the active involvement of workers in the development of these guidelines gives them more powers than we might think obvious. The way we present discretionary spaces needs to account for these nuances.

Through the academic endeavours of this work, I hope to reconcile the findings of legal scholars with those of public administration.[8] The latter often point to the fact that street-level bureaucrats hold significant discretion in how they execute their job, especially when it is up to them to manage their workflow as well as the relations with those they interact with.[9] The former, however,

7 For recent examples of similar research on discretionary policy implementation see Barbara Oomen, Moritz Baumgärtel, Sara Miellet, Elif Durmus, and Tihomir Sabchev, 'Strategies of divergence: local authorities, law, and discretionary spaces in migration governance' (2021) 34 *Journal of Refugee Studies* 3608; Helene O.I. Gundhus, 'Shaping migrants as threats: multilayered discretion, criminalization, and risk assessment tools' (2021) 10 *International Journal for Crime, Justice and Social Democracy* 56; Hannes Schammann, Danielle Gluns, Christiane Heimann, Sandra Müller, Tobias Wittchen, Christin Younso and Franziska Ziegler, 'Defining and transforming local migration policies: a conceptual approach backed by evidence from Germany' (2021) 47 *Journal of Ethnic and Migration Studies* 2897.

8 Stavros Zouridis and Vera Leijtens, 'Bringing the law back in: the law-government nexus in an era of network governance' (2020) 4 *Perspectives on Public Management and Governance* 118.

9 Bernardo Zacka, *When the state meets the street: public service and moral agency* (Harvard University Press 2017).

place greater emphasis on the legal restraints that are imposed on nations as the most important tool for assessing how bureaucratic work is done.[10] But the truth is, as usual, at some halfway point. This book enters in this discussion by showing that, while rules provide the basic framework for action, there must also be some leeway allowing for flexibility in implementation. Practically, there are great analytical benefits to paying more attention to where this flexibility lies. For those working in the field of asylum, does discretion manifest itself in different standards of proof used when assessing applications? Or is it exercised only to fill information gaps in institutional provisions regulating systematic asylum application assessments? The opening chapters argue that formal discretion is a specific type of ambiguity – an intentional one – which is meant to give implementers the power to interpret provisions in a way that best reflects the needs of the specific tasks they are trying to solve.

Finally, attention must be given to the effects of temporality, specifically on differences in policy outputs in old and new EU Member States. Scholars have already warned against expecting one model of public administration research to fit all national and historical contexts as constants,[11] even in the case of the Common European Asylum System, where the 'rules of the game' are spelled out in a common set of directives and regulations. Organisational features specific to asylum do not happen in a vacuum; they are dependent on the historic development of the state's institutions, and the legacies of the past play a role in the way institutions are designed today.[12] In the Netherlands, for example, the rules of the CEAS have been entrenched in national procedures, particularly by the country's direct involvement in shaping Europe's asylum system since its inception. This, it should be noted, in spite the fact that there is no constitutional weight given to the effect of international law in national policy development. In Romania, on the other hand, international law is constitutionally recognised as a source of authority. Yet, as one of the last members to join the EU, Romania simply adopted the rules of CEAS as they had already been established and negotiated.

Given the complexity of the CEAS, there are many points at which ambiguities may arise and noncompliance occur. This confers heightened importance

10 Arne Niemann and Natascha Zaun, 'EU refugee policies and politics in times of crisis: theoretical and empirical perspectives' (2017) 56 *Journal of Common Market Studies* 3.

11 Turo Virtanen, 'Context in the context – missing the missing links in the field of public administration', in Christopher Pollitt (ed.) *Context in public policy and management: The missing link?* (Edward Elgar 2013).

12 Heinrich R. Greve and Hayagreeva Rao, 'History and the present: institutional legacies in communities of organizations' (2014) 34 *Research in Organizational Behavior* 27.

to the process by which gaps of information necessary for performing specific tasks are settled, therefore fulfilling the delivery of services to the clients of bureaucracy. Figuring or delegating interpretation of ambiguities has implications that cannot be overlooked when discussing policy harmonisation and implementation in the European Union. But how exactly do these ambiguities arise? Or, more specifically, where is their source? Before going further, I consider it important to address where ambiguity and discretionary implementation begin – both in time and in legal documents.

2 The CEAS: A Long Journey to Ambiguous Complexity

Potential differences in implementation among Member States can be attributed to a specific type of public and political discourse,[13] creating unique contexts within which policy development takes place. Moreover, images of asylum seekers cramming onto boats and risking their lives to reach Europe have given rise to framings such as 'refugee crisis,' 'migration crisis,' or 'Mediterranean crisis.' Usage of these terms has permeated discourse at the European level, leading to what Moreno-Lax has recently described as a 'crisification' of policy responses. Yet, it is the Union's policies themselves that have given asylum seekers no choice but to pursue hazardous and illegal ways of protecting their livelihoods, and have therefore given credibility to the image of the invading hordes of potential refugees.[14] The fact that access to refuge is dealt with in an ambiguous manner by EU law, coupled with specific policies in respect to Schengen visas and carrier sanctions, among many others, have left those needing asylum with very few options for securing other means of adequate protection. The ambiguity of EU law has thus bestowed onto Member States a lot of flexibility in choosing how to adapt the CEAS to their own context.[15] Demetriou takes this argument one step further, by noting that such measures,

13 Cathryn Costello and Minos Mouzourakis, 'The Common European Asylum System: Where Did It All Go Wrong?' in Maria Fletcher, Ester Herlin-Karnell, and Claudio Matera (eds), *The European Union as an Area of Freedom, Security and Justice* (Routledge 2017).

14 Ibid 264–265.

15 Violeta Moreno-Lax, 'Must EU Borders Have Doors for Refugees? On the Compatibility of Schengen Visas and Carriers' Sanctions with EU Member States' Obligations to Provide International Protection to Refugees' (2008) 10 *European Journal of Migration and Law* 315.

which leave asylum seekers at the margins of protection, can be categorised as a general strategy of "prevention through deterrence."[16]

The roots of ambiguity in the CEAS can nevertheless be traced to the features of the multilevel system of governance inherent to the European system of asylum, something reflected in the scholarly work on the matter. Many studies have analysed (and criticised) each individual regulation and directive encompassed by the CEAS,[17] as well as many others not encompassed by the system yet relevant to asylum policy, such as the forced return directive[18] or the 2015 relocation and redistribution scheme.[19] Other EU mechanisms have also been scrutinized, most notably the work of Court of Justice of the European Union,[20] but also policy documents released by the European Commission, Council, or Parliament.[21] Many of these works take on a critical tone, but few

16 Olga Demetriou, 'Complementary Protection and the Recognition Rate as Tools of Governance: Ordering Europe, Fragmenting Rights' (2022) 48 *Journal of Ethnic and Migration Studies* 1264.

17 Agnes Hurwitz, 'The 1990 Dublin Convention: A Comprehensive Assessment' (1999) 11 *International Journal of Refugee Law* 646; Cathryn Costello, 'The Asylum Procedures Directive and the Proliferation of Safe Country Practices: Deterrence, Deflection and the Dismantling of International Protection?' (2005) 7 *European Journal of Migration and Law* 35; Françoise Comte, 'A New Agency Is Born in the European Union: The European Asylum Support Office' (2010) 12 *European Journal of Migration and Law* 373; Hemme Battjes, 'Subsidiary Protection and Other Alternative Forms of Protection' in Vincent Chetail and Céline Bauloz (eds) *Research Handbook on International Law and Migration* (Edward Elgar 2014); Cathryn Costello and Minos Mouzourakis, 'The Common European Asylum System: Where Did It All Go Wrong?' in Maria Fletcher, Ester Herlin-Karnell, and Claudio Matera (eds) *The European Union as an Area of Freedom, Security and Justice* (Routledge 2017).

18 Directive 2008/115/EC of the European Parliament and of the Council of 16 December 2008 on common standards and procedures in Member States for returning illegally staying third-country nationals.

19 Council Decision 2015/1601 establishing provisional measures in the area of international protection for the benefit of Italy and Greece [2015] OJ L248/80. See Diego Acosta Arcaranzo, 'The Good, The Bad and The Ugly in EU Migration Law: Is the European Parliament Becoming Bad and Ugly?' in Elspeth Guild and P. E. Minderhoud (eds) *The First Decade of EU Migration and Asylum Law*, (Martinus Nijhoff 2012); Simas Grigonis, 'EU in the Face of Migrant Crisis: Reasons for Ineffective Human Rights Protection' [2017] *International Comparative Jurisprudence*.

20 Gregor Noll, 'Formalism v. Empiricism: Some Reflections on the Dublin Convention on the Occasion of Recent European Case Law' (2001) 70 *Nordic Journal of International Law* 161.

21 Dallal Stevens, 'Asylum, Refugee Protection and the European Response to Syrian Migration' (2017) 9 *Journal of Human Rights Practice* 184; Florian Trauner, 'Asylum Policy: the EU's 'Crises' and the Looming Policy Regime Failure,' (2016) 38 *Journal of European Integration* 311.

reach any concrete conclusions regarding the role of discretionary implementation in the level of harmonisation achieved. Indeed, this may be largely because there is no one image of what a harmonised system should look like. On the other hand, this work will not attempt to argue for or against the merits of harmonised policies in the EU. It will not address whether harmonising policies is desirable. Rather, it is understood here that regardless of the normative arguments for or against harmonisation, the EU has pursued this strategy in building the Union's approach to asylum seekers, and Member States have implemented this in their own ways.

As will be argued in a later subchapter, even the assertion of the European Commission that harmonisation has failed is built on an incorrect perspective that equates harmonisation with uniformity. Nevertheless, the literature listed above has tried to stitch together stages of the entire multilevel process in order to better understand why, for example, the national and institutional levels interact in the way they do,[22] or why the EU relates in specific ways with the national level in this policy area.[23] Givens and Luedtke make an argument regarding asylum policy harmonisation, and the effects of issue salience and intergovernmental bargaining, but one that explains the EU level and the actors involved in the bargaining.[24] Gill takes the opposite approach, by looking at specific spatial and temporal aspects affecting how asylum-sector decision makers conduct their jobs, but nothing above.[25]

As much as these scholars have elevated our understanding of certain aspects of this process, insight into the way multilevel governance affects the implementation of asylum policies from beginning to end still lacks. This is largely because many studies conducted thus far have isolated and looked at specific instances in the policy process, but fewer at its entirety. This implies the need for an analysis that considers the country specific contexts in which its implementation takes place across Europe. For this reason, I will argue, a strict reliance on the concept of legal harmonisation is limited in the amount of insight it can offer. A public administration lens calibrated to understand

---

22 Nora Dörrenbächer, 'Frontline Uses of European Union (EU) Law: a Parallel Legal Order? How Structural Discretion Conditions Uses of EU Law in Dutch and German Migration Offices' (2017) 38 *Journal of Public Policy* 455.

23 Philipp Genschel and Markus Jachtenfuchs, 'From Market Integration to Core State Powers: The Eurozone Crisis, the Refugee Crisis and Integration Theory' (2017) 56 *Journal of Common Market Studies* 178.

24 Terri Givens and Adam Luedtke, 'The Politics of European Union Immigration Policy: Institutions, Salience, and Harmonization' (2004) 32 *Policy Studies Journal* 145.

25 Nick Gill, 'Presentational State Power: Temporal and Spatial Influences over Asylum Sector Decisionmakers' (2009) 215 *Transactions of the Institute of British Geographers* 215.

the nuances of discretionary implementation will shed light on the way harmonised policies play out at the street-level of governance. Afterall, a policy meant to secure fundamental rights is successful only when those rights are delivered, or when non-deliverance is justified by its being done through a proper bureaucratic procedure.

Nonetheless, the importance of the legal tools for analysis cannot be minimised. Afterall, the obligations and responsibilities of the EU in this policy area are enshrined in Art. 78(1) of the Treaty on the Functioning of the European Union (TFEU). The first half of this article states that "the Union shall develop a common policy on asylum, subsidiary protection and temporary protection with a view to offering appropriate status to any third-country national requiring international protection and ensuring compliance with the principle of non-refoulement." Even more, actors such as the Court of Justice, whose competence lies firmly in the judicial sphere, exemplify the fact that legal tools of analysis cannot simply be relegated to lower echelons of importance in a study such as this. As such, a starting point needs to be found. The second part of Art. 78(1) states that the "policy must be in accordance with the Geneva Convention of 28 July 1951 and the Protocol of 31 January 1967 relating to the status of refugees, and other relevant treaties."

The 1951 Geneva Convention Relating to the Status of Refugees ('the Geneva Convention'), Resolution 2198 (XXI) adopted by the United Nation General Assembly in 1966, and the 1967 Protocol Relating to the Status of Refugees are a perfect starting point for showing the complex and ambiguous nature of today's asylum system in Europe. After all, not taking the Geneva Convention and its subsequent resolutions and protocols into account would ignore the very mechanisms and inspirations upon which the CEAS was built. In a 2014 Information brochure of the European Commission, the first mention in the document is that the granting of asylum "is an international obligation under the 1951 Geneva convention on the protections of refugees."[26]

It is in the 1951 convention that the very definition of what a refugee is comes up. According to Article 1, Section A, Paragraph 2, the term refugee applies to any person who

> As a result of events occurring before 1 January 1951 and owning to well-founded fear of being persecuted for reasons of race, religion, nationality, membership of a particular social group or political opinion, is outside the country of his nationality and is unable or, owing to such fear, is

26 Commission, 'A Common European Asylum System' (2014).

> unwilling to avail himself of the protection of that country; or who, not having a nationality and being outside the country of his former habitual residence as a result of such events, is unable or, owing to such fear, is unwilling to return to it.

This definition only becomes relevant today once its supplement from the Protocol Relating to the Status of Refugees (1967) is taken into account. This amended the Geneva statement to exclude the words "as a result of events occurring before 1 January 1951 and…", as well as "… as a result of such events." In essence, the 1967 Protocol, which was placed into discussion by the United Nations General Assembly Resolution 2198 (XXI), ensured that the protections dictated by the Geneva Convention in 1951 applied to all refugees, not only those directly affected by the events of the Second World War.

There are many principles which might not be covered by the Geneva Convention explicitly, and the document does take this possibility into account. In *Recommendation E* it expresses the "hope that the Convention relating to the Status of Refugees will have value as an example *exceeding its contractual scope* and that all nations will be guided by it in granting so far as possible to person in their territory as refugees and who would not be covered by the terms of the Convention, the treatment for which it provides," (*emphasis added*). In solidarity with this expression of hope, European legislation interprets the Convention outside its contractual scope as well. In cases where asylum seekers do not meet the principles established by the Convention as necessary to be granted refugee status, yet they are nevertheless deemed in need of protection, they should be granted the status of 'subsidiary protection', as defined by EU legislation.[27] This is likely what the architects of Recommendation E had in mind (or hoped) would happen as a result. But as early as 1951, the birthdate of modern international standards for protection, ambiguity served as a building block. A certain degree of vagueness was used to allow countries the possibility of a more favourable treatment for those seeking protections.

Many concepts and principles from these fundamental documents are found not only in the European asylum system, but in other similar systems around the world.[28] The principle of *non-refoulement*, for example, is one of the chief concepts upon which the CEAS is built. This is governed by Article 33, Paragraph 1, which states that

---

27 Steve Peers, *EU Justice And Home Affairs Law* (Oxford University Press 2016), 233.

28 The Geneva Convention has been used as basis for several other refugee protection instruments, such as the 1969 Organization of African Unity Convention governing the Specific Aspects of the Refugee Problem in Africa or the 1984 Cartagena Declaration.

> No Contracting State shall expel or return ("refouler") a refugee in any manner whatsoever to the frontiers of territories where his life or freedom would be threatened on account of his race, religion, nationality, membership of a particular social group or political opinion.

Fifty years after the adoption of the Convention Relating to the Status of Refugees, in the 2001 UNHCR Declaration reaffirming the principles of 1951 Refugee Convention, non-refoulement is categorised as a core principle of asylum systems, and a concept "whose applicability is embedded in customary international law." The same statement was reiterated by the UNHCR in an introductory note to the 60 Year Anniversary publication of the Convention, specifying that "the principle of non-refoulement is so fundamental that no reservations or derogations may be made to it." In the specific context of the European Union, protection from *refouler* is a key element in both the Dublin Regulation and the Qualification Directive of the Common European Asylum System. The concept has been interpreted in many ways in its implementation, not always to the benefit of those seeking asylum. Moreno-Lax, for example, makes the case that *non-refoulment*, in the way it is used today, only applies to asylum seekers reaching European shores, and it thus manages to leave many unprotected.[29] Much of the EU's asylum system is built to allow for loose interpretation of provisions. This ambiguity allows for a skirting of *non-refoulment* guarantees using mechanisms such as carrier sanctions, which place part of the burden of border controls on airlines transporting passengers, thus not allowing some asylum seekers to reach European shores and benefit from protection.

The Convention also introduced, with a clear historical context in mind, the mechanisms for dealing with potential over-burdening that states may be subjected to in times of crisis. "Considering that the grant of asylum may place heavy burdens on certain countries," the Preamble reads, "and that a satisfactory solution of a problem of which the United Nations has recognised the international scope and nature cannot therefore be achieved without international co-operation." No specific burden-sharing mechanism is proposed here, yet the acknowledgement that some countries can potentially face a higher degree of pressure gives justifications for certain mechanisms to be enacted as states find it necessary.[30] Aside from Article 78(3) TFEU, whereby in cases

29 Violeta Moreno-Lax, 'Must EU Borders Have Doors for Refugees? On the Compatibility of Schengen Visas and Carriers' Sanctions with EU Member States' Obligations to Provide International Protection to Refugees' (2008) 10 *European Journal of Migration and Law* 315.

30 Cathryn Costello, 'The Asylum Procedures Directive and the Proliferation of Safe Country Practices: Deterrence, Deflection and the Dismantling of International Protection?'

of mass arrivals "the Council, on a proposal from the Commission, may adopt provisional measures for the benefit of the Member State(s) concerned," the paragraph of the Geneva Convention preamble gives further justification to the European Union's decision to enact, in 2015, the mechanism which attempted to remove some of the pressure felt by primary recipient countries of asylum seekers through a redistribution of those granted refugee status among all Member States.

There are many other instances where the principles of the Convention and the way in which the EU has applied them create a breeding ground for ambiguity and vagueness. For instance, Article 31, which prohibits Contracting States from imposing penalties on account of illegal entry into their territories upon people whose intention is to seek protections. Visa systems, however, are also enforced through carrier sanctions, not just at the border of the Contracting State. Asylum seeker cannot make a claim to protection without undertaking dangerous travels, because in the absence of visas, they will not be allowed to board any regular form of transportation. "Asylum systems start their functioning only once [asylum seekers] can be considered to have reached state territory,"[31] yet EU policies enforce *a priori* punishments of illegal attempts to enter the territory of any member state, in what seems to be a contradiction to Article 31 of the Geneva Convention.

The convention's Article 31, as a matter of fact, provides the setting for a curious example of the Union's decisions of what rules of the Geneva Convention to follow *ad-literam*. In a court case before the Court of Justice of the European Union (CJEU), the German courts made a request for an interpretation of Article 31 in the case of Mohammad Ferooz Qurbani, who was accused of using the services of people smugglers and fake documents. The CJEU decision states that it can only

> provide interpretations by way of preliminary rulings ... only to rules which are part of EU law ... [and] in the present case, although several pieces of EU legislation have been adopted in the field to which the Geneva Convention applies as part of the implementation of a Common European Asylum System, it is undisputed that the Member States have retained certain powers falling within that field, in particular relating to the subject-matter covered by Article 31 of that convention. Therefore,

(2005) 7 *European Journal of Migration and Law* 7 35, 38; see also Eiko Thielemann, 'Why Asylum Policy Harmonisation Undermines Refugee Burden-Sharing' (2004) 6 *European Journal of Migration and Law* 47.

31 Moreno-Lax (n 29) 317.

> the Court does not have jurisdiction to interpret directly Article 31, or any other article, of that convention.[32]

This case serves as a perfect example of why a vague interpretation and application of certain principles regarding asylum is inherent to the multilevel system of governance through which the policy is applied. The Common European Asylum System intends to apply standards of the Geneva Convention to many different Member States, each with their own institutional legacies and unique contexts, and each retaining certain powers of interpretation and implementation.

As a result of this complex system, each level involved in the process of asylum retains certain rights and discretions derived from the ambiguity found and accumulated along the way. This ambiguity, while valuable in reaching consensus, also means that it manifests itself differently depending on different national contexts. History, institutional designs, or even the legal framework that dictates how public servants must conduct themselves will add their own layer of ambiguity. Focusing on only one section of the process, and treating the rest as constants, will only identify where ambiguity lies at that stage, but it will not be able to explain how this ambiguity is created or perpetuated, and how ultimately it is used to construct the discretionary space of the bureaucrat charged with implementing the policy.

While policy distortion can take place anywhere, since rules of the game are constantly renegotiated at any level of governance,[33] everything preceding the moment of practical implementation is just an establishment of the expectations of how a decision should be made. If the goal of the Union is to eliminate differences of policy implementation across jurisdictions, then a perfectly harmonised system should see the bureaucrat being given a rulebook based only on the mechanisms proposed by the CEAS in making asylum decisions. As the preceding paragraphs show, policies are fraught with ambiguity, shaped by both the EU and national level.[34] The European Union reacted to ones

32 Case C-481/13 *Criminal proceedings against Mohammad Ferooz Qurbani* [2014].

33 Christopher Lord and Paul Magnette, 'E Pluribus Unum? Creative Disagreement about Legitimacy in the EU' (2004) 42 *Journal of Common Market Studies* 183.

34 Joëlle Bastien, 'Goal Ambiguity and Informal Discretion in the Implementation of Public Policies: the Case of Spanish Immigration Policy' (2009) 75 *International Review of Administrative Sciences* 665; Fulya Memisoglu and Asli Ilgit, 'Syrian Refugees in Turkey: Multifaceted Challenges, Diverse Players and Ambiguous Policies' (2016) 22 *Mediterranean Politics* 317; Izabela Jędrzejowska-Schiffauer and Peter Schiffauer, 'New Constraints on Mobility in Europe: Policy Response to European Crises or Constitutional Ambiguity?' (2017) 10 *Journal of International Studies* 9; Rianne Dekker, 'Frame Ambiguity

encountered in the Geneva Convention, but in its own approach it opened other avenues of ambiguity. This dynamic passes its way down the policy process until it reaches the street-level. This is eventually manifested in the discretionary space that street-level bureaucrats must navigate to make decisions. These are the public servants who interact directly with asylum seekers during personal interviews, who assess the information provided during the asylum procedure, and who provide the reasoning behind decisions being made. The bureaucracy surrounding the CEAS is fascinating because it encompasses case workers, border guards, correctional officers, legal counsellors, interpreters, lawyers, social housing officials, and many other street-level bureaucrats both in the public and non-governmental sector. Yet, only public servants that deal with claims to asylum are directly involved with the deliverance of fundamental human rights. It is because of these specificities that the administration of asylum bureaucracy is deserving of particular focus.

---

in Policy Controversies: Critical Frame Analysis of Migrant Integration Policies in Antwerp and Rotterdam' (2016) 11 *Critical Policy Studies* 127.

CHAPTER 2

Discretionary Implementation: Ambiguity and the Work of Street-Level Bureaucrats

Understanding how asylum procedures are constructed for bureaucrats in the context of multilevel governance and administration requires understanding what is meant when we speak of discretionary implementation. Given the high number of asylum applications that Europe has witnessed in recent years, especially during the so-called 'refugee crisis' in 2015–2016, it is important for academia to tackle the internal workings of migration regimes and attempt to explain how and why asylum is granted or denied by street-level bureaucrats at the borders of Europe, and how this fits into the larger context of the CEAS. Equally important, on the other hand, is to visualize the stakes. Take the example of Imad Al-Tamimi, who had arrived in Sweden in 2009, and after waiting for over seven years for the country's asylum bureaucracy to reach a final decision regarding his case, described the process as "lethal," allowing asylum claims to be decided based on the personal views and biases of the state worker handling the case.[1]

The following sections fit into a trend within the study of migration regimes which is beginning to catch increasingly more traction: focusing on micro-level situations and examining how border regimes (specifically asylum) manifest themselves at the intersection between local society and migratory movements.[2] The bias that Al-Tamimi saw as playing a role in deciding his case is indeed important in understanding how asylum is granted in general. But equally important is understanding the importance of the bureaucrat's conflicting roles and the information used to reach decisions.

1 Hiba Dlewati, 'Asylum Seekers Stranded in Swedish Bureaucracy' *National Geographic* (22 June 2016) https://blog.nationalgeographic.org/2016/06/22/asylum-seekers-stranded-in-swedish-bureaucracy/.

2 Andreas Pott, Christoph Rass, and Frank Wolff, *Was Ist Ein Migrationsregime?* (Springer VS, 2018).

 | DOI:10.1163/9789004700826_003

1 Discretionary Implementation in Multilevel EU

According to the EU, one way to prove that harmonisation has not been reached in the establishment of asylum policies is through the vastly different recognition rates for citizens from the same countries of origin.[3] For example, "with regard to the differences between recognition rates, data for the third quarter of 2016 shows that the recognition rates for asylum-seekers from Afghanistan varied from 97% in Italy to 0% in Bulgaria."[4] A similar trend can be observed in the type of protection granted to those in need: Member States such as Ireland, Greece, Lithuania, Luxembourg, and Slovenia usually grant refugee status to all Syrians who received a favourable decision, while Spain, Cyprus, Malta, Sweden, Czech Republic, and Hungary almost always granted subsidiary protections.[5] Even further differences can be noticed in access to rights and residence permits, or even cessations of protections already granted. Yet, there are several pitfalls to using the above-mentioned metrics as an image of the success of a common policy for asylum in the EU, the main one being that asylum is an individual right, not a group one. Indeed, some conclusions may be drawn from general acceptance rates by country, but these by themselves are not enough evidence that harmonisation has or has not occurred. Through an assessment of discretionary implementation, we can provide an explanation of policy convergence in the EU which cannot be addressed by focusing only on recognition rates. Pierre Georges Van Wolleghem and Hakan G. Sicakkan, in their recent research, show that administrative effectiveness and experience can greatly impact recognition rates. As far as explanations go, it is in the administrative set up that we are guided to look.[6]

That is not to say that recognition rates do not play a role in making some inquires into the Europeanisation of asylum policies across Member States of the European Union. Many studies had put forward the hypothesis that countries would tighten admission restrictions to ensure that harmonisation would not lead to an increase in applications lodged on their territories. However, using UNHCR data from 1999–2010, Toshkov and de Haan show that, despite

3 Commission, 'Towards a Reform of the Common European Asylum System and Enhancing Legal Avenues to Europe' (Communication) COM(2016) 197 final.

4 Olga Demetriou, 'Complementary Protection and the Recognition Rate as Tools of Governance: Ordering Europe, Fragmenting Rights' (2022) 48 *Journal of Ethnic and Migration Studies* 1264, 1268.

5 Differences between the types of protections will be discussed in detail in later chapters.

6 Pierre Georges Van Wolleghem and Hakan G. Sicakkan, 'Asylum seekers in the machinery of the state: administrative capacity vs. Preferences. Recognition rates in EU member states' (2023) 24 *European Union Politics* 348.

expectation, attempted harmonisation of asylum policies in the EU has not led to such a race to the bottom, neither in terms of the overall recognition rates of receiving countries, nor of asylum seekers from specific 'sending' countries.[7] Still, the authors accept the limitation that, while important to assess if overall rates of acceptance have decreased, their analysis does "not take into account other important aspects like the quality of the border facilities, the length and fairness of the decision process, etc."[8]

In some cases, lowering recognition rates have also been proposed to have a deterrent effect on the number of applications received.[9] Yet, the success of making such claims veritable is limited. If this relationship could be proven strong in the context of the EU, governments could, theoretically, control the number of future applications through the number of positive rates of recognition. Studies show that the effects of such an approach, while visible, are also minimal.[10] As such, using recognition rates as a policy instrument is argued to have no discernible effect on asylum application flows, as there is evidence to show that asylum policies appear to be somewhat insulated from the political rhetoric that advocates diminishing recognition rates as a tool for migration control.

While keeping these considerations in mind, this book looks at the procedures that take place before policy output – i.e., the procedural aspects of the CEAS that can shed a light on the fairness or quality of the norms based on which decisions are made. Interest into this process up until this point, both academically and from a practice-oriented point of view, has taken an overwhelmingly black-letter approach. This book makes the argument that for a proper analysis of the success or failure of the implementation of certain policies which emanate from the EU, street-level influence must be given equal analytical weight as black-letter approaches. But our view should not be limited by the constraints of the CEAS. While an aim of this study is to use literature on the street-level of bureaucracy in order to develop an understanding of the administrative aspect of discretionary implementation, it is also important to keep in mind that the asylum process begins in the asylum seekers' home

7 Dimiter Toshkov and Laura de Haan, 'The Europeanization of Asylum Policy: an Assessment of the EU Impact on Asylum Applications and Recognitions Rates' (2013) 20 *Journal of European Public Policy* 661.

8 Ibid, 670.

9 Thomas Holzer, Gerald Schneider, and Thomas Widmer, 'The Impact of Legislative Deterrence Measures on the Number of Asylum Applications in Switzerland (1986–1995)' (2000) 34 *International Migration Review* 1182, 1205.

10 Dimiter Toshkov, 'The Dynamic Relationship between Asylum Applications and Recognition Rates in Europe (1987–2010)' (2013) 15 *European Union Politics* 192.

country, where European Union foreign policy, externalisation of borders, and other instruments, such as carrier sanctions and visa policies, play a great role in determining the path any person wishing to receive protection undertakes.[11] Of course, the purpose here is not to analyse those policies and instruments that affect asylum seekers before they reach Europe, but it is important to visualise the magnitude and reach of the EU's bureaucracy in this policy area. In truth, these procedures are not at all new or innovative; rather, they represent the culmination of several years of policymaking, aimed at deterring the flow of asylum seekers.[12] Understanding them will also help to understand where the European Union has failed, according to some of its most vehement critics but also to practitioners of the field, in enacting uniform asylum policies.

Traditionally, creating a Common European Asylum System is seen as something that happens when countries adopt the measures determined at the EU level, i.e., in transposition.[13] There is little heed given in such approach to the role that implementation, and therefore street-level bureaucrats, play in the policy process.[14] Policy creation and implementation are both part of the same process, and not separate activities of governance. Consequently, there is value in analysing creation and implementation together, one not being able to have developed the specific way it has independent of the other. Writings on multilevel governance echo this thought. Beyond the belief that international law impacts national legal orders, and national legal developments are exerting a bottom-up influence on the evolution of international legal order,[15] it is becoming more and more apparent that the concepts of policy creation and implementation are, in a multilevel system more than any other, intrinsically intertwined.[16] Still, administration and governance are often treated as separate entities. This framing leaves something to be desired about the role that

11 Steve Peers, *EU Justice And Home Affairs Law* (Oxford University Press 2016) 232–234.

12 Cathryn Costello and Minos Mouzourakis, 'The Common European Asylum System: Where Did It All Go Wrong?' in Maria Fletcher, Ester Herlin-Karnell, and Claudio Matera (eds) *The European Union as an Area of Freedom, Security and Justice* (Routledge 2017), 263.

13 Peter Hupe, 'What Happens on the Ground: Persistent Issues in Implementation Research' (2014) 29 *Public Policy and Administration* 164.

14 Peter Hupe and Michael J Hill, "And the Rest Is Implementation.' Comparing Approaches to What Happens in Policy Processes beyond Great Expectations' (2015) 31 *Public Policy and Administration* 103.

15 Jan Wouters and Ramses A. Wessel, 'The Phenomenon of Multilevel Regulation: Interactions between Global, EU and National Regulatory Spheres' (2008) 4 *International Organizations Law Review* 259.

16 Nupur Chowdhury and Ramses A. Wessel, 'Conceptualising Multilevel Regulation in the EU: A Legal Translation of Multilevel Governance?' (2012) 18 *European Law Journal* 335.

bureaucrats have in the policy process, by treating administration as a separate entity from policy formation.[17]

Even when the issues of the type of policies implemented are considered, whether they be welfare, regulatory, or any other, the way the policy process should be approached does not change. These distinctions are not all that relevant once we move away from a legalistic analysis of the concept of policy harmonisation. As Majone defines it, harmonisation means "making the regulatory requirements or governmental policies of different jurisdictions identical or at least more similar."[18] Leebron, who Majone uses as the starting point of his analysis, makes the claim that harmonisation equals the reduction in differences in laws and policies of different jurisdictions – a typical black-letter approach which places the onus of harmonisation entirely on a centralized authority, and looks at the outcome only in legal terms.[19] Later in his work, however, Majone goes on to claim that a great part of his considerations of policy harmonisation come from a perspective of efficiency of delivering welfare benefits to individuals.[20] In this case, implementation of policies is key to understanding attempts at harmonisation. It is the act of delivery that matters.

The work of bureaucrats, then, cannot be viewed as neutral – their work has an active effect on the policy outcome. Understanding the norms to which they must comply is crucial, beyond strictly legal approaches. Some of the literature specific to immigration in the EU has understood the importance of including street-level bureaucrats' actions in the policy process. In a sense, a distinction is drawn between legal transposition and practical implementation,[21] and both are dependent on the tensions found between the different levels of governance. Legal transposition of European requirements will be negotiated with national political preferences, with a domestic-centric approach always being the priority for national governments.[22] A practical implementation then goes even further down in the national arena, to the street-level, where if there is ambiguity found between national policies and EU requirements, the discretion of frontline implementers becomes a key factor in deciding how a

17 Woodrow Wilson, 'The Study of Administration,' (1887) 2 *Political Science Quarterly* 197.

18 Giandomenico Majone, 'Policy Harmonization: Limits and Alternatives' (2014) 16 *Journal of Comparative Policy Analysis: Research and Practice* 4.

19 David Leebron, 'Lying down with Procrustes: An Analysis of Harmonisation Claims' in Jagdish Bhagwati and Robert Hudec (eds) *Fair Trade and Harmonisation* (MIT Press, 1996).

20 Majone (n 18) 14.

21 Eva Thomann and Fritz Sager, 'Toward a Better Understanding of Implementation Performance in the EU Multilevel System' (2017) 24 *Journal of European Public Policy* 1385.

22 Terri Givens and Adam Luedtke, 'The Politics of European Union Immigration Policy: Institutions, Salience, and Harmonization' (2004) 32 *Policy Studies Journal* 145.

policy is implemented.[23] This is a clear understanding that a policy process broken down and whose parts are evaluated independent of each other will suffer deficiencies of analysis: transposition depends on national political contexts, and implementation depends on the level of ambiguity found between the levels of governance.

Neither of the two can be analysed without the other providing a clearer context. Thomann and Sager agree that there is a need "to explore the relevant properties of policies and institutions creating different implementation dynamics, as well as the conditions under which implementers implement EU law correctly and effectively."[24] The focus on ambiguity becomes key, as often policy success is highly dependent on the level of ambiguity found at the implementation level.[25] The sections that follow will assess how discretion and ambiguity interact in a system defined by a multilevel architecture of policy implementation, leading to a clear picture of what discretionary implementation is.

Discretionary implementation is defined here as *the process through which street-level bureaucrats make decisions in their day-to-day work, on issues fraught with ambiguity, yet within the bounds of expected legal and institutional behaviour*.[26] This definition relies on several building blocks. First, it concerns specifically those decisions made by frontline workers in policy implementation. Secondly, it assumes that ambiguities are ever present, and it is up to street-level bureaucrats to settle these. Lastly, the definition places this analysis at the intersection of legal and practical implementation, bringing insights from law and public administration in the same study.

In public administration, the biggest problem posed by 'discretion' comes from the challenges it poses to the belief about the duties, limits, and responsibilities of public institutions. The very essence of representative democracy is that authority should be found only with those directly responsible to the electorate, often leading to the identification of discretion as a cause for concern in the policymaking process. Studies in implementation literature, in fact, point

---

23 Nora Dörrenbächer, 'Europe at the Frontline: Analysing Street-Level Motivations for the Use of European Union Migration Law' (2017) 24 *Journal of European Public Policy* 1328.

24 Thomann and Sager (n 21) 1400.

25 Eva G. Heidbreder, 'Strategies in Multilevel Policy Implementation: Moving beyond the Limited Focus on Compliance' (2017) 24 *Journal of European Public Policy* 1367, 1376.

26 For an exploration of the interplay between discretion and ambiguity, see Karl Heyer, 'Keeping migrants at the margins. Governing through ambiguity and the poiltics of discretion in the post-2015 European migration and broder regime' (2022) 97 *Political Geography* 102643.

to discretion as a factor that can potentially lead to discrepancies between policy goals and outcomes.[27]

But perceptions of discretion are often dependent on the framing with which the problem is presented, making the concept both necessary and problematic, depending on the approach taken. When presented in terms of administrative efficiency, more discretion is called for. Conversely, its framing in terms of abuse of discretionary powers leads to a call for political or legislative control.[28] In reality, despite any reservation to the concept's presence in administrative structures, "administrative agencies exercise tremendous discretion in relation to elected officials and courts, and public managers exercise tremendous discretion in relation to policy mandates and bureaucratic rules."[29]

The extent to which discretion is, or should, be allowed does not follow objective criteria, but rather depends on the social or political events of the time.[30] In the context of the EU, the amount of discretion granted can be dependent on the political priorities not only of the national public officials, but of decision-makers at different levels of governance within the Union and in Member States. Discretion must be understood generally in context-rich settings,[31] and the context of asylum policy in the EU is highly dependent on the system of multilevel governance within which it is implemented. In this sense, some argue that discretion in public bureaucracies should be taken as policy entrepreneurship,[32] something that would make street-level bureaucrats policymakers themselves.

Before diving into the policy-making power of these bureaucrats, however, a few lines should be spent discussing specifically the implications that multilevel governance have on administrative discretion in immigration policies. Decision-making capacity in the EU is located at several levels, from the supranational, down to the national and sub-national levels. This means that while

27 William F. West, 'Structuring Administrative Discretion: The Pursuit of Rationality and Responsiveness,' (1984) 28 *American Journal of Political Science* 340.

28 Marc Holzer and Kaifeng Yang, 'Administrative Discretion in a Turbulent Time: An Introduction' (2005) 29 *Public Administration Quarterly* 128, 131.

29 Ibid 128.

30 Alasdair Roberts, 'Administrative Discretion and the Access to Information Act: An 'Internal Law' on Open Government?' (2002) 45 *Canadian Public Administration* 175.

31 Ralph S. Brower, Mitchel Y. Abolafia, and Jered B. Carr, 'On Improving Qualitative Methods in Public Administration Research' (2000) 32 *Administration & Society* 363, 383.

32 Bien Baez and Mitchell Y. Abolafia, 'Bureaucratic Entrepreneurship and Institutional Change: A Sense-Making Approach' (2002) 12 *Journal of Public Administration Research and Theory* 525.

states have given up some of their sovereignty in specific fields – e.g., immigration and asylum – there is now an interconnectedness between the different levels, whereby political developments at one level impact levels above and below.[33] In such a framework, not only do developments at the supranational level have a trickle-down effect that can be observed at the sub-national level, but vice-versa as well. If the extent to which discretion is allowed depends on the political priorities at different levels of governance, then the way bureaucrats implement asylum policy can have effects on the entire system, just as the decisions made at the supranational level do.

Such a perspective to multilevel governance is not new in literature on the topic. It is true that some see the 'Europeanisation' of immigration policies as a top-down process that gives supremacy to the EU, making institutions such as the Court of Justice or the European Commission activists of this trend;[34] counterarguments to this approach point to a voluntary ceding of sovereignty by Member States toward EU institutions. This is done with the purpose of strengthening control over migration as a policy field – a transgovernmentalist approach to European integration. This approach is what allows "local" policy actors to enter into cooperation with EU levels of governance.[35] This model comes close to what we expect based on multilevel governance, with EU, national, and subnational level systemically connected, without one having undue control over the other. This multilevel approach, however, also allows for the option of decoupling to happen – whereby misalignment of interests can lead to conflicts, as has been the case in the resistance given by Visegrad countries in implementing asylum measures that responded to the 2015 'refugee crisis.'[36]

What this means is that the way decisions are made at all levels – including the street-level of governance – can have an impact on the entire system, since multilevel settings are interconnected and interdependent. Understanding the discretionary powers of implementation that bureaucrats have helps shed light on how their actions influence a policy that is developed and implemented in

---

33 Neill Nugent, *The Government and Politics of the European Union* (Palgrave Macmillan 2017).

34 See the typologies of Europeanisation of immigration policies developed in Andrew Geddes and Peter Scholten, 'Policy Analysis and Europeanization: An Analysis of EU Migrant Integration Policymaking' (2013) 17 *Journal of Comparative Policy Analysis: Research and Practice* 41.

35 Andrew Geddes and Peter Scholten, *The Politics of Migration & Immigration in Europe* (Sage 2016).

36 Peter Scholten and Rinus Penninx, 'The Multilevel Governance of Migration and Integration' in Blanca Garcés-Mascareñas and Rinus Penninx (eds) *Integration Processes and Policies In Europe: Contexts, Levels and Actors* (Springer Open 2016).

such a context. For this, we must understand that those working on the front-line of asylum policy do more than simply play by the rulebook that has been written;[37] in a way they are co-designers of the system. This is why, aside from strict legal rules, other factors must be accounted for in the shaping of everyday working practices, such as the administrative routines, decisions paradigms, or workplace socialisation.[38] If we take to understand, then, how street-level bureaucrats both interpret and apply the written rules based on the administrative and multilevel context, we are looking at the actions of these public officials as part of those very political motivations that shape the structure of multilevel administration.[39]

The extent to which those interacting directly with asylum seekers can be seen as more than just applying law, but are part of the policy-making process, can be observed when it comes to credibility assessments of applicants. While we would expect legal considerations to be the driving factors behind assessing claims to international protection, it is the *credibility* of an asylum seeker's story that decides his or her fate – it is, more often than not, the deciding element in asylum cases, and this takes place in "the vacuum left by human rights formalism."[40] As the asylum procedure described in later chapters shows, it is evidentiary assessments, and not material law that decide if someone does or does not receive international protection in a EU Member State. And while guiding principles for such assessments are given, there is no coherent legal approach to evidentiary assessment, leaving the door open for discretionary implementation.[41]

This is why international refugee law looks different in jurisdictions – even if they are meant to apply the same principles – because these ideals are taken from the high-tower of international law to the "mundane form of bureaucratic decision making."[42] Each state reacts differently to EU asylum policies, and in

37 Oivind Fuglerud, 'Constructing Exclusion. The Micro-Sociology of an Immigration Department' (2004) 12 *Social Anthropology* 25, 29; Maybritt Jill Alpes and Alexis Spire, 'Dealing with Law in Migration Control' (2013) 23 *Social & Legal Studies* 261, 267; Tobias G. Eule, Lisa Marie Borrelli, Annika Lindberg and Anna Wyss, *Migrants before the Law: Contested Migration Control in Europe* (Palgrave Macmillan, 2019).

38 Laura Affolter, 'Shaping Administrative Practice: The Institutional Habitus' (2020) in Laura Affolter, *Asylum Matters* (Palgrave Macmillan 2020).

39 Ibid.

40 Gregor Noll, 'Asylum Claims and the Translation of Culture into Politics' (2006) 41 *Texas International Law Journal* 491, 497.

41 Gregor Noll, *Proof, Evidentiary Assessment and Credibility in Asylum Procedures* (Brill Nijhoff 2005).

42 Rebecca Hamlin, 'International Law and Administrative Insulation: A Comparison of Refugee Status Determination Regimes in the United States, Canada, and Australia' (2012) 37 *Law & Social Inquiry* 933, 962.

many cases the actual human rights considerations of determining refugee status do not play the most important role. Furthermore, front-line bureaucracies are the interpreters and enforcers of migration policies, making street-level bureaucrats agents of legal globalisation. In some cases, where administrative insulation exists and detailed guidance is given to those analysing claims, decisions made are seldom contradicted. On the other hand, in cases where administrations are not insulated and political decisions have narrowed the definition of who deserves or not to be a refugee, many claims become ambiguous because political regimes cannot adapt to changing global conditions in any consistent manner.[43] "Bureaucratic justice is conceptualised and organised differently in different states, and so states vary in how they draw the line between refugee and nonrefugee."[44]

Asylum seekers are "migrants in search of a category",[45] one which must be conferred by the agents manning the administrative structures in the countries where the asylum seekers land. These adjudicators are tasked with giving out a coveted asset, yet different systems frequently lead to divergent conclusions, even in cases that have similar patterns.[46] Yet, despite the reality that international refugee law manifests itself differently depending on the administrative structures of the countries where it is implemented,

> People are often surprised and even outraged by the fact that decision-makers interpret – rather than just "apply" – rules when putting them to use in specific situations. Therefore, it seems crucial to continue stressing the important role that discretionary practices play in administrative decision-making. Discretion is what makes law work. It necessarily forms part of law in practice.[47]

Even more, while literature does tend to suggest that street-level agents are conservers of institutional values, we cannot assume they are mere vessels of such values. This is so because of their own set of ideals, and because "the bonds of supervision and principal-agent obligation break down long before authority reaches down to the front lines."[48] When their ideals match the ones

43 Ibid. See the examples of the United States as an administration influenced by political interference in the definition of refugee, vs. Canada, where administrations are insulated from such interventions.

44 Ibid 963.

45 Rebecca Hamlin. *Let me be a refugee.* (Oxford University Press 2010) 3.

46 Ibid 7.

47 Affolter (n 38), 5.

48 Heidbreder (n 25).

of the institution within which they operate, and the information needed to make decisions is complete, there is little risk of workers becoming noncompliant with the requirements that come from their role as bureaucrats. What made street-level bureaucrats identify with clients and make decisions beneficial for them was the idea that interactions between similar groups created bonds. "While public administration and government may aspire to certain ideals, they cannot exist in an ideal world. Social equity is realized when put to practice, not when discussed in principle."[49]

Let's step out of the street-level for one moment, and analyse the claims presented above by considering the entire governance structure. In a multi-level system, we notice that "decision outcomes often differ from the outcomes preferred by at least some member states. Such differences between preferred and actual outcomes can be thought of as member states' 'incentive to deviate' when implementing EU legislation."[50] In other words, when we look at multi-level governance and administration, we start to notice several points at which we can expect deviation from the intended policies – i.e., non-compliance. But "full compliance is a broader concept, which includes appropriate policies by national agencies, and even appropriate behaviour by street-level bureaucrats delivering services to citizens."[51] On the other hand, Maynard-Moody and Musheno describe what incentives a street-level bureaucrat might have to deviate from legislation. They, and much of the rest of the literature, talks of positive reasons for this sort of non-compliance: identifying with the community which they serve. In other words, being members of the same in-group as their clients.[52]

This problem can be best pictured by the way the term 'client' is used. A client, or a consumer of public services delivered by bureaucracies, must strike a balance between asserting their rights, and but also adjusting expectations according to the deficiencies of bureaucracies.[53] For this reason, one prominent way to describe street-level bureaucrats is to equate them "with public services with which *citizens* interact," (emphasis added), but also through the

49 Steven Maynard-Moody and Michael Musheno, 'Social Equities and Inequities in Practice: Street-Level Workers as Agents and Pragmatists' (2012) 72 *Public Administration Review* S16, S21.

50 Robert Thomson, Rene Torenvlied, and Javier Arregui, 'The Paradox of Compliance: Infringements and Delays in Transposing European Union Directives' (2007) 37 *British Journal of Political Science* 685, 686.

51 Ibid.

52 Maynard-Moody and Musheno (n 49).

53 Michael Lipsky, *Street-Level Bureaucracy: Dilemmas of the Individual in Public Services* (Russell Sage Foundation 2010), xvi.

restraints placed upon them in interactions with citizens.[54] This, however, is fundamentally different when asylum seekers are the consumers of the services, as the assertion of rights is balanced against expectations formed on the spot, not through a long-standing relationship with service management that citizens have.

Michael Lipsky, whose 1980 work entitled *Street-Level Bureaucracy* is considered a seminal reading by students of public administration, defines the street-level bureaucrat as a public service worker "who interacts directly with citizens in the course of their jobs, and who have substantial discretion in the execution of their work." This, combined with the approach of who a client is, reinforce the idea that clients are, by the definition of the bureaucracies that they interact with, citizens. In short, in Lipsky's own words, these workers "hold the keys to a dimension of citizenship."[55] This approach, however, reveals several assumptions that are less valid if the client is not treated as a citizen. Firstly, there is an explanation of bureaucracies as the target of controversies because they face the backlash of clients who feel disadvantaged by changes in policies. Clients of asylum bureaucracies have little power to provide such backlash as the one described by Lipsky.[56]

Belabas and Gerrits touch somewhat upon this dilemma in their study of discretion of street-level bureaucrats in implementing integration policies of immigrants. The authors no longer use the term "citizen-client", but focus rather only on the client, while explicitly claiming that their work "builds on Lipsky's research and motives of street-level bureaucrats who interact directly with *citizens* when implementing and delivering public policies."[57] But, their emphasis on decision making of street-level bureaucrats still focuses greatly on positive connections with the client: high client motivation, extreme personal distress of the client, and negative assessment of the policies as related to how they affect the client in terms of fairness and practicality are considered to be motives for bureaucrats to make use of their discretionary space. The theory

---

54 Ibid xvii.

55 Ibid 3–4.

56 Ibid 10. On page 23, Lipsky also illustrates the problem of depending on citizenship to define client: "street-level bureaucrats, like everyone else, have personal standards of whether or not someone is deserving [...] Clearly discretion provides opportunity to intervene on behalf of clients as well as to discriminate against them,". If this is the case, it would be worrisome to assume that citizenship does not matter when determining when and how benefits should be delivered.

57 Warda Belabas and Lasse Gerrits, 'Going the Extra Mile? How Street-Level Bureaucrats Deal with the Integration of Immigrants' (2015) 51 *Social Policy & Administration* 133, 134.

of street-level bureaucracy must consider that conflicts between in-group and out-group can have a negative spillover effect on policy implementation.

If the above-mentioned characteristics of bureaucratic decision making in relation to asylum seekers are correct, we are then dealing with discretionary implementation at the bureaucratic level not only in terms of policy frameworks, but also in the context of intergroup conflict. The assistance of bureaucrats in attempting to provide the best-case outcome for the citizen-client is a representation of in-group defence: coordinating for the 'defence' of the group to which they belong. When these bureaucrats are faced with deciding the fate of out-group members, however, there could be an expectation that in-group defence no longer plays a role, and even more important, out-group aggression has a potential to do so.[58] Nonetheless, the simple absence of the citizen-client dynamic should not be treated as an assumption that intergroup conflict is used in bureaucratic decision making. It only serves to illustrate how principles outside of legal guidelines can manifest themselves at the street-level. Indeed, while citizenship may not be a way to create a positive bond with the client, other factors may be. The bureaucrat may still favour certain clients based on belonging to other groups, defined by gender, ethnicity, religion, or other factors. The absence of the citizen-client bond still makes this relationship one deserving of special attention, but not one that is predefined in terms of expected interactions. The consideration does provide, nevertheless, another opportunity for observing ambiguities: in the negotiation of new linkages with those served by asylum bureaucracies. For this reason, it is important to contextualise the general working conditions of bureaucrats with the specific of working in asylum policies.

Street-level bureaucracies are crucial elements of the policy process: they are charged with translating legal texts into implementable regulations, while at the same time adapting the requirements of those texts to the shifting realities on the ground. As indicated above, because of the crucial role that these institutions play, Michael Lipsky's work on *Street-Level Bureaucracy* represents the foundation on which a great number of public administration studies are built. Discretion is built into Lipsky's definition of what a bureaucrat is. The term, then, can be best defined as the set of options available to these public servants for making a decisions, with reliance on any such option still conforming to a pre-determined expectation of outcome,

58 Carsten K. De Dreu et al., 'In-Group Defense, out-Group Aggression, and Coordination Failures in Intergroup Conflict' (2016) 113 *Proceedings of the National Academy of Sciences* 10524.

i.e., still legally compliant.[59] Such characterisation, particularly regarding the amount of discretion granted to street-level bureaucrats, comes from Lipsky's account of the job of these public servants: the conditions of work, the need to ration resources, stressful relations with clients, or ambiguous goals and performance standards all lead to discretionary practices, which may manifest themselves as rationing services, exerting control over their clients, or the development of particular client-processing mentalities specific to the job. The following sections will explore these concepts of street-level bureaucracy and discuss how practices change in cases of emergency, a situation of particular interest to asylum management.

The fact that the work of street-level bureaucrats is characterized by high levels of discretion needed to be able to deliver policy implies that an aggregate of their individual actions adds up to agency behaviour.[60] If we consider Lipsky's argument that "relationships between policy deliverers and managers are conflictual and reciprocal, [then] policy implementation analysis must question assumption that influence flows with authority from higher to lower levels."[61] Organisational autonomy categorically influences the role of bureaucrats in the policy process, and the capacity of bureaucrats to resist organisational pressures is paramount in assessing implementation. Such capacity can be categorised by threats of noncompliance or of withholding cooperation (absenteeism or quitting). By holding such leverage over their managers, Lipsky argues, street-level bureaucrats don't only implement, but they also make policy.

The two-way street of dependence, whereby workers are dependent on managerial decision and managers are dependent on the job delivery of their subordinates, incentivizes managers to pay attention to worker preferences if there is reciprocity in job performance. This dynamic is bound to be affected by crisis situations, and Lipsky's work does not lose sight of this. He addresses what happens in such cases, and how agencies define and adapt to emergency practices. First in their toolbox for handling urgencies, street-level bureaucracies must determine the categories of the emergency and when clients fit said categories, thus allowing for prioritization of resources.[62] Emergencies, from an organizational perspective, cannot exist outside of the relationship between bureaucracy and client. Procedures adopted have the purpose of (1) aiding

59 Robert B. Cialdini and Noah J. Goldstein, 'Social Influence: Compliance and Conformity' (2004) 55 *Annual Review of Psychology* 591, 592.

60 Lipsky (n 53), 13.

61 Ibid 25.

62 Ibid 138.

with the rational allocation of resources, (2) facilitating resource mobilisation, (3) allowing to treat part of the caseload comprehensively when treating all cases fully cannot be done, (4) permitting agencies and street-level bureaucrats to make exceptions, and (5) allowing for the provisions of resources to those who threaten smooth implementation, thus avoiding unsatisfied clients to discredit the agency. Emergency procedures thus allows for legitimate ways to make exceptions, while also giving street-level bureaucrats even more of a say over their work practices, conferring on them the power to select clients for preferential treatment.[63] Emergency procedures, then, differ from regular triage procedures because they do not seek to address the cases most in need of intervention, but rather those that are most likely to respond to the intervention, as assessed by the street-level bureaucrat.

The two concepts that are vital, equally so for regular policy implementation and for emergency procedures, are resource allocation and strategies for rationing services. In regular situations, bureaucrats already constrained by the costs of obtaining information relative to the resources available, and by the frequency with which decisions must be made. Time and an adequate ratio between workers and clients are resources vital to job performance. Since this implies a strong relationship between case load and efficiency with which resources can be used, it only makes sense that the introduction of emergency procedures as described above help manage caseloads in order to achieve optimal efficiency in delivery of services and benefits. Resources needed for job performance can also be personal, such as experience or training. In some cases, however, a lack of personal resources is also attributable to the nature of the work: "some jobs cannot be done properly, given the ambiguity of goals and the technology of particular social services." In situations of upheaval, characterised by unpredictability and even uncertainty when it comes to the finality of intervention, such ambiguities are inherently exacerbated. Clear job objectives, Lipsky argues, must be taken equally as necessary personal resources in assessing policy implementation.

The problem for Lipsky is that these resources, as well as material resources such as proper funding, are inadequately present in street-level bureaucracies. Workers in these institutions have access to little information, must handle large caseloads with little time and under high stress, and must always operate with a certain lack of clarity when it comes to objectives. This is because demand for public services increases to meet supply. When resources, and therefore number of services, are increased, demand also increases. But according to the

63 Ibid 139.

definition discussed above, it is these very deficiencies that emergency procedures seek to address. Lipsky himself first gives us a glimpse with his analysis of police officers. The behaviour of this group of street-level bureaucrats can be best explained by "their felt need to avoid danger." The description of police officers' work situations is appropriate here because their jobs are largely influenced by emergency situations. The police force faces unpredictable yet constant threats. Much of a police officer's job is centred around assessing which situations may be more threatening than others, and the constant presence of physical danger creates tremendous amounts of stress. This unpredictability also affects how services are rationed. Unlike bureaucracies where a sense of urgency is not present, workers in police forces have little control over workflow because intervention must be done according to need.[64]

What also becomes evident is that the power to ration service delivery is limited for street-level bureaucrats on the frontlines of emergencies. In regular situations, costs of service, queuing strategies, or even personal routines of individual bureaucrats all affect how service delivery is allocated. These are the practices that serve as a triage of clients. As already mentioned, however, the rationale behind triage shifts in emergencies, or in bureaucracies that deal with emergency-like workflows: rather than serving those in need, rationing must serve those most likely to respond positively to bureaucratic intervention. While a police force, which usually deals with emergencies, relies on actors such as dispatchers to ration services and ensure that officers are not assigned more cases than they can handle, such straightforward mechanisms do not exist in asylum bureaucracy. The reasoning, as further chapters will show, lays in the need for an individual assessment of every application for asylum. Triaging can only be done once at least a preliminary assessment has been conducted. The diminished power over client triage and the unpredictability of the workflow makes emergency bureaucratic procedures equally important for asylum case workers as for police officers.

The tenets of emergency bureaucratic procedures from street-level bureaucracy only refer to procedures implemented by one organisation in dealing with crises. Upheavals, however, can take place on any level, form the personal to an entire system, and they are characterised by situational disorder that cannot be dealt with effectively with the usual procedures and where procedural mechanisms are overwhelmed.[65] In some cases, nonetheless, "crisis

64 Ibid 29–33.

65 Gerald Caplan, *An Approach to Community Mental Health* (Routledge 2011). See also Tan Ngoh Tiong, 'Crisis Theory and SARS' (2004) 14 *Asia Pacific Journal of Social Work and Development* 7.

management efforts cut across organisational boundaries."[66] When this happens, crisis intervention, or actions taken in order to help a system adapt and respond to specific crises, means harnessing resources and developing emergency procedures for an entire system.[67] Like what has been observed when assessing the working conditions of bureaucrats, crisis management literature acknowledges the severe strain that emergencies impose of resource management and levels of stress among workers.[68] From a managerial point of view, "an incident or event must pose a threat to the organization's reputation and viability to be considered a crisis."[69] Some also suggest that, in dealing with these crises, both at the strategic and operational level, 'bureau-political' tensions fulfil various positive functions, much as Lipsky argues that the conflictual relationship between workers and managers creates a balance between job performance and worker preferences.[70]

Interestingly, for Lipsky this dynamic is not inherent to crisis management. Indeed, he sees the powers of workers diminishing in emergency situations by the abandonment of regular triage procedures, and he does not purport any similar sacrifices to be made managerially. For crisis-management scholars, the competition for advantages is not something to shy away in times of crisis, as it is considered that crisis management must have the discretion to derogate from established procedures in order to foster adaptation.[71] This is what is known as the adaptive approach, or a framework that emphasises creativity and flexibility in crisis management operations. Some scholars claim that crisis responses are hindered by not relying on an adaptive approach, and choosing instead to follow a traditional bureaucratic model, defined as a "command-and-control model with centralized decision-making and communication systems that promote a hierarchical structure that is strictly rigid."[72] This same conclusion is reached by those looking at adaptive responses in the

66 Christine M. Pearson and Ian I. Mitroff, 'From Crisis Prone to Crisis Prepared: a Framework for Crisis Management' [1993] *Academy of Management Perspectives* 48.

67 Tan Ngoh Tiong, 'Crisis Theory and SARS' (2004) 14 *Asia Pacific Journal of Social Work and Development* 7, 8.

68 Pearson and Mitroff (n 66), 49.

69 Ibid.

70 Uriel Rosenthal, Paul Hart, and Alexander Kouzmin, 'The Bureau-Politics of Crisis Management' (1991) 69 *Public Administration* 211.

71 Alastair Stark, 'Bureaucratic Values and Resilience: an Exploration of Crisis Management Adaptation' (2014) 92 *Public Administration* 692, 702.

72 Kyujin Jung, Minsun Song, and Han Woo Park, 'Filling the Gap between Bureaucratic and Adaptive Approaches to Crisis Management: Lessons from the Sewol Ferry Sinking in South Korea' (2017) 52 *Quality & Quantity* 277, 282.

context of resilience, or the collection of actions through which "governments have sought to improve their responses to crises [stemming from] an understanding that crisis management must be adaptable."[73]

As this section shows, the conditions of work then depend largely on the environment of the bureaucrats: the ambiguity found in the jobs, the relationships with managers, the resources and client processing techniques, are all relevant factors in how the work of street-level bureaucrats is carried out. But these factors must act upon the bureaucrat somehow to affect the way decisions are – or potentially may be – affected. These conditions of work create the discretionary space within which implementation takes place. They represent the 'breeding ground for ambiguity' described in role conflict theory, an approach that allows for individual considerations to be factored into an analysis of agency behaviour.

2 The Breeding Ground for Ambiguity in Multilevel Governance

Ambiguity has many different definitions, depending on which strand of literature defines it. Most research has been conducted by focusing on behaviour of individuals in decision-making. The concept has been defined in terms of the quantity and determinacy of information available for decisions, whether this is over the clarity of available information,[74] its precision,[75] or a lack of consensus over its applicability.[76] For others, ambiguity has less to do with the availability of information, but rather to its relevance, reliability, and source credibility.[77] In other cases, ambiguity has also been conceptualised as a process-oriented term: one which looks at the level of experience of decision makers in dealing with ambiguous decisions, or the motivation behind being involved in making the decision in the first place.[78]

Literature has also looked at ambiguity in terms of how it can be mitigated, either by choosing the best-outcome scenario or dealing with ambiguity

73 Stark (n 71) 692.

74 Ching Leong and Neng Qian, 'Ambiguity, bureaucracy and certainty: The ABCs of enabling water self-sufficiency' (2016) 35 *Policy and Society* 165.

75 Dale Whittington and Xun Wu, 'Water resource development on the Ganges: moving beyond ambiguity' (2013) 15 *Water Policy* 1.

76 Vicki Eaton Baier, James G. March and Harald Saetren, 'Implementation and ambiguity' (1986) 2 *Scandinavian Journal of Management Studies* 197.

77 Kristin Taylor, Stephanie Zarb and Nathan Jeschke, 'Ambiguity, Uncertainty and Implementation' (2021) 3 *International Review of Public Policy* 100.

78 Michael Hill and Peter Hupe, *Implementing public policy* (2nd edn., Sage 2009).

by putting in place contingency plans. In attempting to look at the effects of dealing with ambiguities, streams of analysis have taken different paths. One such path involves assessing if actions taken to mitigate ambiguity involve norm violation, while in other cases it was more concerned with effects ambiguity may have at different levels of administration. The latter of these effects involves assessing the externalities relevant to each level, and if (or how) ambiguity is interconnected with the choices made at other levels.

The interconnectedness of these ambiguities is particularly important when considering the multilevel structures in which EU asylum policy takes place. The days of asylum policy being the sole competency of the state have long passed in the EU. Ever since asylum policy entered the European policy agenda in the 1990s, EU Member States have formalised rules to address the issues they deemed necessary. The 1992 Maastricht Treaty established the first broad framework for intergovernmental cooperation under EU auspices, and by 1997 the European Union was provided with a strong legal basis to act on the matter. By the time the Lisbon Treaty entered into force, immigration policy was already a core policy area of the EU, making the field a strongly Europeanised one. This involved strong transfer of powers away from the central governments, toward the Court of Justice and the EU Parliament, although Member State participation in the Council and through various working groups still gives national governments a say in the way asylum policy is developed.

Policy implementation in multilevel settings can only be judged when all ambiguities associated with implementation have been settled. If discretionary implementation is the process through which street-level bureaucrats make decision on issues fraught with ambiguity, then we cannot judge how the CEAS is enforced during the stage of transposition, if the transposed legislation builds a discretionary space for the agents charged with implementation. The ambiguities inherent to discretionary spaces represent uncertainties of what policy demands. This is especially the case in policy areas in which street-level agents have a large enforcement role, such as policies that target immigrant communities.

This field has already seen some focus from academia in recent years, concluding, indeed, that enforcement structures with high discretion give street-level bureaucrats the responsibility of settling their own the lack of information necessary for making job-related decisions. Inversely, structures with small discretionary spaces have clear guidelines for street-level bureaucrats on how to settle any potential lack of information necessary for decision-making. Low discretion points to low ambiguity because those charged with enforcement can find the information needed to conduct their job in the structure within which they are embedded.[79] As research has already shown in the Netherlands, where ambiguities are dealt with early in the policy process, street-level bureaucrats have clear guidelines for filling any gaps of information.[80] Romania's enforcement of the CEAS, where unlike the Netherlands the bureaucracy is described as *deconcentrated*, would indicate that the street-level must deal with higher levels of ambiguity and wider discretionary spaces which can potentially affect implementation results, although academic studies in the specific area of asylum still lack.

Literature has addressed the subject of ambiguities from several angles. Zielonka[81] portrays ambiguity as resulting from unclear objectives of policies, while Room[82] points to ambiguity as a benchmarking tool of policy success. Yet, the success or failure of integration has hinged on the built-in ambiguity of the process. This was seen as providing the solutions for bridging differences between Members States that emerged because of the schism between federalists and intergovernmentalists, differences of the functional scope of integration, and even divergences of national agendas. Yet, these gains are offset by the fact that ambiguity was at times perceived as indicating a lack of priority, since it leads to the creation of policies based on the lowest-common denominator between Member States, not as a result of a cost/benefit analysis.

The above arguments refer to two different forms of ambiguity. First, we see what could be called *intentional ambiguity*, or the ambiguity purposefully built into a system to provide the implementer discretion in how certain goals are achieved. Ferraro and De Capitani refer to this as "creative ambiguity," claiming that "legal clarity comes later and very often only after the intervention of national and European judges who will inevitably be called to solve the problems of its interpretation and implementation."[83] Secondly, we see also *unintentional ambiguity*, when provisions from the same policy or from several different policies provide conflicting information regarding expectations. These can also come from institutional deficiencies, or inter-institutional conflicts. National legislators can't always be assumed to correctly (and in a timely

79 Jan Beyers and Jarle Trondal, 'How Nation States 'Hit' Europe: Ambiguity and Representation in the European Union' (2004) 27 *West European Politics* 919.

80 Nora Dörrenbächer, 'Frontline Uses of European Union (EU) Law: a Parallel Legal Order? How Structural Discretion Conditions Uses of EU Law in Dutch and German Migration Offices' (2017) 38 *Journal of Public Policy* 455.

81 Jan Zielonka, 'Ambiguity as a Remedy for the EU's Eastward Enlargement?' (1998) 12 *Cambridge Review of International Affairs* 14.

82 Graham Room, 'Policy Benchmarking in the European Union' (2005) 26 *Policy Studies* 117.

83 Francesca Ferraro and Emilio De Capitani, 'The New European Border and Coast Guard: Yet Another 'Half Way' EU Reform?' (2016) 17 *ERA Forum* 385, 387.

manner) transpose EU directives, while sometimes national norms of implementation are not in accordance with EU law, leading to ambiguities between different guidelines emanating from different authorities.[84]

Ambiguity could then be generally defined as any provision that contributes, intentionally or not, to the building of the implementer's discretionary space. While it can be assumed then that ambiguity is an integral-part of the policy-making process,[85] there is a clear differentiation that must be kept in mind between intentional or unintentional ambiguities, as the former serves as a tool for integration, while the latter can lead to unpredictable implementation outcomes. Beyers and Trondal point to this unpredictability when it comes to unclear instructions and objectives of national bureaucrats working in European settings. This implies that dilemmas regarding where authority lies, whose interests should be represented, and how conflict should be resolved make the practice of bureaucratic representation uncertain. "Under these ambiguities actors may either fall back on familiar and traditional roles or, under certain conditions search for new roles."[86]

Focusing on ambiguities as building blocks of discretionary spaces allows us to create a metric for which discretionary provisions can be traced at every level of governance, since transposition actors delegate discretion to practical implementers.[87] The intended results of the Common European Asylum System are based on bureaucratic procedures. As such, understanding how these are built cannot ignore the process that takes place between transposition and implementation, namely the passing of discretion horizontally, from the legislative to the executive branches of government, and also vertically, down the hierarchical ladder of administration.

3 Role Theory and Ambiguity

I have referred several times now to the 'roles' that a bureaucrat fills. This is because a more precise understanding of how ambiguity manifests itself organisationally can be found in role theory. Because the rules of game can be

84 Dörrenbächer (n 80).

85 Nikolaos Zahariadis, 'Ambiguity and Choice in European Public Policy' (2008) 15 *Journal of European Public Policy* 514, 515.

86 Beyers and Trondal (n 77), 926.

87 Nora Dörrenbächer and Ellen Mastenbroek, 'Passing the Buck? Analyzing the Delegation of Discretion after Transposition of European Union Law' (2017) 13 *Regulation & Governance* 70.

changed or revisited at any point,[88] policy is decided and negotiated at every step, and agenda building, policy creation and implementation therefore collapse into each other.[89] Decision-making, in other words, is not something simply found in the political arena, because the political arena and administration cannot be divided by a clear line. Justifications for making decisions are crucial in policy implementation at all levels.

Yet, Hupe and Hill claim that if we treat the work of street-level bureaucrats as "a presupposed residual in goal achievement [we pay] little attention to political dimensions, like ambiguity and conflict."[90] The work of Kahn, Wolfe, Quinn, and Snoek, which set the foundations for role conflict theory, means to tackle exactly the issues identified as being ignored by treating implementation as separate in the policy process: role conflict and role ambiguity. This unearths a need to identify how certain institutions are created, and perpetuated, and how individuals fit into these institutions, transcending any analysis that would otherwise focus only on one level of governance and decision-making. Indeed, role expectations, or the expectations of a particular response that add up to norm compliance, are determined by the broader organizational context.[91]

Firstly, however, we must establish exactly what is meant by *role behaviour, role conflict,* and *role ambiguity,* as these are the terms at the centre of this theoretical lens. Khan et al. assert that by role behaviour, "we mean behaviour which is system relevant (not necessarily congruent with the expectation and requirements of others), and which is performed by a person who is accepted by others as a member of the system."[92] Behaviour congruent with bureaucracy, therefore, and an acceptance of a person as being part of bureaucratic apparatus, confer upon a person the role of bureaucrat. Role-conflict, on the other hand, can manifest itself in two distinct categories: intrinsic and extrinsic to the organization. Intrinsic role conflict refers either to situations in which norms and rules originating from one point (usually a superior) are contradictory, or situations when different pressures originate from different points – for example, from supervisor on one end and subordinates on the other. Extrinsic

88 Christopher Lord and Paul Magnette, 'E Pluribus Unum? Creative Disagreement about Legitimacy in the EU' (2004) 42 *Journal of Common Market Studies* 183.

89 Charles E. Lindblom and Edward J. Woodhouse, *The Policy-Making Process* (Prentice Hall 1993).

90 Hupe and Hill (n 14), 103.

91 Robert L. Kahn et al., *Organizational Stress: Studies in Role Conflict and Ambiguity* (Wiley 1964), 31.

92 Ibid 18.

role conflict, or more specifically inter-role conflict,[93] refers to the pressure associated with the conflict between membership to one organisation and association to other groups. In a simplistic example, Khan et al. talk about the pressure that arises when organization role requires that a person work late, while membership to a family unit require that they go home early. A more complex version of extrinsic role-conflict is *person role conflict,* or the pressure arising when role requirements and personal values are in contradiction, or otherwise said, when role requirements violate individual moral standards.

Finally, there is the concept of role ambiguity, which arises from the needs that a person has for information to perform their job. As a result, ambiguity can also come in two different forms. Objective ambiguity, or a condition of the environment, or subjective ambiguity, as a condition of the individual person. Objective ambiguity refers to the context in which workers find themselves, while subjective ambiguity to the psychological responses to that context. "The influence of [objective ambiguity] on a particular individual constitutes his subjective (experienced) ambiguity in that particular situation."[94] A lack of clear, consistent information, or the improper communication of such information, results in objective ambiguity. The extent of availability of this information then leads to the person's reaction. When objective ambiguity is high, expected role behaviour may be unclear, leading to a higher discretionary space where the important aspect in decision making becomes the personal reaction of the individual to the ambiguous environment.

The concepts of role behaviour, role conflict, and role ambiguity create the lenses which inform the analysis conducted in this work. One point needs to be emphasized: both the argument presented by Hupe and Hill regarding policy processes and implementation, and the arguments of Khan et al. regarding role theory show a great need, when attempting to analyse policy success (irrespective of the yardstick used to measure that success), of analysing that policy at each level of governance. Bringing the theoretical discussion back into the fold of the empirical scope of this project, when looking at how the implementation of asylum policies takes places across the EU, it has been shown that there is a distinct need to understand how the table is set for bureaucrats to implement the requirements of the CEAS at the street-level. This means understanding how policies are developed, how the national contexts shape the way these are transposed, how organisational (and legal-administrative)

93 Ibid 18–21. There is also inter-sender and intra-sender conflict, which deal with different pressures coming from within the organization. In this case these distinctions are important, but they will be considered when analysing organizational culture.

94 Ibid 22.

norms affect decision-making, and finally how personal biases and/or preferences both toward clients and toward the governing authorities guide the way bureaucrats respond to objective ambiguity.

Critics of the approach of treating the bureaucrat as being influenced by contradictions between individual factors and institutional ideals might point out that in their function, any role other than that of bureaucrat is – or should at least be – irrelevant. This approach treats the bureaucrat as if being enclosed in a sort of Weberian 'iron cage', removed from any other ideals, identities, or considerations. Role theory allows us to notice that other identities not only matter, but they are necessary in making decisions in ambiguous environments. In practice, then, compliance depends on information gathered from many different roles. The line of reasoning presented here should allow for a study of the effects of this relationship. Yet, from a normative point of view, this would mean that the other roles of bureaucrats may be a good thing from the point of view of effectiveness, but it may block reaching an objective that was decided in a democratic way. "Street-level workers occupy the bottom tier of our public and private bureaucracies, and yet their actions shape the public's experiences with the state and assessments of the state's legitimacy."[95] Even if the definition of citizenship is expanded and taken to include the broader concept of 'European citizen,' the premise remains unchanged: the ideals of an institution will be weighed against the ideals that come with belonging to other roles, and ambiguity will push workers to make decisions based on the outcome of such reflection.

Some attention should also be given to the argument that the discretionary space observed for bureaucrats is how the system is supposed to work. This is, for example, what is referred to as street-level bureaucrats dealing with 'cases of hitch,' or 'cases of trouble.'[96] Essentially, slight conflicts between practices and circumstances cause cases of hitch, where bureaucrats are forced to make minor adjustments for proper implementation. Other cases, those of trouble, are deeper conflicts between norms and institutional performance, when a re-examination of assumptions about practice is needed. In both cases, it shows use of the discretionary decision-making as a means for controlling political decisions that do not align to reality on the ground. Much evidence has been presented to show this kind of reasoning on behalf of bureaucrats in different

95 Maynard-Moody and Musheno (n 49) S19.

96 Ibid S18.

fields.[97] Take, for instance, the example below which analyses the interactions of education bureaucrats with immigration policy. It was concluded that

> teachers and school leaders are attempting to help students feel safe at school and support them when they may actually be unsafe at home, on public transportation, or walking in their community … [There] was intentional resistance on the part of the school personnel to ensure that a student would continue to have the opportunity to learn and the freedom to pursue her education. It is clear that it is unsafe for immigrant students to participate in direct action or active resistance to the current administration. However, these teachers are no longer remaining politically neutral or encouraging passive acceptance.[98]

While the case study above only looks at one community in the U.S.A., "the problem of reconciling democratic values with the unavoidable bureaucratic discretion that plagues democratic theory at the domestic level looms even larger in the global case."[99]

This chapter has shown how policy implementation can be understood by looking the discretionary space within which street-level bureaucrats manoeuvre. Certainly, a policy can look much different in implementation than in adoption, making the study of what happens between the two difficult.[100] Part of these difficulties arise from a treatment of the policy objectives as a given: a belief that its architects both know what they want, and that what they want is communicated unambiguously. There seems to be an assumption that "policy makers can choose the level of clarity of a policy, that policies are ambiguous because of some form of inadequacy in policy making. … In fact, policies are negotiated in a way that makes the level of clarity no more accessible to

97 James F. Spriggs, 'Explaining Federal Bureaucratic Compliance with Supreme Court Opinions' (1997) 50 *Political Research Quarterly* 567; Paul Teske and Julie Laumann, 'Principals, Agents, and the Impact of Regulatory Federalism on the Savings-and-Loans Crisis of the 1980s' (2003) 3 *State Politics & Policy Quarterly* 139; Meredith I. Honig, 'Street-Level Bureaucracy Revisited: Frontline District Central-Office Administrators as Boundary Spanners in Education Policy Implementation' (2006) 28 *Educational Evaluation and Policy Analysis* 357.

98 Chandler P. Miranda, 'Checks, Balances, and Resistance: The Impact of an Anti-Immigrant Federal Administration on a School for Immigrant Teenagers' (2017) 48 *Anthropology & Education Quarterly* 376, 383.

99 Allen Buchanan and Robert O. Keohane, 'The Legitimacy of Global Governance Institutions' (2006) 20 *Ethics and International Affairs* 405, 417.

100 Baier, March, and Saetren, (n 76) 197.

arbitrary choice than other vital parts of the policy."[101] Talk of the concept of implementation usually leads to images of consistent and clear norms simply being executed as they were envisioned. This approach creates the problems that fog our understanding of what happens between policy adoption and implementation.

The trends in literature discussed in this chapter point to the fact that bureaucratic discretionary implementation is critical in an analysis of how the push and pull in EU policy integration manifests itself in practice. The ordinary arrangement of selecting a constrained number of agents who can make decisions in the interest of a large, heterogeneous polity is entangled on account of the indistinct character of the EU's boundary limitations with different institutions of government inside its own territory. "It is precisely because discussions on the rules of the game are not the province of a given entity that they can occur at any time or place in the system" – including during the phase of bureaucratic implementation.[102] A larger discretionary space, which presents gaps in information necessary for making decisions, can either help implementation in local contexts, or it can lead to noncompliant behaviour. All of this points to bureaucratic decision-making as a process guided not only by the norms of bureaucratic institutions, but also by considerations unrelated to explicit job requirements.

101 Ibid 205.

102 Lord and Magnette, (n 88) 197.

CHAPTER 3

The Common European Asylum System

The first step in understanding the bureaucratic discretionary implementation of asylum policy means thoroughly understanding what the Common European Asylum System is, what it isn't, and how its construction may or may not be conductive to ambiguous transpositions. Originally, the CEAS was thought of as a set of minimum standards for asylum procedures in the context of enforcing the idea of a European Union without internal frontiers. The need of a common system of rules and procedures for asylum emerged at the same time as the Single European Act (SEA) established the single market. The SEA's establishment of a European market without frontiers meant that border checks within the EU had to be abolished, and new strategies for managing a borderless Union were needed. This necessity was cemented in 1992, when the Maastricht Treaty called for the EU "to promote economic and social progress which is balanced and sustainable, in particular through the creation of an area without internal frontiers."

What these changes in the fundamental scope of action of the EU meant was that with the abolition of internal border, the role of external borders had to be redefined. Asylum had to be approached now not as a matter of individual Member State competences, but rather as a policy whose implementation had to be coordinated with other European neighbours. The sections that follow will try to trace exactly the development of the CEAS as it is today, but understanding the larger conversations taking place in Europe at the time, particularly the re-negotiation of the scope of the Union, is crucial to understanding the motivations behind the measures proposed.

While the first official mention of the need to establish a Common European Asylum System was made in Tampere, at the European Council Meeting in October 1999, harmonisation of the EU's asylum policies has been called for since much earlier. When the Tampere conclusions claim that the Council has "agreed to work towards establishing a Common European Asylum System, based on the full and inclusive application of the Geneva Convention,"[1] it built on a call for harmonisation of asylum policies that went back as far as 1986. And while the Tampere Council conclusions and the subsequent legislation

1 Council of the European Union 'Presidency Conclusions, Tampere European Council' 15–16 October 1999.

 | DOI:10.1163/9789004700826_004

that emerged had placed focus and emphasis on the rights of asylum seekers, earlier discussions from the European Council, detailed below, show a development of asylum policies whose starting point is based on a need for exclusion, not protection of rights.

One of the earliest mentions of a common approach to asylum in an official EU document is from the European Council Conclusions from December 1986. Concerted action is called for so that "the right to asylum is not abused."[2] It was decided here that asylum should not be granted for economic and financial reasons, and that cooperation is needed in conducting extraditions, dealing with document forgery, and for preventing illegal immigration. The first mention of asylum, then, does not come in the context of upholding the Geneva Convention or offering adequate protections, but it is strongly guided by arguments linked to security and national sovereignty. Referring to the larger discussions regarding the Sigle European Act, these arguments make sense. The December 1986 Conclusions open by stating that the "Member States which have not already done so aim to ratify the Single European Act in time for it to enter into force on 1 January 1987."[3] It is in this context of a growing call for cooperation in an unprecedented number of fields, coupled with a changing dynamic of internal borders and sharing of competences needed to develop the necessary "cohesion in the implementation of the internal market and other community policies," that led to the motivations behind establishing coherent asylum policies. At that time, the focus was not on international protection; it was rather on ensuring that the new system of no internal borders could be implemented without a hitch. By 1989, 10 years before Tampere took place, the Council officially calls for harmonised asylum policies, by asking for an inventory of national policies of asylum, visas, and the crossing of external frontiers, "with a view of achieving harmonisation."[4] This first call for harmonisation immediately led to what is the cornerstone of today's CEAS: the 1990 Dublin Convention for determining the state responsible for examining applications for asylum.

While the SEA, and the measures necessary to achieve its implementation, guided the necessity of establishing a common asylum policy, the Treaty on European Union (TEU), signed in Maastricht, 1992, ensured that a legal basis was created on which a truly harmonised system could be established. Article K

2 Council of the European Union 'Presidency Conclusions, London European Council' December 6, 1986.

3 Ibid 1.

4 Council of the European Union 'Presidency Conclusions, Strasbourg European Council' December 8–9, 1989.

established "the need for cooperation in the fields of justice and home affairs," while K.1 explicitly states that "for the purposes of achieving the objectives of the Union, in particular the free movement of persons, and without prejudice to the powers of the European Community, Member States shall regard [asylum policy] as a matter of common interest." Furthermore, the Declaration on asylum annexed to the treaty states that "the Council will consider as a matter of priority questions concerning Member States' asylum policies, with the aim of adopting, by the beginning of 1993, common action to harmonise aspects of them." It is expected, then, that calls for much more cooperation in the field should intensify, but also that cleavages emerge because of increased demand for cooperation. And, as the previous chapter argued, such cleavages are often resolved by relying on discretion.

Indeed, during the early 1990s the EU's calls for harmonisation became more frequent and more explicit, and even more so after 1992. In 1990, this time at the Council Meeting in Rome, the European Union Council called for a review of how asylum activities at the national level can be brought into the ambit of the union and made clear the need for a harmonised policy on the right to asylum. By 1991, at the initiative of the German delegation, an immediate and preparatory measure was required from Member States regarding the work required for harmonisation. These are clearly done in anticipation of the importance that such policy will play in the maintenance of the border-free Union, which happened officially in 1992 with the TEU.

Since the TEU made asylum a matter of common interest, the surrendering of sovereignty in a field that had been until recently untouched began to simmer. By 1993, as the plans for closer cooperation on asylum began to grow, difficulty in reaching actionable agreements were also becoming apparent. The conclusions from the December council meeting explicitly congratulates the plan of action in the field of Justice and Home Affairs, and it reaffirms the commitment to a tighter cooperation for asylum policies, while also "bearing in mind Member State's reservation on the implementation of common action regarding asylum."[5] Furthermore, the developments of the early 1990s were still centred on the goal of protecting a border-free union, rather than a delivery of human rights. Yet, by the middle of the decade, as another Treaty revision was underway, a shift started to occur.

Over the years following these earliest calls for cooperation and harmonisation, the topic of asylum was a near constant present on agenda discussions

5 Council of the European Union 'Presidency Conclusions, Brussels European Council' December 10–11, 1993.

of the Council. However, by 1998 other elements that deviate from the original goals and needs of a common asylum policy start to emerge. Calls for temporary protection schemes, Eurodac system for fingerprinting, and a decision to establish the High-Level Working Group on Asylum and Migration[6] indicate that now more humanitarian rationales are slowly beginning to motivate action. The text of the Treaty of Amsterdam Amending the Treaty on European Union helps understand this change in focus. For the first time, the Treaty now calls not only for asylum policy as a way of maintaining the internal market and free movement of persons, but also for adopting measure in accordance with the Geneva Convention and the 1967 protocol. The measures of the mechanism for determining the Member State responsible for reviews an application, minimum reception standards, qualification standards and procedures standards are all, with the Treaty of Amsterdam, given a legal basis to move forward.

These developments led to the Tampere Council Meeting in 1999, the same year the Treaty of Amsterdam was set to go into force. As a way for adhering to the calls for action set out by the new TEU, the Common European Asylum System is mentioned by name for the first time. Once again, the original motivations behind the system emerge, with an acknowledgement that the Union must "develop common policies on asylum and immigration, while taking into account the need for a consistent control of external border to stop illegal immigration and to combat those who organise it and commit related international crimes." The balance is struck, however, at least compared to the first mention of harmonised asylum from 1986. The Geneva Convention and the principle of non-refoulment are invoked as building blocks of the Common European Asylum System, shifting the discourse more toward granting of protections as the principal motivators behind the CEAS.

The following sections in this chapter will explain, in detail, what elements make up the CEAS, what motivated the emergence of these mechanisms, and how they developed over time. While all of the CEAS instruments will be explained, the Asylum Procedures Directive and the Qualifications Directive will be subjected to extended attention, as these two documents are crucial for assessing the discretionary decision-making powers given, eventually, to street-level bureaucrats.

---

6 Council of the European Union 'Presidency Conclusions, Vienna European Council' December 11–12, 1998.

1 Dublin Regulation

With the CEAS officially becoming a policy goal of the European Union, the Dublin Convention passed in the early 1990s and which entered in force in 1997 would now be seen as one of the founding legislative documents of the system. From this first Dublin Convention, until its third iteration from 2013, the scope of the regulation was greatly expended, often representing the evolving discourse that was taking place on the continent. Since the Dublin Convention, this legislation was meant to lay down the principles upon which the state responsible for analysing an asylum application is supposed to be determined. With the establishment of the border-free Schengen zone it became clear that other than ensuring the integrity of the border-free Union, a mechanism for preventing asylum shopping was also needed. Asylum shopping refers to an asylum seeker choosing countries based on perceived benefits of being a refugee in that place, rather than an urgent need for protection. Dublin II, adopted in 2003, reaffirmed this criterion, while also expanding on the protection of rights. Furthermore, given the Treaty developments that happened in the late 1990s, Dublin II brought the mechanism for determining a Member State responsible for assessing an asylum application firmly within the confines of EU law. It was also with Dublin II that the EURODAC system for fingerprinting was introduced, thus adding another moving part to an already complex system.

Dublin II did expand greatly on the details that the Dublin Convention left vague. Special protections for unaccompanied minors and a more comprehensive definition of 'family member' were introduced. Changes also included prioritizing unaccompanied minors with family members in a Member State and clarifying the responsibility of processing asylum applications for family members with false identities or counterfeit documents. Dublin III, on the other hand, expanded greatly on many of the issues that Dublin II proposed, and aimed for much deeper integration of competences. This new regulation also clarifies and makes explicit the hierarchy criteria for determining a state responsible, affirming that family reunification is the first and foremost consideration that needs to be made when assessing a state responsible for handling a claim to asylum. 'Stateless persons' are also specifically covered in this iteration for the first time. The evolving complexity of the larger asylum system that Dublin III is a part of also becomes more apparent. Article 3, for instance, now claims that the sending of an applicant back to a Third Country should be done in accordance with Directive 2013/32/EU (Procedures Directive), whereas Dublin II called for this action to be done in accordance with the 1951 Convention Relating to the Status of Refugees.

Despite this expansion in scope, Dublin still faces several criticisms for perceived shortcomings in how it tackles the issues it means to regulate. Some argue that since migratory routes of asylum seekers are focused on a handful of countries along the external borders, the EU must be aware of the effect that Dublin has on burden-sharing, considering that the requirements of Dublin III were partially suspended during the 2015 crisis of mass arrivals.[7] Namely, the argument is that Dublin hinders those countries that lie at the external borders and are first point of entry on major migratory routes. Furthermore, Dublin aims to stem the practice of asylum-shopping, while such a strategy of seeking protection may be entirely justified from the point of view of the asylum seeker. Asylum seekers might have motivations based on linguistic, ethno-cultural, religious, or professional reasons to believe they are better suited to thrive in a certain country. The fact that such "factors are not taken into account suggests that the normative focus of EU refugee protection rules has shifted away from the refugee."[8] Legal developments in the EU during this time, however, would point to the opposite: The Union now has the legal tools not only to implement asylum policy for the sake of maintaining an internal market, but also for ensuring proper adherence to the principles of the Geneva Convention. If focus is shifting away from the refugee, it is purposefully receding to the original motivations behind the CEAS.

As shown in earlier sections, the EU never really focused its rules to the benefit of the refugees in the first place, but rather in fighting illegal migration, trans-border crime, and protecting the integrity of frontiers.[9] In a study for the European Parliament drafted by Guild, Costello, Garlick, and Moreno-Lax,[10] the authors argue that, as long as this mechanism is entirely based on coercion, it will be incapable of serving as a solution to the problems of burden-sharing or offering adequate protection. A problem such as this suggests as solution the restructuring of the entire asylum system that does a better job a redistributing responsibility. This means that it must be thought about how to approach burden sharing in a way that shows solidarity with the Member States most likely

7 See for example Nevena Nancheva, 'The Common European Asylum System and the Failure to Protect: Bulgaria's Syrian Refugee Crisis' (2015) 15 *Southeast European and Black Sea Studies* 439.

8 Ibid 444.

9 Eiko Thielemann and Carolyn Armstrong, 'Understanding European Asylum Cooperation under the Schengen/Dublin System: a Public Goods Framework' (2013) 22 *European Security* 148.

10 Elspeth Guild, Cathryn Costello, Madeline Garlick, and Violeta Moreno-Lax, 'Enhancing the Common European Asylum System and Alternatives to Dublin' [2015] *CEPS Papers in Liberty and Security in* Europe no. 83.

to receive large numbers of applications, but also with the asylum seekers. Brekke and Brochmann,[11] meanwhile, have found in their work that migrants, despite their wish apply for asylum in a second country, are often restricted by the Dublin Regulation. The preferences of migrants do not always match to the Dublin requirements, thus creating a tension between supranational conventions and a fair management of asylum seekers. It should be noted that some of the early criticisms of the Dublin Convention were eventually addressed by the European Union. Hurwitz claimed, before Dublin II was proposed, that the Convention "does not include applications for humanitarian protection, the conditions for family reunification are too strictly defined, and most importantly the difficulty of providing strong evidence of illegal entry into the Member States renders the Convention useless in many cases."[12] These criticisms have been addressed, to one degree or another, in the second and third iterations of the Dublin mechanism.

2 EUAA and EURODAC

Implementing the Dublin Regulation, as well as ensuring that granting of asylum is done in a fair and responsible manner, is highly dependent on the workings of two CEAS mechanisms whose specific aim is to assist Member States in meeting their asylum obligations: the European Union Agency for Asylum (EUAA, formerly the European Asylum Support Office, or EASO) and the European Dactyloscopy (EURODAC) mechanism. Both, whether they are an institution, as the former, or a fingerprint database as the latter, have as purpose is to aid national bureaucracies to reach an equitable decision in cases of asylum.

2.1 *The European Union Agency for Asylum* (EUAA)

For the analysis here, it is important to look at the effect that EASO has had on discretionary implementation. As predecessors to the EUAA, this institution, which was set up in 2011 by Regulation (EU) 439/2011, was intendent to act as a centre for expertise on asylum, giving support in particular to countries who find themselves under a lot of pressure from large influx of potential refugees.

11 Jan-Paul Brekke and Grete Brochmann, 'Stuck in Transit: Secondary Migration of Asylum Seekers in Europe, National Differences, and the Dublin Regulation' (2015) 28 *Journal of Refugee Studies* 145.

12 Agnès Hurwitz, 'The 1990 Dublin Convention: A Comprehensive Assessment' (1999) 11 *International Journal of Refugee Law* 646.

The agency itself had limited personnel and financial resources, as well as no decision-making powers in terms of asylum applications. Nevertheless, EASO and the EUAA have become crucial in the debate taking place regarding who should have control over territorial borders, and according to which standards should access to third country nationals be given into the European space of social positions.[13] While EASO played a central role in providing necessary information to bureaucratic actors, such as information of what are considered safe third countries, the existence of this institution added a level of ambiguity in everyday decision making of street-level decision makers. Since inter-sender conflict refers to the ambiguity emerging from pressures and expectation from different points, EASO and the EUAA have added another layer of expectations of role behaviour. By having to interact with these EU level institutions, "bureaucratic actors are engaged in complex relational positioning which are indicative of the dynamics of power and counter-power surrounding the institutionalisation of a European asylum administrative field."[14]

The original ideas for establishing EASO go back as far as 2004, 7 years before the agency actually became operational.[15] The reasoning behind its creation, as it was promoted by traditional recipients of asylum seekers, most notably Germany, the UK, France, and the Netherlands, was that an institution such as EASO was needed in order to push for the harmonisation of asylum standards. The argument was that the lack of harmonisation was what led to an uneven distribution of asylum seekers in the countries previously listed. On the other hand, southern European countries insisted on maintaining divergent standards of asylum, citing this as a counterweight to the burdens they endured as countries that constituted Europe's external borders.[16] Regulation (EU) 439/2010, which calls for EASO's establishment, reflects this push and pull between countries. Recital 14 of the Preamble stated that EASO should have no powers to interfere in the decision making of Member States' asylum authorities, while allowing EASO to be a hub for expert knowledge necessary for implementing Europe's asylum standards.

---

13 Stephanie Schneider and Carolin Nieswandt, 'EASO – Support Office or Asylum Authority? Boundary Disputes in the European Field of Asylum Administration' (2018) 43 *Österreichische Zeitschrift Für Soziologie* 13, 15.

14 Ibid.

15 Françoise Comte, 'A New Agency Is Born in the European Union: The European Asylum Support Office' (2010) 12 *European Journal of Migration and Law* 373.

16 Steffen Angenendt and Roderick Parkes, 'A New Impulse for EU Asylum Policy? The Potential of the European Asylum Support Office' [2010] *Stifung Wissenschaft Und Politik Comments no. 21.*

With the 2015 crisis of mass arrivals on European shores, however, EASO's role, both practical and perceived, altered drastically. Expert missions were now deployed to hotspots in Italy and Greece, with personnel now playing an active role in the assessment of applications. While it is still the role of national administrations to make formal decisions, EASO staff has been actively involved in the interviewing and evidence assessment.[17] During the same time, members of the European Parliament's LIBE committee had referred to EASO as the main coordinator of the Common European Asylum System. Echoing these perceptions, the European Commission submitted in 2016 a Proposal for a Regulation on the European Union Agency for Asylum, thus repealing Regulation 439/2010 which established EASO. Part of the proposed reform of the CEAS, such a measure gave the European Union Agency for Asylum an enhanced mandate which would enable it not only to provide support to Member States, but also to reinforce and complement individual asylum and receptions system. In other words, it got more decision-making powers, including the possibility of involvement in the entire or parts of procedure for international protection at the administrative stage.[18]

Even with this reform, the constitutional struggles described by Adler-Nissen, which could also be relevant to the EUAA's role, are not resolved.[19] Specifically, the issue of exercise of sovereignty remains unaddressed, and thus ambiguity regarding the CEAS' implementation persists.

> In line with the subsidiarity principle, the CEAS entails a Europeanisation of legislative and judicative functions, but operates on the assumption that executive functions, and administrative discretion in the taking of individual asylum decisions in particular, should remain with the competent authorities of the member states.[20]

This points to an understanding of sovereignty in the context of European asylum policy as not only being defined as the differentiation of boundaries between states, but also between different levels of governance, on one hand,

---

17 Evangelia Tsourdi, 'Bottom-Up Salvation? From Practical Cooperation towards Joint Implementation through the European Asylum Support Office' (2016) 1 *European Papers* 997.

18 Commission, 'Proposal for a Regulation of the European Parliament and of the Council on the European Union Agency for Asylum' COM(2016) 271 final.

19 Rebecca Adler-Nissen, 'Symbolic Power in European Diplomacy: the Struggle between National Foreign Services and the EU's External Action Service' (2013) 40 *Review of International Studies* 657.

20 Schneider and Nieswandt (n 13) 18.

and on the other hand between political, bureaucratic, and legal spheres of influence. Still, the EU does not hold the power to confer rights to those seeking protection.

In this case, the work conducted by bureaucrats must be seen in the context of boundaries delimitated by European spheres intersecting domestic ones. Since the EUAA's influence is supposed to extend only to the point where domestic administrative discretion begins, the discretionary space of the bureaucrat is crucial in understanding where said boundary lies. Concepts such as 'Europe' or 'domestic' must be organic in the case of implementing the CEAS, as their reach is determined by the discretionary space of the bureaucrats. The very existence of the EUAA means that the actions of street-level bureaucrats must be conceptualized not as a rigid set of procedures, but as position-takings within a field of possibilities.[21] Indeed, there seem to be several argumentative similarities between the conceptualisation of position-takings within a field of possibilities, as referred to by Schneider and Nieswandt, and decisions made based on role conflicts within a discretionary space. The most relevant here, however, is the fact that decisions made are a result of reactions to the environment in which the work is performed, i.e., the subjective ambiguity referenced by role conflict theorists.

In their conclusions regarding the work of the EASO in relation to domestic actors of administration, Schneider and Nieswandt show how their position-takings argument is a mirror image role conflict theory. Belonging to an EASO network used to represent a different role than that of belonging to a domestic bureaucracy. Information emanating from this role, then, aided bureaucrats in navigating the ambiguities of asylum administration. From this perspective,

> cooperation with or via the EASO provides important symbolic resources for navigating the grey zone between politics and 'pure' administration in their own particular work contexts. ... where and how national civil servants work on maintaining or shifting boundaries depends not only on their belonging to a particular national authority but also on the specific types of capital they have accumulated in the course of transnational cooperation.[22]

The EUAA, as EASO's successor, then serves not only as a formal hub for expertise aimed at helping national administrations make decisions. The agency can

21 Ibid 18–20.

22 Ibid 31–32.

also be conceptualised as a role creator, providing information to street-level bureaucrats to make decisions in ambiguous national frameworks.

2.2 *EURODAC*

Regulation (EU) No 603/2013 on the establishment of Eurodac for the comparison of fingerprints, or the Eurodac Regulation, is a tool used for the effective application of the Dublin Regulation. Essentially, Eurodac is a fingerprinting database established originally in 2003, is meant to provide a way for authorities to be able to identify if an asylum applicant has previously lodged an application in another member state, thus facilitating the implementation of Dublin. According to Article 1 of Regulation (EU) 603/2013,

> a system known as "Eurodac" is hereby established, the purpose of which shall be to assist in determining which Member State is to be responsible pursuant to Regulation (EU) No 604/2013 for examining an application for international protection lodged in a Member State by a third-country national or a stateless person, and otherwise to facilitate the application of Regulation (EU) No 604/2013 under the conditions set out in this Regulation.

As a result, this database includes fingerprints, gender, and the date and location where information was recorded. When a new set of data is taken, this is submitted to the Eurodac central unit, which immediately compares this to all data previously gathered. If a positive match is found, then the relevant authorities that submitted the new information will be able to tell where and when the asylum applicant's information was previously taken.

While Eurodac itself is more of a technological tool to aid in the implementation of the Common European Asylum System, an expansion of the scope of this tool has been in the works. The first iteration of the Regulation, passed in 2000, only allowed for the database to be used strictly for asylum purposes. The current version, however changed the primary purpose, which was to verify the first country of asylum where a claimant filed a request for protection. It now allows police forces and Europol access to the database so that fingerprints can be compared for police investigations, as well as registration of irregular migrants.[23]

---

23 Lehte Roots, 'The New EURODAC Regulation: Fingerprints as a Source of Informal Discrimination' (2015) 5 *Baltic Journal of European Studies* 108.

The potential infringement on privacy and data protection are, at least on paper, dealt with in Regulation (EU) 603/2013. Article 12, for example, specifies that all data stored from asylum seekers must be erased after 10 years. Meanwhile Article 13, calls for the immediate erasing of data if the asylum seeker becomes a citizen of any Member State. Furthermore, Chapter VI spells out explicitly the necessary steps that must be followed for a request for fingerprint comparison to be made (Article 19), as well as the conditions upon which access may be granted to national authorities (Article 20), or Europol (Article 21). Finally, Articles 23 and 24 call for lawful, efficient, and up to date gathering and transmission of data, while Article 29 spells out the rights of the data subject. These include being aware of the purpose of data collection, who the requesting authorities are, and the right to access the data referring to him or her.

Nevertheless, Eurodac is still more than a simple electronic tool. As Tsianos and Kuster claimed, "Eurodac is de facto an instrument for managing migration and regulating mobility ... in consequence, we understand Eurodac as both a technology work that breaks down the body of migrants into data streams and as part of Europe's border."[24] The database, as such, fits perfectly within the definition of a digital border, but not a definition that delineated between the technological and the physical aspects of border control. Rather, Eurodac should be regarded as a digital aspect of existing societal norms. After all, digitalisation is a part of the larger societal structures and institutions in which it is developed and is as much a result of social construct as of technological advances.

3 Receptions Conditions Directive

The Reception Conditions Directive, formally known as Directive 2013/33/EU of 26 June 2013 laying down standards for the reception of applicants for international protection, is a mechanism meant to "apply during all stages and types of procedures concerning applications for international protection, in all locations and facilities hosting applicants and for as long as they are allowed to remain on the territory of the Member States as applicants," (Recital 8). Several instances make the provisions of the Receptions Conditions Directive unapplicable, according to Article 3: requests for diplomatic or territorial asylum

24 Vassilis S. Tsianos and Brigitta Kuster, 'Eurodac in Times of Bigness: The Power of Big Data within the Emerging European IT Agency' (2016) 31 *Journal of Borderlands Studies* 235, 236.

submitted to representations of Member States, or when the provisions of Council Directive 2001/55/EC on temporary protection in the event of a mass influx are applicable.

The latter of the two permissible situations for derogations is of particular interest, and not only because the provisions of the temporary protection directive were not activated even during the 2015 crisis of mass arrivals. In fact, the first time these were used was 21 years after the Directive was passed, as a response to the Russian invasion of Ukraine in 2022. At the time when the Reception Conditions Directive was recast, Directive 2001/55/EC was the mechanism that the EU had in place to deal with a hypothetical mass influx. It makes sense, for the purposes of clarity and specificity, for the drafters to reference the legislative mechanism in place for burden sharing in cases of mass arrivals. Nonetheless, many other mechanisms for dealing with such crises have been developed since, and likely many more will be developed. If the principle behind Article 3(3) stands, then the EU does not consider the obligations of the Receptions Conditions Directive to be necessary if mechanisms for dealing with mass influx of displaced persons are active.

Member States have several obligations that emerge because of this directive. They must inform applicants of any benefits and obligations they have regarding reception conditions (Art. 5), and within three days of the lodging of an application, authorities must issue a document that recognises the status of asylum seeker (Art. 6). On the other hand, Article 7 gives countries the right to restrict the area of movement of an asylum seeker, but the "assigned area shall not affect the unalienable sphere of private life and shall allow sufficient scope for guaranteeing access to all benefits under this Directive." Furthermore, mechanisms for assessing individual request to leave said area must be in place.

The Directive, in fact, lays down many of the standards for benefits that are ever present in policy and academic debate. Several articles lay down the grounds based on which an applicant may be placed in detention, the guarantees that must be made for detained applicants, the conditions for detention, as well as the requirement that "the health, including mental health, of applicants in detention who are vulnerable persons shall be of primary concern to national authorities," (Art. 11). Family unity is kept as the guiding principle when housing is provided (Art. 12), medical screening is required only on grounds of public health (Art. 13), and education, employment, vocational training, and healthcare must all be provided to applicants (Arts. 14–16, 19).

Material conditions are, however, among the key elements of the Directive, and these were so in the early iterations of the CEAS as well.

> The policy of the Directive is to emphasise these material conditions since they are apt to determine the asylum seeker's 'well-being and ... ability to start the integration process.' Article 13 [of the first iteration] establishes the grounds for the welfare of asylum seekers from their first day of arrival and is crucial in setting basic reception conditions.[25]

The practical applicability of such material conditions has been subjected to questioning from the very beginning. Several reports point to problems in implementation. Particularly with its initial applicability in the UK, an EU Member State at the time, consultations regarding the implementation of the Directive yielded doubts about the ability to meet the levels of material assistance prescribed, including adequate healthcare. Furthermore, it was reported in 2005 that the material conditions were at least somewhat provided. This includes caveats that housing centres are often at capacity, and that healthcare was limited in certain countries especially for those whose applications had been rejected.[26] Given the discussion that Europe has had since the 2015 crisis, these are the issues that practitioners have in fact identified as most problematic today.[27] From the perspective of the asylum seekers, this translates to a life "characterized by uncertainty, passivity, powerless, and gradual disqualification."[28]

4 Qualifications Directive

To be able to understand the construction of the discretionary space of bureaucrats, there must be an assurance that the same type of discretionary space is analysed – i.e., that the breeding ground for ambiguity is kept within the same policy realm. This will be done by focusing on officials involved in making first instance decisions regarding granting or rejecting an application for international protection. While this means analysing legislation regulating one specific aspect of the asylum system, it is important to note that two

25 Richard Plender, 'EU Immigration and Asylum Policy – The Hague Programme and the Way Forward' (2008) 9 *ERA Forum* 301, 307.

26 Ibid 309–310.

27 See Charles O'Sullivan and Delia Ferri, 'The Recast Reception Conditions Directive and the Rights of Asylum Seekers with Disabilities: Opportunities, Challenges and the Quest for Reform' (2020) 22 *European Journal of Migration and Law* 272.

28 Marko Valenta and Berit Berg, 'User Involvement and Empowerment among Asylum Seekers in Norwegian Reception Centres' (2010) 13 *European Journal of Social Work* 483.

distinct EU Directives govern this step of decision making. Unlike Regulations, tracking how Directives are filtered through country-specific systems would provide for opportunities to analyse how national contexts shape the absorption of European standards, thus ruling out an analysis based on the Dublin Regulation. It is here that lies that opportunity to observe how the discretionary space of bureaucrats is constructed not only directly through the discretion given in national systems, but also by the ambiguity that is inherent to EU Directives.[29] Meanwhile, the scope of the Receptions Conditions Directive falls outside of the traditional realm of asylum granting/denying decisions. As such, the remainder of this chapter will take an in-depth look at the Asylum Procedures Directive and the Qualifications Directive.

I will employ frame analysis which will point to the emergence of a framework for multilevel implementation of the CEAS, which I can then use to identify ambiguities in these directives. This will include ambiguities found in specific clauses of the directives, or those arising from conflicts between directive clauses and other sources of information. The first questions that must be addressed, however, are how to identify ambiguities, and what does this work consider to be an ambiguous clause? An ambiguous clause in legislative documents refers to a provision or section that is unclear, vague, or open to multiple interpretations, leading to potential confusion or disputes in its application. Building on the exploration in the second chapter, this book takes ambiguous clauses to be those that contain imprecise language, conflicting terms, or inadequate specification of conditions. This allows for the possibility that different individuals or entities may interpret the language in divergent ways. Identifying ambiguous clauses in legislative documents involves a meticulous analysis, including close reading, definition of key terms, consideration of context, and seeking legal guidance, i.e., in the case law of the CJEU.

Identifying ambiguities in the two directives, then, will follow two steps: first, a literal analysis will be done to point out where discretionary and non-discretionary clauses lie according to the wording. The second step, which the following chapter will handle, goes further in depth and looks at how the Court of Justice of the EU interprets ambiguities that arise in implementation, at time providing context from interpretations by other institutions, be them judicial (such as the European Court of Human Rights), or executive (like EASO or EUAA). Ambiguities do not only lie in linguistically discretionary clauses. In many cases, wording that at first glance seems non-discretionary is

29 See Robert Zbiral, Sebastiaan Princen, and Hubert Smekal, 'Differentiations through flexibility in implementation: Strategic and substantive use of discretion in EU directives' (2022) 24 *European Union Politics* 102.

fraught with interpretative ambiguity. In these cases, the case-law of the Court, through the preliminary procedure, serves as a tool to identify ambiguities that a black-letter analysis cannot.

Directive 2011/95/EU of the European Parliament and of the Council, also known as the Qualifications Directive, was first adopted in 2004, and originally had as its purpose to "lay down minimum standards for the qualification of third country nationals or stateless persons as refugees or as persons who otherwise need international protection and the content of the protection granted." In the current iteration of this Directive, however, the purpose was no longer to lay down minimum standards, but rather to "lay down standards for qualification of third country nationals ... as beneficiaries of international protection, for uniform status of refugees or for persons eligible for subsidiary protection." By removing the term "minimum standards," the European Union signalled that they are no longer interested in pursuing policy approximation, but rather a clear path toward harmonisation.

The first substantial implication of this Directive is that it is the first multinational tool used to harmonise what complementary protection is – "subsidiary protection" in EU terms. This is important because, ever since the passing of the 1951 Convention Relating to the Status of Refugees, states have been confronted with the reality that not every person seeking protection fits into a pre-established category. European states have often times shown great awareness of this dynamic and have usually allowed many that do not neatly fit into a refugee category to receive protection, nonetheless. Yet, until 2004 this sort of protection varied largely from one country to the next.[30] By introducing the term 'subsidiary protection,' the EU sought to bring under one umbrella a strategy for granting protections that was used more widespread than any of the conditions stipulated in 1951. With the passing of the Qualifications Directive, not only were the requirements of the 1951 Convention Relating to the Status of Refugees codified into European legislation, but complementary protections were also beginning to be approximated; no longer would the subsidiary protection regime be left to be implemented without any guidance.

This is crucial because it meant that countries, by the very historical nature of institutional development, had to adapt different realities. While all Member States were already obligated to abide to requirements of the 1951 Convention, it was in the field of this complementary protection that harmonisation could prove more difficult, as the different practices of the time meant that there was

30 Jane McAdam, 'The European Union Qualification Directive: The Creation of a Subsidiary Protection Regime' (2005) 17 *International Journal of Refugee Law* 461.

no emerging model of governance that could be adapted to all Europe. States that were already members of the European Union had to adapt to a uniform system of subsidiary protections. Nonetheless, no new system of protections was created. Ultimately, the Qualifications Directive simply aimed at harmonising existing concepts and methods of subsidiary protection – creating a patchwork of best-practices.[31] It was, by all accounts, a codification of existing approaches to subsidiary protection. States that partook in the creation of this Qualification Directive, i.e., all states that were EU members before 2004, saw a system moulded around what was already in practice. Any of the states that came with the 2004, 2007, or 2013 enlargements adopted a system which was not designed to integrate any of the practices found in their respective institutions.

Such a distinction becomes crucial when analysing the implementation of these acts. The 2004, 2007, and 2013 waves of EU enlargement included countries from the former communist bloc, which came with a very particular style of governance and administration. "If 'complementary protection' describes the role of human rights law in broadening the categories of persons to whom international protection is owed beyond article 1A(2) of the Geneva Convention, then 'subsidiary protection' is a regionally-specific political manifestation of the broader legal concept."[32] If wide differences in implementation of subsidiary protection existed in Member States before 2004, these differences would likely have been much greater had the countries of the later waves of enlargement been considered.

4.1 *The Qualification Directive at First Glance: A Literal Analysis of Discretionary Clauses*

One form of ambiguity, as Chapter 2 argues, is intentional: the discretionary powers built into the Directives as a way for Member States to tailor implementation to national contexts. Such discretion can be observed in the wording of the provisions: the so-called "may" clauses, as opposed to the non-discretionary "shall" clauses. It needs to be noted, nevertheless, that the simple existence of a "shall" clause does not make a provision unambiguous or clear in its objectives. These can still be subject to judicial misunderstandings or improper implementation. It does, however, provide a starting point in identifying the objectives of the EU in drafting this regulation. At least on

31 Ibid 437.
32 Ibid 465.

paper, it is in this analysis that the intention to grant discretionary powers to national authorities is uncovered.

The Qualifications Directive is composed of a total of 177 provisions, spread over 42 articles. Of these, 97 are directly relevant to the issuance of first instance decisions on claims to international protection. Interestingly, of these relevant ones, only 12 grant verbal discretionary powers. These range from provisions which give "simple permissions to act" to "permission to act with reference to national order." In terms of frames of action identified, the discretionary provisions emerge from four: definitions of terminology, supporting evidence, claim processing, and national security. On the other hand, six other frames for action are identified, each composed of non-discretionary clauses. These are actors for protection, content of protection, time parameters, particularly vulnerable applicants, obligation of non-refoulment, and requirement of qualified workers for the implementation of the Directive.

In more specific detail, there are 6 different types of discretionary powers granted. Table 1 lists all different discretionary powers granted, while Table 2 lists the non-discretionary obligations encountered in provisions of first instance decision. These can be categorised as either 'permission' given (i.e., discretion granted to chose certain ways to acting), or obligations (i.e., no discretion to deviate from prescription). Within each, these permissions or obligations can be qualified: done so only within the context of national legal order, only when certain conditions are met, only to adopt more favourable conditions, etc.

Diving further into the provisions of this Directive, a total of 10 different frames of action are identified. A frame of action is considered any overarching theme that a provision governs, thus allowing for a grouping of clauses. While the ten frames are named in the previous paragraph, Table 3 below lists these, alongside the number of provisions that can be grouped into this category based on the taxonomy developed.

From a purely literal analysis, the Qualifications Directive conveys its objectives and how these must be reached. Afterall, with only 12 provisions granting discretionary powers, two of which have to do with the permission to adopt more favourable conditions, such an inference may not seem too far-fetched. That being said, the preliminary ruling procedure of the Court of Justice of the European Union shows that not only are the ambiguities in how to use discretionary powers in the implementation of the discretionary provisions, but a lot of interpretative ambiguity can also be found in provisions pertaining to actors of protection, content of protection, particularly vulnerable applicants, non-refoulment, and other frames which, in a literal reading, convey

TABLE 1 Discretionary provisions in dir. 2011/95/EU

Discretion granted	Number of provisions found in directive 2011/95/EU
Simple permission to act	1
Simple permission to act with reference to national legal order	2
Simple permission to act with certain conditions	4
Simple permission to act under international law and with certain conditions	1
Permission to adopt more favourable conditions	2
Permission to use certain interpretations of terms	2

non-discretionary calls to action. More on this will be explored in the following chapter.

5 Procedures Directive

Directive 2013/32/EU of the European Parliament and of the Council on common procedures for granting and withdrawing international protection, or the Procedures Directive, is a mechanism developed by the European Union in 2013 with the expected goal of both aiding harmonisation efforts and guaranteeing applicant's rights. While at the time of this writing a the EU is in the process of passing a reformed version of the Procedures, namely the Asylum Procedures Regulation, the analysis in this book will focus on the effects of Directive 2013/32/EU, as this is the document that has influenced bureaucratic implementation in the ten years between 2013 and 2023.

The Directive itself establishes proper procedures based on several different considerations. Protection for children or for the family unit, for example, is the most widely appealed to principle, with Articles 7, 11, 14, 15, 25, 31 and 33 all establishing procedures in dealing with these categories of applicants. Another common component of this directive is the reliance on other mechanism of

TABLE 2 Non-discretionary provisions in dir. 2011/95/EU

Non-discretionary obligation	Number of provisions found in directive 2011/95/EU
Obligation to act	19
Obligation to act with reference to national legal order	2
Obligation to act with certain conditions	10
Obligation to act under international law/other EU mechanisms	7
Obligation to act under international law and with certain conditions	2
Obligation to not deviate from the Directive	5
Obligation to use certain interpretation of terms	28
Obligation to use certain interpretation of terms under certain conditions	1
Obligation to act with permissive implementation[a]	11

a "Obligation with permissive implementation" is a hybrid provision: it contains both a non-discretionary and a discretionary clause. More examples of hybrid provisions will be explored in the analysis of the Procedures Directive.

the CEAS, or other international asylum legislation and tools. Article 4, for example, spells out the relationship between authorities bound by the procedures of this directive, and trainings received from EASO (at the time of its passing), requiring that "Member States shall take into account the relevant training established and developed" by such European level entities. Article 37, meanwhile, calls for consultations with EASO to take place in determining which countries are considered safe countries of origin. In total, 6 articles of this Directive spell out the proper procedures in determining Safe Countries of Origin or Safe Third Countries.

Most of the directive, however, deals not with issues specifically defining who should get asylum, as that is the purview of the Qualifications Directive.

TABLE 3 Frames of action in dir. 2011/95/EU

Frame of action	Number of provisions
Definitions	36 – 2 discretionary – 34 non-discretionary
Supporting Evidence	17 – 4 discretionary – 13 non-discretionary
Actors of Protection	4 (all non-discretionary)
Content of Protection	4 (all non-discretionary)
Particularly Vulnerable Applicants	5 (all non-discretionary)
Non-Refoulment	1 (non-discretionary)
Claim Processing	12 – 2 discretionary – 10 non-discretionary
Security	14 – 4 discretionary – 10 non-discretionary
Time Parameters	2 (both non-discretionary)
Qualified Workers	2 (both non-discretionary)

Most of this directive, in fact, spells out administrative procedures for reviewing an application for asylum. In Articles 14, 31, and 33 we find information regarding how accelerated procedures should be carried out. Article 31(8) claims that, if certain criteria are met, "Member States may provide that an examination procedure in accordance with the basic principles and guarantees of [the Directive] be accelerated or conducted at the border or in transit zones." Similarly, Articles 6, 17, 24, 25, 31, and 43 deal with the speed in which the review of an application must be made, and the time in which a decision must be reached. These cover the speed with which an application for international protection must be registered (Article 6), the time allowed for clarifications to be made following an interview (Article 17), speed with which the need for special procedural guarantees must be assessed (Article 24), speed with which an unaccompanied minor must be assigned a representative (Article 25), establishing a 6-month time-limit on the examination of an application (Article 31), or the 4 week time period within which border examination procedures must take place (Article 43). The Directive also sets down the rules for what rights and responsibilities applicants have, as well as the competent authorities reviewing applications, or how proof of persecution must be handled by those reviewing each case.

The Procedures Directive has received its fair share of criticisms. Costello, writing about the first iteration of the Procedures Directive in 2005, points out that due to governments' dispute over the existence of a right to asylum in any particular country, policies are developed with the intent to deflect asylum seekers, rather than provide wider possibilities for protection.[33] The argument, according to Costello, is that the focus on first country of asylum, safe third country, and safe country of origin that we see in the 2005 version of the Directive undermine access to and the integrity of asylum procedures.[34] Safe third country practices, for instance, threaten to place an unevenly heavy burden on new Member States and the countries neighbouring the newly enlarged EU (in 2005). The Directive's failure of addressing the issues of effective protection and meaningful links as a means of transferring asylum applicants elsewhere, and leaving Member States the possibility to, effectively, lower standards of protection offered, make this Directive unable to comply with the principle of *non-refoulment.* Lastly, in a nod to the legacy of how the CEAS came to be developed, Costello argues that the Directive also allows border control issues to trump protection issues, returning yet again to a motivation for refugee management based on security concerns, rather than the need to offer protections.

The recast version of the Asylum Procedures Directive, from 2013, followed much for the same approach as the 2005 Directive. Much like the Qualifications Directive, the scope now shifted from an establishment of minimum standards, to "establishing common procedures for granting and withdrawing international protection," (Article 1). The main difference between the two versions is that the latter of the two strengthens greatly the procedural guarantees that the 2005 version addressed loosely. Applicants are now allowed to submit clarifications following an interview, and new categories of potentially vulnerable applicants were introduced as deserving of special procedural guarantees.[35] The weaknesses identified by Costello in the first version of the directive,

33 Cathryn Costello, 'The Asylum Procedures Directive and the Proliferation of Safe Country Practices: Deterrence, Deflection and the Dismantling of International Protection?' (2005) 7 *European Journal of Migration and Law* 35.

34 Ibid 36.

35 Samantha Velluti, *Reforming the Common European Asylum System – Legislative Developments and Judicial Activism of the European Courts* (Springer 2014).

however, were not fully addressed. The issue of "safe country of origin," is still used to justify the use of accelerated procedures (Article 36). We begin to see a push-and-pull between different motivators behind the requirements of the Directive: the notion of unfounded and abusive claims to protection on one hand, yet the acknowledgement that some migrants are particularly vulnerable and thus deserving of special attention on the other hand.[36]

As the Qualification Directive reflected a patchwork of different systems found across EU, the Procedures Directive reflects similar compromises between political actors and other non-state actors. "The risk of failing common standards and the principles of international refugee law is thus not only a matter of implementation but is already inherent in the directive's design."[37] This means that, while trying to achieve harmonised procedures, the implementation of the Procedures Directive, and indeed of the entire CEAS, is still very much the purview of national administrative structures and political inclinations.

5.1 *Untangling the Procedures Directive: A Literal Analysis of Provisions*

The Asylum Procedures Directive is divided in six chapters, the most notable of which for the current research is Chapter III: Procedures at First Instance. Nevertheless, as the analysis of the Qualifications Directive exemplified, even provisions unrelated to first instance decisions can help in identifying difficulties in interpretation of the Directive in general. Chapter I, entitled General Provisions, establishes everything from the Purpose of the Directive (Article 1), to who the responsible authorities are (Article 4), and the permission to adopt more favourable provisions (Article 5). Chapter II: Basic Principles and Guarantees, enumerates several guaranteed rights and responsibilities of applicants and competent authorities, such the right to remain in the Member State while applications are examined (Article 9), the requirements for a decision by the determining authority (Article 11), to the right to legal assistance (Article 22). Chapter IV, on the other hand, enumerates the procedures for the withdrawal of international protection, while Chapter V details in just one article (Article 46) the right to an effective remedy (appeals procedure), another guaranteed right that is directly related to the requirements of the EU Charter.

36 Cathryn Costello and Emily Hancox, 'The Recast Asylum Procedures Directive 2013/32/EU: Caught between the Stereotypes of the Abusive Asylum-Seeker and the Vulnerable Refugee' in Vincent Chetail, Philippe de Bruycker, and Francesco Maiani (eds), *Reforming the Common European Asylum System: the New European Refugee Law* (Brill Nijhoff 2016).

37 Karin Schittenhelm, 'Implementing and Rethinking the European Union's Asylum Legislation: The Asylum Procedures Directive' (2019) 57 *International Migration* 229.

Finally, Chapter VI, General and Final Provisions, is a mirror image of the final two chapters of the Qualifications Directive, establishing the requirements of inter-institutional cooperation (Article 49), transposition (Article 51) and the entry into force of the Directive (Article 54). Yet the aspect of procedures that deals only with the examination of an application is indeed the one most relevant here.

Following the Asylum Procedures Directive can lead competent authorities to several types of decisions, from a simple granting of protection to a rejection of such an application. Yet, these represent ends on a spectrum of decisions, not a binary choice. Article 32, for example, allows for Member States to consider applications as unfounded if the applicant does not qualify in accordance with the Qualifications Directive, or the instance in which an individual application can be categorised as inadmissible. Lastly, Article 39 even provides that no examination must be conducted in cases where the applicant is seeking to enter the Member State's territory from a safe-third country. Interestingly, there is no article in the Asylum Procedures directive that explicitly enumerates how refugee or subsidiary protection status should be issued. If such a status is granted, this is done only in accordance with Articles 13 and 18 of the Qualifications Directive. The Procedures Directive, in turn, details how to properly reject or not examine an application while maintaining the principle of *non-refoulment*.

In the case of the Asylum Procedures Directive, the literal analysis is even less indicative of the actual level of discretion really granted. Given the remarkably high complexity of this Directive, such analysis provides only a snapshot of discretion, while once again interpretive ambiguity is ubiquitous. Looking verbally at what kind of discretionary powers are given and in what cases is discretion withheld, the Asylum Procedures Directive has 414 relevant provisions spread over 54 articles. Of these, 333 are relevant to first-instance decisions, meaning that a great portion of the provisions must be taken into account during the procedures for reaching a decision at first instance. Of these, a total of 122 provisions use some variation of a 'may' clause, which means that approximately half of first instance provisions of this directive give discretionary powers, or permission to act.

Most of the relevant first instance provisions that grant discretionary powers come from 17 frames, out of 25 total frames identified. These include protection against *refoulment*, border procedures, security, or obligations of applicants, among many others. Interestingly, is that in certain frames we observe no discretion given verbally whatsoever. Access to effective remedy, for instance, has no discretionary provisions. As the analysis from the CJEU will show, however, this is also one of the frames that is most widely subjected to the preliminary

TABLE 4 Discretionary provisions in dir. 2013/32/EU

Discretion granted	Number of relevant provisions found in directive 2013/32/EU
Simple permission to act	32
Simple permission to act with reference to national legal order	12
Simple permission to act with certain conditions	55
Simple permission to act under international law	5
Simple permission to act under international law and with certain conditions	4
Permission to adopt more favourable conditions	1
Permission to choose between the rules	1
Permission to derogate	4
Permission to derogate under certain conditions	7
Permission to Delegate	1

procedure. Of the approximately 200 non-discretionary provisions, almost all frames identified have some sort of non-discretionary provisions. The only case where this does not happen is "security." This indicates that when it comes to making decisions based on national security or public order, in theory Member States have complete discretion in making decisions.

Table 4 breaks down the different types of discretionary powers granted by the Procedures Directive, and Table 5 does the same of the non-discretionary obligations.

From a purely literal analysis, the Asylum Procedures Directive shows a fairly even split between discretionary and non-discretionary provisions. Unlike in the Qualifications Directive, where only 12 provisions granted discretionary powers verbally, the Procedures Directive spread discretion and lack of it over the entire directive, with the notable exception being decisions made under the frame of "security." It is worth noting that this Directive also has 10

TABLE 5 Non-discretionary provisions in dir. 2013/32/EU

Non-discretionary obligation	**Number of relevant provisions found in directive 2011/95/EU**
Obligation to act	138
Obligation to act with reference to national legal order	9
Obligation to act with certain conditions	18
Obligation to act under international law/other EU mechanisms	15
Obligation to act under international law and with certain conditions	1
Obligation to use certain interpretation of terms	20

hybrid provisions, which call for permissive implementation with restrictions (3 provisions), obligation with permissive implementation (2 provisions), and obligation with exceptions (5 provisions). These add to the document's complexity, and this will further be uncovered in the analysis that follows.

This chapter shows that in order to understand how ambiguities make their way in national legislation and bureaucratic practice, first we need to investigate the goals of CEAS and how they developed over time. The earliest calls for harmonisation of asylum policies across Europe concerned with a protection of borders and the internal market, rather than of those in need. In fact, at the earliest Council meetings where this issue was brought up, the conclusions explicitly referred to the need to ensure that asylum is not abused, indicating a deterrence-oriented policy development. Nonetheless, even if deterrence-oriented, those early calls did make it clear that asylum is now a matter of common interest, hence the need for harmonisation. Preparations for implementation of the Treaty of Amsterdam in the late 1990s further emphasized the cleavages among Member States, clearly reluctant to cede sovereignty over border policies. These were now supplemented by a new focus on international protection as a humanitarian matter. Goal ambiguity as to the exact objectives of the system was becoming entrenched in the rules that national actors perpetuated.

The Dublin system is perhaps the perfect example of this. From the Dublin Convention to Dublin II, it can be observed that *the objectives of the Union are a moving target, shifting from deterrence to protection*. Dublin II, for instance, sought to strike a balance between preventing asylum shopping, i.e., limiting movement, while also expanding the rights of applicants. By Dublin III, even more protections are ensured, although the coercive roots dating back to the Convention are still present. This goal ambiguity will be crucial in understanding how national systems implement the rules of the CEAS, especially in the context of ever-increasing calls for harmonisation.

The importance of attention given to discretionary implementation is also evident in the Qualifications and Asylum Procedure Directives. The shift from "minimum" to "common" standards, as well as the introduction of subsidiary protection, shows that asylum is brought more and more into the ambit of European Union policymaking. Implementation, nonetheless, happens at the street-level, and for that to take place ambiguities must be addressed. While the Qualifications Directive expands the scope of protection across the Union, the Asylum Procedures Directive has been criticised for its focus on deterrence-oriented procedures. Because some EU Member States participated in the construction of this system, while latecomers merely adopted an already existing set of rules, harmonising processes through which such goal ambiguities are addressed is crucial in their implementation. The following chapters will explore further the ambiguities in these two directives, by focusing on ambiguities that exist beyond strict literal observations.

CHAPTER 4

Interpretive Ambiguities: Case Law and Guidance

The previous chapter highlighted that, even when considering the formal discretion awarded by specific provisions of the CEAS, other forms of ambiguity persist and hinder straightforward interpretation. In a traditional governing system, this would be enough to give pause to anyone trying to address the level of success of asylum policies. In the EU's multilevel system of governance, nevertheless, this ambiguity is compounded by the process of transposition at the domestic level. As such, it is worth to elucidate how EU institutions themselves perceive the implementation of this system at the national level. Through reports pf EU institutions, and through the case law of the Court of Justice of the European Union, we can see what other ambiguities exist, beyond those found through a strict textual analysis.

1 The Union's Approach to National Implementation Post-2015

In the 2016 Annual Report on Migration and Asylum, immediately following what has been perceived as a 'refugee crisis,' a large portion was dedicated to the first chapter on International Protection and Asylum, while less was said about Legal Migration, Integration, or Securing Europe's Borders. By the 2018 report, however, Legal Migration is framed as the main frame of action chosen by the EU, leaving the issue of international protection in the background. A quick glance at the report itself shows why. In the area of legal migration, the Commission adopted a Communication on 'Enhancing legal pathways to Europe,' launched the Fitness Check on Legal Migration, and spearheaded the contact group on legal migration as a forum where Member States could openly debate the Directives on migration. Moreover, by the end of 2018 several other Directives were meant to be transposed by Member States, giving the Commission justification for enhanced monitoring of national systems. These include the Seasonal Workers Directive (2014/36/EU), Intra-corporate transfers Directive (2014/66/EU), and the recast Students and Researchers Directive ((EU)2016/801), with the latter being the subject of infringement procedures against 17 Member States for non-transposition.[1]

1 European Migration Network, *Annual Report on Migration and Asylum 2018* (2019), 5.

 | DOI:10.1163/9789004700826_005

By contrast, no such pro-active attitude is observed in the 2018 report regarding the developments around international protection and asylum. If anything, the report itself highlights not what the European Commission has done in this area, but rather what Member States are doing independent of EU requirements:

> The vast majority of Member States and Norway introduced changes to their national asylum procedures, reception conditions and to the rights and obligations of persons seeking international protection. In terms of (access to) asylum procedures, legal changes inter alia made it possible for authorities to seize and analyse data storage media (e.g., smart phones) from asylum seekers and increased the applicants' duty to cooperate. A trend was observed in some Member States towards improving accessibility to legal counselling for applicants of international protection. Multiple Member States reported on the resumption of transfers of non-vulnerable individuals to Greece under the Dublin Regulation, as well as on expanding lists of safe countries of origin. With regard to reception conditions, several Member States initiated legislative changes inter alia to reduce reception costs for the public, while policy changes mostly aimed at better managing capacity in the face of fluctuating numbers of applicants. The rights and obligations of beneficiaries of international protection were also subject to legal changes in a few member States, relating particularly to labour market access and access to public benefits and services.[2]

While it could be argued that the Commission is trying to make the case that their approach of building asylum policies based on the lowest common denominator yields results, the other side of that coin would show that several of these actions at the national level represent a breaking down of the bonds of supervision to an extent that risk non-compliance.

In a context where the CJEU has made several rulings based on a strict interpretation of the right to privacy, an increase in the applicants' duty to cooperate, including through the enhancement of state powers by allowing seizure and analysis of storage media, could be seen as inviting violations to principles advanced by the Court.[3] Furthermore, especially since the signing of the

2 Ibid 6.

3 See Case C-473/16 *F v. Bevándorlási és Állampolgársági Hivatal* [2018]; Case C-652/16 *Nigyar Rauf Kaza Ahmedbekova and Rauf Emin Ogla Ahmedbekov v Zamestnik-predsedatel na Darzhavna agentsia za bezhantsite* [2018].

EU-Turkey Statement in 2016, there is still an ongoing debate about Greece's ability to provide appropriate reception conditions to asylum seekers, meaning that the resumption of transfers cannot be taken as an indicator of success in it of itself.[4] A similar argument can be made for the expansion of lists for safe countries of origin, as the flaws of overreliance on these factors has already been pointed out.[5] As such, from 2016 until presently, or at least recently, a change in the Commission's prioritisation seems to have taken place. The lack of action highlighted in the Annual Report from 2018 points either to a deadlock in decision-making, but perhaps also to a reallocation of Union resources to migration policies that are capable of building winning coalitions.

Legislative procedures at the European level for reforms to the CEAS are still ongoing, although, as of early 2024, an end seems to be in sight. Deadlock has been observed particularly when it comes to reforming Dublin and the Asylum Procedures Directive. In the 2018 Annual Report on Migration and Asylum, Member States are praised for the actions taken in adopting the necessary legislation for the implementation of the Asylum Procedures Directive in the reference period, something they were legally compelled to do.[6] As a further sign of improvements, the report also notes Greece's action in changing the legislation regarding reception conditions, an area where severe shortfalls were identified in the past. Nevertheless, despite the legal developments which the European Commission report presents as a success in correctly implementing the CEAS (i.e., adhering to harmonised practices), several reports still indicate that Greece is falling short of meeting its reception conditions obligations.

Certain changes in practice, not only in legislation, are also emphasized through this report. This includes, for instance, the expansion of capacity of reception centres in Member States where this was needed, or the downward readjustment of capacity where the number of asylum seekers has decreased compared to previous years. Changes in practice also included new agreements between competent authorities and legal associations for ensuring better representation and counselling for asylum seekers and introducing pilot counselling schemes. Many other changes in practice are enumerated, but one thing stands out from this report as compared to the one published only 2 years previous, which detailed the state of affairs in 2016: a clear switch in focus from

4 For an overview of the reception conditions on the Greek islands, see Konstantinos Tsitselikis, 'Refugees in Greece: Facing a Multifaceted Labyrinth' (2018) 57 *International Migration* 158.

5 Cathryn Costello, 'The Asylum Procedures Directive and the Proliferation of Safe Country Practices: Deterrence, Deflection and the Dismantling of International Protection?' (2005) 7 *European Journal of Migration and Law* 35.

6 European Migration Network, *Annual Report on Migration and Asylum 2018* (2019), 21.

the need for a strong push from the European level toward the responsibility of individual Member States to correctly implement, and therefore harmonise, the CEAS.

Regarding what changes were implemented at the national level, the 2016 report opens by stating that "changes in national legislation were underpinned in some Member States by the requirements of the CEAS."[7] Meanwhile, there is also a list of changes made that were not "motivated by the need to implement the EU asylum *acquis,"* highlighting an odd approach. These legal changes are listed as being introduced by Member States who had more favourable provisions and chose to align themselves to the EU "minimum standards."[8] Despite the CEAS allowing for Member States to introduce or retain more favourable provisions, the EU then did not criticise this race to the bottom, but rather framed it in a way that would highlight the harmonising power of the CEAS instruments. For example, a legislative amendment from Finland, which got rid of the national protection category of 'humanitarian protection' is described in terms of efficiency. Since this is a national, not EU, category, the Commission argues, it is irrelevant "in light of the increasing take up of subsidiary protection." This is even more puzzling when considering that in a Quality Assurance Tool developed by the EASO in 2018 and updated by the EUAA in 2021, one of the indicators to be assessed is that "where applicable, additional protection grounds (e.g., humanitarian grounds) are applied correctly."

The way the EU is framing the discussion in 2018 as compared to 2016 indicates that there is much more reliance placed on the initiatives that individual Member States take without a strong push from the EU. Whether this is a strategy meant to break through gridlock or a sign that the EU will no longer take a lead role in the implementation of Article 78 TFEU is not a question that this work tries to answer. What it does make clear, nonetheless, is that seeing the implementation procedures at the national level bears a strong weight on understanding how the CEAS is implemented today, how the 2015 'refugee crisis' has affected this implementation, and, perhaps most importantly, how harmonisation of asylum policies is pursued today.

This becomes even more pertinent when considering the reforms that are being brought to the existing legal framework. The policy documents of the European Commission help us understand the motivation behind legal norms. The Court itself looks at the importance of motivations behind legislative initiatives. In case related to social security payments to immigrants, the court

7 European Migration Network, *Annual Report on Migration and Asylum 2016* (2017), 15.
8 Ibid 16.

stated that the Regulation in question[9] is the result of legislative development reflecting, in particular, "the intention of the EU legislature to extend the entitlement to family benefits to other categories of person aside from employed persons."[10] Intentions, then, play a crucial role in the interpretation of legislation. These can be found best in policy documents free from the technical language of legal documents.

Take, for instance, the European Commission's Communication to the European Parliament entitled "Towards a Reform of the Common European Asylum System and Enhancing Legal Avenues to Europe,"[11] which set the groundwork for what is today the Pact on Migration and Asylum, i.e., the reform proposal of the CEAS. It is in this document that the Commission first establishes what it considers are the weaknesses that have led to a lack of harmonisation of asylum procedures. In only two places does the Commission identify national-level indicators that it considers as proof of an un-harmonised system. In one footnote (footnote 14), the Commission points to uneven recognition rates of similar groups of asylum seekers in different Member States, while later the document also makes the claim that Member States do not make use of the 'cessation of status' article in the Qualifications Directive. Regarding the Procedures directive, the document only points to European level indicators, such as the amount of discretion written into the Directive. As such, the Commission proposes that all reforms continue to harmonise the CEAS, particularly by strengthening the Dublin Regulation, giving the Asylum Procedures Directive and the Qualification Directive more weight by making them Regulations, and expanding EASO's mandate to have a policy-implementing role. Essentially, the Commission is proposing to push the street-level of implementation closer to the European level of governance.

With this proposal the Commission continues to attempt to strike a balance between the border states most burdened by mass flow of asylum seekers, and those European countries whose economic conditions also attract many seeking international protection. In an effort to placate the former, the Commission promised to strengthen the fight against secondary movement within the EU, while at the same time it sought to ensure solidarity and fair sharing of responsibility, even if this should be done by "moving to a new [Dublin] system based

9 Regulation (EC) No 883/2004 of 29 April 2004 on the coordination of social security systems [2004] OJ L166/1.

10 See Case C-322/17 *Eugen Bogatu v Minister for Social Protection* [2019].

11 Commission, 'Communication from the Commission to the European Parliament and the Council: Towards a Reform of the Common European Asylum System and Enhancing Legal Avenues to Europe' COM(2016) 197 final.

on a distribution key."[12] We see in this approach the same considerations at play when the EASO was established: traditional countries of asylum seeking to limit secondary movement, while border states want to see more burden-sharing mechanisms enacted.

Pursuing a strategy based on placating both sides, however, does not address what could be the largest issue of the system. Many of the discretionary provisions included now are a result of the push-and-pull between diverging positions, and ambiguity in the documents can be attributed to the need of the Commission to ensure that each Member State can apply the legal norms within their own national context. If any proposed reforms are developed following the same dynamic, which the Commission indicates to be the case in the 2016 Communication to the European Parliament, the ambiguous and discretionary clauses will not necessarily have been addressed. Rather, all that would be achieved is a move of the level at which the street-level operates.

The Pact on Migration and Asylum presented by the European Commission in September 2020[13] shows where these proposed reforms are headed, particularly after more than 8 years of gridlock on getting the entire package passed. Most emphasis going forward is placed on border procedures and quick returns of unsuccessful applicants. One of the most eye-catching proposals is the introduction of a screening procedure that "should be applicable to all third-country nationals who are present at the external border without fulfilling the entry conditions or after disembarkation, following a search and rescue operation." This would apply to those applying for international protection as well as if they do not have authorisation to cross an external border. This screening should consist in a preliminary health check, identity check, registration of biometric data, and a security check.

The Commission also creates a constant link between quicker and more efficient decisions, both on awarding international protection where this may be the case, or alternatively on carrying out expulsions of rejected applications. The proposal for a new Asylum Procedures Regulation, from 2016, is amended in this sense, now to include a border expulsion procedure, and calling for the decision on rejecting an application for asylum to automatically include an expulsion order. An appeal against a decision is thus also an appeal against an order to leave the territory of the Member State. Eurodac is also proposed to be expanded to include photos and other personal data, as well as to

12 Ibid 6.

13 Commission, 'Communication from the Commission to the European Parliament, the Council, the European Economic and Social Committee and The Committee of the Regions on A New Pact on Migration and Asylum' COM 2020(609) final.

become interoperable with other electronic databases, such as the Schengen Information System.

By far the most anticipated proposal in this new Pact was that of dealing with the fair sharing of the responsibilities created by mass movements of people. The term 'solidarity' has often been used in this case: if the EU's single market have created the conditions of prosperity and stability that serve as a pull factor of migration, it should be the EU as a whole that shares the administrative burden of processing the claims of those seeking international protection. Solidarity, however, has been heavily politicised since 2015, when the Commission 'imposed' solidarity requirements on its Member States, while a very vocal group, particularly Hungary and Slovakia, argued in favour 'voluntary solidarity.' Anticipating a similar rebuke, the Commission now proposes 'flexible solidarity,' trying to frame it simultaneously as permissive and obligatory, and by giving Member States options in what type of contributions to the fulfilment of this obligation they would like to make, while at the same time introducing ambiguity by making expectations diverse and unclear.

2 Case Law

While the instruments of the Common European Asylum System compose the core of the European approach to the management of asylum policies, there is a heavy reliance on the Court of Justice of the European Union (CJEU) to aid with CEAS implementation. In 2014, for example, it was the CJEU which reiterated that "the Geneva Convention constitutes the cornerstone of the international legal regime for the protection of refugees and that the provisions of the [Qualifications] directive were adopted to guide the competent authorities of the Member States in the application of that convention on the basis of common concepts and criteria."[14] As this case shows, and given the principles of international law that the Europe's asylum system is rooted in, the first competency of the CJEU is to use the principles of international law, such as the Geneva Convention, in shaping its own interpretations of European legislation grounded in those same principles.

Many examples, unrelated to field of asylum, exemplify that the CJEU has taken international law in a way that parallels the approach to internal law,

14 Case C-604/12 *H.N. v Minister for Justice, Equality and Law Reform and Others* [2014].

or the law within the European Union.[15] As such, the Court has employed a restrictive approach to the interpretation of international law in judgements. Eckes points out in several other instances of how the Court has often ruled in favour of a restricted effect of international law in the European legal order.[16] In what could be one of the most infamous cases, *Kadi*, the Court refused to give effect to a United Nations Security Council resolution, since "it is not for the Community judicature, under the exclusive jurisdiction provided for by Article 220 EC, to review the lawfulness of such a resolution adopted by an international body, even if that review were to be limited to examination of the compatibility of that resolution with *jus cogens*, but rather to review the lawfulness of the implementing Community measure."[17]

Yet the Court's approach has been more liberal when dealing with cases of protection of human rights. Today, it draws inspiration from three formal sources of human rights law: the European Convention of Human Rights (ECHR), the EU Charter of Fundamental Rights, and the "general principle of EU law," or principles derived from national constitutions or other treaties to which Member States are parties.[18] The ECHR has traditionally been used by in several European countries as a way of mediating deficiencies in national protection of fundamental rights. As such, the Convention provided significant reference on how the Court interpreted human rights, having been treated often as a singular source of inspiration. Such inspiration was attempted to be made formal in the Treaty on European Union (TEU) article 6(2), calling for the EU to accede to the ECHR. The Court, however, blocked this ascension in 2014, citing the necessity of maintaining the supremacy of EU Law.[19] While the Convention did indeed serve as a special source of inspiration, the CJEU was not prepared to forego EU autonomy over the laws it had to interpret. The second source of inspiration for the Court in matter of human rights is the Charter of Fundamental Rights, which, according to TEU Article 6(1) has the same legal value as the treaties of the EU. As a result of this, the CJEU has established

15 Christina Eckes, 'International Law as Law of the EU: The Role of the ECJ' in Enzo Cannizzaro, Paolo Palchetti and Ramses A. Wessel (eds), *International Law as Law of the European Union* (Martinus Nijhoff 2011).

16 Ibid.

17 Joined Cases C-402/05 P and C-415/05 P, *Kadi and Al Barakaat International Foundation v Council and Commission* [2008] I-06351.

18 Paul P. Craig and Grainne De Burca, *EU Law: Text, Cases and Materials* (Oxford University Press 2015), 380.

19 Adam Łazowski and Ramses A. Wessel, 'When Caveats Turn into Locks: Opinion 2/13on Accession of the European Union to the ECHR' (2015) 16 *German Law Journal* 179.

clearly that the principal basis on which the CJEU will judge cases of human rights violations will be this Charter.[20]

Seeing how the Court approaches cases where international law plays a role is crucial given the role that the Geneva Convention has played in the development of the CEAS. As with the ECHR, the Convention has frequently been used and cited in cases dealing with the Directives of the European asylum system. Several cases, for instance, refer to the Geneva Convention as the cornerstone of the international legal regime for the protection of refugees.[21] In one of the more widely known ones, *Bolbol*, the Court cited that

> it is apparent from recitals 3, 16 and 17 in the preamble to the [Qualifications] Directive that the Geneva Convention constitutes the cornerstone of the international legal regime for the protection of refugees and that the provisions of the Directive for determining who qualifies for refugee status and the content thereof were adopted to guide the competent authorities of the Member States in the application of that convention on the basis of common concepts and criteria.

Moreover, we also observe in Joined Cases C-411/10 and C-493/10 that the Court uses the Geneva Convention often for determining the definitions of terms crucial to the Common European Asylum System, such as *non-refoulment.* "The Common European Asylum System," the Court claims, "is based on the full and inclusive application of the Geneva Convention and the guarantee that nobody will be sent back to a place where they again risk being persecuted. Article 18 of the Charter and Article 78 TFEU provide that the rules of the Geneva Convention and the 1967 Protocol are to be respected."

Other courts in Europe have also ruled extensively, and resulting in heavy criticism, on certain aspects of the CEAS, particularly the Dublin system. Decisions taken by the European Court of Human Rights (ECtHR) have put the effectiveness of Dublin under question. In *T.I. v* UK, the court heard the case of a Sri Lankan national whose application for asylum had been rejected

20 Craig and De Burca (n 18) 381.

21 See, e.g., Joined Cases C-175/08, C-176/08, C-178/08 and C-179/08, *Aydin Salahadin Abdulla, Kamil Hasan, Ahmed Adem, Hamrin Mosa Rashi and Dler Jamal v Bundesrepublik Deutschland* [2010] I-01493; Joined Cases C-57/09 and C-101/09, *Bundesrepublik Deutschland v B & D* [2010] I-10979; Case C-31/09, *Nawras Bolbol v Bevándorlási és Állampolgársági Hivatal* [2010] I-05539; Case C-364/11, *Mostafa Abed El Karem El Kott and Others v Bevándorlási és Állampolgársági Hivatal* [2012]; Case C-604/12, *H.N. v Minister for Justice, Equality and Law Reform and Others* [2014].

in Germany and had intended to apply again in the UK. Under the Dublin Convention, the UK courts ruled that Germany must take charge of the applicant, and that the UK could not review the application as it would undermine Germany's application of the Geneva Convention. As a result, the ECtHR ruled that, despite evidence of persecution, and even though German courts did not recognize non-state actors as agents of persecution, the United Kingdom could send the applicant to the first country of application, since there is no basis to assume that the latter would fail to fulfil its obligation under the Geneva Convention. Similarly, *K.R.S. v.* UK followed the same reasoning of inter-state trust, where even though several actors such as the UNHCR had recommended the suspension of Dublin transfers to Greece due to a lack of quality in asylum procedure,[22] the ECtHR ruled that there is an inherent presumption of safety in all countries that are parties to the Geneva Convention.

Yet, in what is perhaps the ECtHR's most (in)famous ruling, in *M.S.S. v Belgium* the Court ruled regarding the case of an Afghan asylum seeker who, after having been fingerprinted in Greece, lodged an application in Belgium. Despite, once again, the UNHCR officially requesting that a transfer to Greece be suspended, the Belgian authorities decided to still send the applicant back to the first country of entry. The Court, in this case, applied contradictory justifications for its conclusions. For Greece, while acknowledging both that Afghanistan is overall an unsafe country, and that the applicant belonged to a particularly vulnerable group, the ECtHR failed to clearly establish that a removal from Greece amounted to a violation of non-refoulment principles. Instead, the Court left it up to Greece to determine this matter.[23] Yet, when the applicant was sent from Belgium back to Greece, the Belgian authorities relied on assurances from the Hellenic Government that the applicant would be able to file a complaint, and that the principle of non-refoulment would be respected. The Court essentially "asserted that, when applying the Dublin Regulation, states must make sure that the intermediary country's asylum procedure affords sufficient guarantees to avoid removal without an evaluation of a risk of refoulment."[24] While for Greece the Court refused to interpret threats to non-refoulment, it condemned Belgium for violations on account of both

22 Violeta Moreno-Lax, 'Dismantling the Dublin System: M.S.S. v. Belgium and Greece' (2012) 14 *European Journal of Migration and Law* 1, 13.

23 Ibid; see also Sílvia Morgades-Gil, 'The Discretion of States in the Dublin III System for Determining Responsibility for Examining Applications for Asylum' (2015) 27 *International Journal of Refugee Law* 433.

24 Moreno-Lax, 'Dismantling the Dublin System' (n 22) 25.

indirect *refoulment* through Greece, but also direct *refoulment* to Greece as was indicated by the UNHCR during the Dublin procedure.

What the *M.S.S.* case also did was establish that countries have, at times, an obligation to activate 'the right to intervention' in cases where an asylum seeker would otherwise be returned to a Member State where there are known deficiencies in asylum procedures. The CJEU, on the other hand, employed restrictive interpretations of the Dublin mechanism, more so than the ECtHR. In cases where there are beliefs that a first country of entry has systematic flaws in the asylum procedures and reception conditions, or where a serious risk of violation of rights in the ECHR is present, a Member State would be obliged to exercise the 'right to intervention,' in accordance with Dublin. Anything less than that interpretation of the limits of the discretionary factors does not fit into the CJEU discreet stance on the obligation of Member States to use the 'right to intervention.'[25] These flaws within this discreet approach became apparent when the Supreme Court of the United Kingdom ruled that the requirement that "only systematic deficiencies in one country's asylum procedures and reception conditions will constitute a basis for resisting transfer to this country cannot be upheld ... the evidence is more likely to partake of systematic failings but the search for such failings is by way of a route to establish that there is a real risk of article 3 [of the ECHR] breach rather than a hurdle to be surmounted."[26]

Case law of the European Union has also interpreted particularities of receptions conditions,[27] Member States' obligations regarding asylum seekers stranded at sea,[28] decisions of expulsion and family reunification,[29] and the 2015 relocation scheme.[30] In order to understand how the rules and norms of the CEAS are applied continent wide, it is important to keep in mind the role that the CJEU plays in how these rules are interpreted. Regarding the

---

25 See Case C-4/11, *Bundesrepublik Deutschland v Kaveh Puid* [2013].

26 Morgades-Gil (n 23) 445.

27 Cathryn Costello and Minos Mouzourakis, 'EU Law and the Detainability of Asylum-Seekers' (2016) 35 *Refugee Survey Quarterly* 47, 55.

28 Violeta Moreno-Lax, 'Seeking Asylum in the Mediterranean: Against a Fragmentary Reading of EU Member States' Obligations Accruing at Sea' (2011) 23 *International Journal of Refugee Law* 174.

29 Diego Acosta Arcarazo and Andrew Geddes, 'The Development, Application and Implications of an EU Rule of Law in the Area of Migration Policy' (2013) 51 *Journal of Common Market Studies* 179.

30 Bruno De Witte and Evangelina Tsourdi, 'Confrontation on Relocation – The Court of Justice Endorses the Emergency Scheme for Compulsory Relocation of Asylum Seekers within the European Union: Slovak Republic and Hungary v. Council.' (2018) 55 *Common Market Law Review* 1457.

CJEU, restrictive interpretations do not have restrictive effects. Rather, the way the CJEU approaches certain aspects has made Member States much more accountable to supranational rule.

3 Interpretive Ambiguities: The Work of the CJEU in Identifying and Dispelling Ambiguities

Understanding the ambiguities found Qualifications Directive of the Common European Asylum System beyond textual ones means understanding first what the motivations behind its development were. This is because, as mentioned in the preceding sections, ambiguities lie not only in language or discretionary powers granted, but also in conflicting information regarding what the goals of policies may be. Before addressing the discretionary powers granted intentionally through legal language, and even further before understanding the unintentional ambiguities from the Qualifications Directives, one must look at the aims and goals of this document. For this, the recitals that comprise of the preamble provide crucial insight into what the Qualifications Directive aims to achieve, and why.

The preamble of a directive is generally considered a crucial tool that Member States can use to interpret the provisions of European law. During the 19th Colloquium of the Association of the Councils of State and the Supreme Administrative Jurisdictions of the European Union of 2004 several rapporteurs emphasized, in the context of the discussions regarding the Treaty Establishing a Constitution for Europe, the importance of preambles. In Germany, for instance, the preamble is deemed to delimit the framework of interpretation, as well as an important tool for shedding light on the reasons and the aims behind particular provisions.[31] Used in an even more specific manner, the Danish Supreme Court determined the scope of Directive 85/337/EEC on environmental impact assessment by making explicit references to the directive's preamble.[32] Similar approaches are also taken by Spanish and British Courts, while Belgian courts use the preamble to aid interpretation only when the text and logic of the Directives are not apparent. Lastly, the Dutch rapporteur had claimed that frequently recourse is taken to preambles in jurisdiction.

---

31 Ernst M.H. Hirsch Ballin and Linda A. Senden, *Co-Actorship in the Development of European Law-Making* (TMC Asser Press 2005), 87.

32 The case involved a Greenpeace claim that the Ministry of Traffic had violated the aforementioned directive.

Nevertheless, preambles are not always clear or helpful in achieving the goals that the rapporteurs above have claimed:

> The Finnish rapporteur observes that, in general, it is felt that the legal status and importance of the preamble remain somewhat unclear – between a legal rule and an explanatory memorandum, which makes it difficult to understand. As a result, the preamble has not been given great relevance in interpretation, although there are some examples where the courts have referred to it. The Austrian Administrative Court every now and then tries to draw conclusions from the preamble, which, however, seldom allows the deduction of a precise answer to a specific question because it is of a too general nature. In France too, this use seems very limited.[33]

As such, the exact nature of the use that the preamble has needs to be interpreted on a case-by-case basis. While the 2004 Dutch rapporteur did make general comments about the way recitals in the preamble are used to elucidate the meaning of European law, it is clear from the commentary above that this is not always the case, or helpful for that matter. The following analysis of the recitals in the Qualifications Directive (and Procedures Directives that follows) will become even more relevant once their use in national contexts is analysed in Chapters 5 and 6.

Recitals generally have no enforcement value, meaning that they can grant no discretionary powers or confer no direct obligation of implementation. As the above claims make clear, recitals in the preamble of directives serve mostly as a framing tool for the actions requested in the legislative tool. The Qualifications Directive is no different, and this framing is often apparent in requests from preliminary rulings from the CJEU. Analysing the preamble to Directive 2011/95/EU through the lens of the Court can provide insight that cannot otherwise be attained by literal readings of any legal text.

Given the low enforcement value of Recitals, their effect on the interpretation and national implementation of a Directive cannot be assessed – it is not a mechanism that can be found by direct reference in transposing legislation. Yet, the use of this tool by the CJEU in reaching or justifying certain decisions can show the general way this section of the Directive affect the interpretation of the rest. CJEU has often referred to recitals as a way to reiterate the fact that the Geneva Convention provides the cornerstone of the international legal

33 Hirsch Ballin and Senden (n 31) 87.

regime for the protection of refugees and that compliance is necessary to the Charter of Fundamental Rights. This is apparent in many cases brought before the Court, such as *B&D; Shepherd; H.T.; Warendorf, Alo & Osso; Lounani; M; X & X,* or *Fathi.*[34]

More than this simple framing of the Directive, courts must also use recitals to justify the competence of the European Union to achieve harmonisation in the area of asylum.[35] In the case *HA v. The Secretary of State for the Home Department*, the Upper Tribunal looks at recitals 1, 10 and 25 to identify the "overarching purposes of the Qualifications Directive." The first of these recitals emphasises the importance of a common policy of asylum on achieving an area of freedom, security, and justice. Recital 10, meanwhile, identifies the importance of the present directive to respect the provisions of the Charter of Fundamental Rights, while finally recital 25 makes explicit the role that international obligations such as the Geneva Convention should play in drawing up criteria for protection.

Another example in which the Court uses recital to frame the larger questions surrounding the interpretation of key provisions of Directive 2011/95/EU can be observed in the case of *F v. Bevándorlási és Állampolgársági Hivatal.*[36] Here, an applicant for international protection in Hungary was denied after authorities conducted several psychological tests, among which the Rorschach test or the so-called 'Draw-A-Man-In-The-Rain' test. The referring court asks the Court of Justice for a preliminary ruling, asking specifically if Article 4 of 2011/95/EU must be interpreted as meaning that it precludes the authority responsible for examining applications for international protection, and if that same article must be interpreted as precluding the preparation and use of a psychologist's expert report. While Article 4 deals broadly with the general assessment of evidence of what amounts to fear of persecution, the Court explicitly uses the Directive's recital 30 in order to make clear that issues relating to gender identity and sexual orientation are indeed among those from which the possibility of seeking advice from experts must be available. Nevertheless, this

34 *B & D* (n 21); Joined Cases C-443/14 and C-444/14 *Kreis Warendorf v Ibrahim Alo & Amira Osso v Region Hannover* [2014]; Case C-472/13 *Andre Lawrence Shepherd v Bundesrepublik Deutschland* [2015]; Case C-373/13 *H. T. v Land Baden-Württemberg* [2015]; Case C-573/14 *Commissaire général aux réfugiés et aux apatrides v Mostafa Lounani* [2017]; Case C-56/17 *Bahtiyar Fathi v Predsedatel na Darzhavna agentsia za bezhantsite* [2018]; Joined Cases C-391/16, C-77/17, C-78/17, *M and Others v Commissaire général aux réfugiés et aux apatrides* [2019].

35 For a more detailed discussion on this matter, see the explanation of *subsidiarity* in Craig and De Burca (n 18) 99–102.

36 *F v. Bevándorlási és Állampolgársági Hivatal* (n 3).

cannot be done unchecked, and the weight given to this advice must still be proportional with the goal.

> In any event, the impact of an expert's report such as that at issue in the main proceeding on the applicant's private life seems disproportionate to the aim pursued, since the seriousness of the interference with the right to privacy it constitutes cannot be regarded as proportionate to the benefit that it may possibly represent for the assessment of the facts and circumstances set out in Article 4 of Directive 2011/95.[37]

Recitals can also be used to exemplify the complexity and intertwining provisions of different Directives of the CEAS. In the *Alheto*[38] ruling, the Court states that "as recital 13 of [Directive 2013/32/EU] states, the approximation of rules under that directive aims to create equivalent conditions for the applications of Directive 2011/95 in the Members States and to limit the movements of applicants for international protection between member states." It is here that we observe a case of recitals from one Directive, namely the Procedures Directive, being used to justify the scope of the implementation specific articles of another Directive, the Qualifications Directive. Moreover, since recital 13 of 2013/32/EU refers to the need for approximation of rules of procedures for granting asylum, and to create the equivalent conditions for the application of the Qualifications Directive, the Court uses this recital to, once again, reassert the competence of the EU in the need for policy harmonisation, and thus for interpreting the scope of 2011/95/EU within the larger context of the Common European Asylum System.[39]

In some instances, nevertheless, case-law has used recitals not as a general framing of the competences of the Union in asylum policy, but to provide interpretation of procedural requirements. In *Ahmedbekova & Ahmedbekov*, the Court was asked, among others, whether:

> Article 4(4) of Directive 2011/95, read in conjunction with recital 36 of that directive, require that the assessment of whether there is a well-founded

37 Ibid para 59.

38 Case C-585/16 *Serin Alheto v Zamestnik-predsedatel na Darzhavna agentsia za bezhantsite* [2018].

39 See also Case C-369/17 *Ahmed v. Bevándorlási és Menekültügyi Hivatal* [2018]; Case C-720/17 *Mohamed Bilali v. Bundesamt Für Fremdenwesen und Asyl* [2019], where recitals are used not only in justifying the competences of the EU in harmonising asylum policies, but also in introducing the differentiation between 'refugee status' and 'subsidiary protection.'

> fear of persecution or a real risk of suffering serious harm be carried out solely on the basis of facts and circumstances relating to the applicant?
>
> [...]
>
> Is [the listed case law] also permissible in the light of considerations relating to the best interests of the child, maintaining the family unit and the right to privacy and family life and the right to remain in the Member State pending the assessment of the application, that is to say, in the light of [...] recitals 9, 11, and 36 of Directive 2011/95
>
> [and]
>
> Does it follow form recitals 16, 18, and 36 [...] of Directive 2011/95 [...] that a provision of national law, pursuant to which the family members of a foreign national who has been granted refugee status are also regarded as refugees in so far as that is compatible with their personal status and there are no reasons in national law for excluding the grant of refugee status, is permissible?[40]

While the Court has often used recitals for the purposes described hitherto, it was now specifically asked to interpret the role that recitals have in framing a specific procedural issue, namely that of ensuring family unity and protecting the rights of child. The CJEU does say that, as it is stated in recital 36, family members of a person at risk will also be vulnerable themselves, as such "in carrying out the assessment of an application for international protection on an individual basis, account must be taken of the threat of persecution and of serious harm in respect of a family member of the applicant for the purpose of determining whether the applicant is, because of his family tie to the person at risk, himself exposed to such a threat." Furthermore, recital 36 is also referenced in establishing that, under the present circumstances, national authorities can adopt more favourable provisions regarding the granting of refugee status to family members of applicants.[41]

Recitals are used to frame the larger competences of the Union in aiming for a more harmonised system of asylum, and only in limited cases do they address ambiguities found in procedural matters of granting refugee status. As mentioned in earlier paragraphs, this is to be expected, as recitals do not contain any demands or permissions for certain actions, but rather general considerations. Ambiguities, nevertheless, still exist, and further analysis of case-law helps identify where these are. While the linguistic analysis of the previous

40 *Ahmedbekova and Ahmedbekov* (n 3), para 43.

41 Ibid paras 51 and 70.

chapter provided a first look, the work of the Court shows that even clauses which might seem unambiguous in writing are subject to much interpretation. This is because often no clear information for reaching a decision can be deduced from the demands found in Directives. As the Court itself said in the case referenced in the preceding paragraph, "Directives 2011/95 and 2013/32 do not specify how to treat the potential interaction between such applications for international protection, which may, in part, concern identical facts or circumstances. Failing specific provisions, the Member States have latitude in that regard." For this, it helps to identify areas of ambiguity by the chapters in which they are found in the Qualifications Directive, and in the following section in the Procedures Directive.

3.1 *General Provisions (Articles 1–3)*

The General Provisions chapter contains three Articles: Article 1, establishing the scope of the Directive, Article 2, setting down the definitions, and Article 3, which allows for the introduction or retention of more favourable provisions. While Articles 1 and 2 are, linguistically, composed of non-discretionary provisions, there have been numerous instances of courts needed to aid with the interpretation of these clauses, particularly those found in Article 2. One such example comes from the case of *B&D*,[42] where the CJEU first addresses Article 2(d), where a 'refugee' is defined as

> A third country national who, owing to a well-founded fear of being persecuted for reasons of race, religion, nationality, political opinion or membership of a particular social group, is outside the country of nationality and is unable or, owing to such fear, is unwilling to avail himself or herself of the protection of that country, or a stateless person who, being outside of the country of former habitual residence for the same reasons as mentioned above, is unable or, owing to such fear, unwilling to return to it, and to whom Article 12 [on exclusion from refugee status] does not apply.

Even discretionary clauses, however, are subject to interpretation by the Court, even if, by their very definition, they are supposed to provide Member States with leeway in implementation (and therefore interpretation). Article 3, which

42 *B & D* (n 21). The ruling was made on the previous Qualifications Directive, namely Directive 2004/83. Articles 1–3 correspond to the Recast Qualifications Directive. The Court references the definition of 'refugee' found in Article 2(c) in Dir. 2004/83. This corresponds to Article 2(d) in Dir. 2011/95.

establishes the right to retain more favourable conditions, is placed under scrutiny in *B&D*. In essence, the CJEU is asked to evaluate whether Article 3 gives the freedom to Member States to award protections to applicants excluded under Article 12 of the Directive. To this, the court upholds the wording of Article 3, but only after it clarifies that such protection cannot be in any way confused with refugee status within the meaning of Directive 2011/95/EU, as it must uphold the definition of 'application for international protection,' in Article 2(g), since this claims that the directive does not preclude anyone from applying for a different kind of protection that falls outside the scope of the directive.[43]

Ahmedbekova & Ahmedbekov, C-652/16, points to another ambiguity found in already discretionary clauses. Through a question posed to for preliminary ruling to the CJEU, the referring court asks if it follows "from recitals 16, 18, 36 and *Article 3* of Directive 2011/95 [...] that a provision of national law [...] pursuant to which the members of the family of a foreign national who has been granted refugee status are also regarded as refugees in so far as this is compatible with their personal status and there are no reasons in national law for excluding the granting of refugee status, is permissible?"[44] In essence, then, the question is if Article 3 must be interpreted as permitting a Member State to provide for an extension of the scope of protection from an applicant to other family members. As such, the Court clarified that indeed, Article 3 must be interpreted as permitting a Member State to extend international protection to family members of applicants, as this is consistent with the rationale of family unity enclosed in the system of international protection.

3.2 *Assessment of Applications for International Protection (Articles 4–8)*

Chapter II, which is composed of Articles 4–8, sets out the rules according to which Members States should assess applications for international protection. These include rules of the assessments of facts and circumstances, including the responsibility of the applicant to substantiate his or her application, and of

43 Similar links can be observed in Case C-542/13, *Mohamed M'Bodj v État belge* [2014], where the definition of 'person eligible for subsidiary protection' in Article 2, as well as the allowance for more favourable provisions in Article 3, is linked to the requirement of Member States to granting social welfare and health care benefits to persons granted leave to live in a country only if such leave were to be regarded as conferring subsidiary status, which in the case at hand it cannot be. See also Case C-562/13, *Centre public d'action sociale d'Ottignies-Louvain-la-Neuve v Moussa Abdida* [2014], and *Shepherd* (n 34).

44 *Ahmedbekova and Ahmedbekov* (n 3) para 43.

the Member State to assess each application on individual merits (Article 4). The Chapter further addresses the possibility of protection needs arising *sur place* (Article 5), a definition of the actors of persecution or serious harm and of the actors of protection (Article 6 & 7), and the possibility that an applicant could have received protection in a specific part of his or her country of origin (Article 8).

While the provisions set out in Chapter I were used largely to give context to other mechanisms of Directive 2011/95/EU, the case-law concerning Chapter II involves many more direct interpretations of reliance on the provisions, and less of their use as contextualisation. Only in *M and Others*[45] does the court state that Chapter II must be used as a guiding set of rules to determine if an applicant has satisfied the material conditions for qualification as a refugee, and thus oblige Member States to provide protection under Article 13 ('Granting of refugee status'). In *Ahmedbekova & Ahmedbekov,* the referring court asks specifically if "Article 4(4) requires that the assessment of whether there is a well-founded fear of persecution [...] be carried out solely on the basis of facts and circumstances relating to the applicant?" and if the same Article 4 "must be interpreted as precluding applications for international protection lodged separately by members of a single family from being assessed in a single procedure, or the assessment of one of those applications from being suspended until the conclusion of the examination procedures in respect of another of those applications."[46] The Court responds that the provisions of this Article must be interpreted as allowing for applications lodged separately by members of a single family to include measures meant to address any interaction between applications, but as precluding those applications from being subject to a single assessment, as well suspending one until the conclusion of another.

Article 4 is the subject of other court cases as well. In *Shephard,*[47] while the interpretation of the article is not requested by the referring court, the CJEU uses it to make clear that competent authorities in Member States must assess all aspects of an application by the individual merits of said application, in this case by assessing the nature of military service in a particular country, and whether this service can be categorised as exposing the applicant to serious harm. Even more detailed, is the request for a preliminary ruling in *Fathi,*[48] where the referring court asks if

45 *M and Others* (n 34).
46 *Ahmedbekova and Ahmedbekov* (n 3).
47 *Shepherd* (n 34).
48 *Fathi* (n 34).

> It follows from Article 4(2) of Directive 2011/95 [...] that an appraisal of the facts and circumstances may be conducted only on the basis of the statements made and the documents presented by the applicant, but it is still permitted to require proof of the missing components covered by the concept of religion as defined in Article 10(1)(b) where:
>
> [...]
>
> National legislation provides that the competent authority must establish all the relevant circumstances for the examination of the application for international protection and the court, should the refusal decision be contested, must point out that the person concerned has not offered and presented any evidence?

In other words, is an applicant required to submit proof in the form of statements or documents of all the components of the concept of the reason for persecution, in this case religion?[49] The Court clarifies that an applicant who claims religion as the reason for persecution cannot be expected make statements or produce documents concerning every component of religion detailed in Article 10, but the applicant must substantiate his or her claims, as "the statements and no more relating to his religious beliefs or membership of a religious community constitute merely the starting point in the process of assessment of the facts and circumstances envisaged under Article 4."[50]

Yet another particular case involving a request for a preliminary ruling on Article 4 is the previously mentioned *F v. Bevándorlási és Állampolgársági Hivatal.*[51] The questions are, essentially, if Article 4 must be interpreted as meaning that it precludes the competent authorities from ordering that an expert report be obtained as a means of assessing the facts of a particular application, and if the use of an expert's report, following a psychological personality test, to assess the veracity of sexual orientation claims is permitted. The court finds that ordering an expert report is not precluded by Article 4, yet the preparation and use a psychological report as the one in the case before the court is prohibited since "the impact of an expert's report [...] on the applicant's private life seems disproportionate to the aim pursued, since the interference with the right to privacy cannot be regarded as proportionate to the benefit that it may possibly represent."[52]

---

49 Ibid para 76. In the CJEU's response, we see ambiguity arising also from specific wordings in the Directive, namely on the interpretation of 'in particular.' This is discussed in the assessment of Chapter III – Qualifications for being a refugee.

50 Ibid para 84.

51 *F v. Bevándorlási és Állampolgársági Hivata* (n 3).

52 Ibid para 59.

The need to clarify aspects relating to Article 4 do not focus on specific wordings, but rather on the interpretation of situations in which the applicability of the Article is put in question. It was observed first that Member States were unsure how to proceed regarding the requirement of an individual assessment of an application in cases where the reason for persecution is the family relations to another applicant,[53] or in cases where the applicant's reason for persecution is the consequences faced for desertion from a voluntary conscription army.[54] Of broader applicability is the interpretation requested in *Fathi*, as this ruling calls for a request on what could constitute credible evidence when assessing the religious-based claims for protection. This, nevertheless, is more an interpretation of Article 10, which lays down the reasons for persecution, than of Article 4.

It should be pointed out that other courts across Europe have also heard cases meant to clarify aspects of the articles that make up Chapter II of this Directive. In a court case at the Metropolitan Court of Public Administration and Labour in Hungary, the court's decision clarified for the national authorities that they had operated a wrong interpretation of Article 5, where they claimed that similar political activities need to be undertaken in the receiving country as in the country of origin. The national court, however, points out that in assessing needs arising *sur place*, Article 5(2) only uses the words "in particular, where it is established that the activities relied upon constitute the expression and continuation of convictions or orientations held in the country of origin." As such, authorities were implementing a much higher standard of proof, essentially denying the proper individual assessment called for in Article 4.

Chapter II is also the subject of a preliminary ruling in the case of *Abdulla*,[55] a well-known cases involving, among others, an interpretation of Articles 4–7. These joined cases involved several applicants from Iraq, which were granted asylum in Germany based on persecution at the hands of Saddam Hussein's authoritative government. Once this government was overthrown by an international military coalition, the referring court argued that the reasons for persecution were no longer valid, thus leading to a cessation of refugee status. Specifically of issue, was Article 4(4), which provides for a relaxation of the burden of proof when previous persecution has already taken place, and article 7(1), insofar as protection could also be considered as being provided by a multinational military coalition.

53 *Ahmedbekova and Ahmedbekov* (n 3).

54 *Shepherd* (n 34).

55 *Abdulla* (n 21).

Specifically, regarding these two interpretations, the Court ruled, on the one hand, that Article 4(4) cannot be used to lessen the burden of proof in the case at hand, as the assessment of new reasons for persecution should be conducted under Article 11(2), namely the assessment of the change in circumstances that may lead to cessation. Moreover, Article 4(4) could only be used when the reasons for persecution has changed, but there are earlier threats that are connected to the newly arisen reason for persecution. Regarding Article 7(1), the Court clarifies that actors of protection may include international organisations controlling the state, including through the use of a multinational military force.

Responding to the ruling, the agency charged by the United Nations with the implementation of the Geneva Convention, the UNHCR, disagreed with the way the Court approached the interpretation of Article 7. "UNHCR has expressed serious concerns about the inclusion of non-State actors and organizations as actors of protection under Article 7(1) of the Qualifications Directive … under international law, international organisations do not have the attributes of a State. In practice, this generally means that their ability to enforce the rule of law is limited."[56] Regarding Article 4(4), the UNHCR sees this as a mirror image of fear of persecution: a low standard of proof should be required when fear of persecution is invoked, and a high standard when the cessation clause is applied. Without making direct reference to Article 11(2), the UNHCR admits, as the Court did, that an assessment of proof when invoking the cessation clause should be done under Article 11.

The UNHCR conflicting opinion on Article 7, nevertheless, is telling. Both the Qualifications Directive and the Asylum Procedures Directive ensure that the opinion of the UNHCR can be considered when assessing an application, particularly as it relates to definitions of safe-third countries or country of origin information. As such, conflicting information is available to Member States when transposing the Directives in their national legislation, but also to competent authorities when attempting to reach a decision.

3.3 *Qualifications for Being a Refugee* (*Articles 9–12*)

Starting on Chapter III , Directive 2011/95/EU begins to move away from more definitory clauses, such as the definitions of who constitutes an actor of protection or of persecution, and into the more substantial attributes of what qualifies as an act of or reason for persecution (Articles 9 and 10), when cessation

56 UN High Commissioner for Refugees (UNHCR), 'UNHCR Statement on the 'Ceased Circumstances' Clause of the EC Qualification Directive' (2008).

of refugee status enters into force (Article 11), or who should be excluded from having their refugee status recognized (Article 12). Unlike the provisions upon which the Court ruled from previous articles, presented above, starting with Chapter III the articles begin being used more and more not only for grounding the reasoning of the Court in the Directive as much as possible, but directly as subjects of preliminary ruling requests.

Fathi showed the Court's interpretation of Article 4, but in the context of Articles 9 and 10. Regarding the acts of persecution mentioned in Article 9 of the Directive, the referring court asks if persecution on the basis of religion (Article 10(1)(b) – *Reasons for Persecution*), can be considered as such if drastic measures are not aimed at one religion in particular, but all religions that are contrary to the religion on which the laws and regulations of the particular country are based. Furthermore, the court also asks, under Article 10(1)(b), if the reason of persecution can exist where the applicant has not produced proof of all the components covered by the concept of 'religion.' The Court, in its ruling, clarifies that Article 10(1)(b) "must be interpreted as meaning that an applicant for international protection who claims, in support of his application, that he is at risk of persecution for reasons based on religion does not, in order to substantiate his claims concerning his religious beliefs, have to submit statements or produce documents concerning all components of the concept of 'religion', referred to in that provision."[57] Furthermore, the Court also interprets Article 9 as including acts which, although don't target one particular religion, still impose corporal penalties on practitioners of any religion contrary to the one of the state, and such penalties are enforced by the domestic authorities.[58]

In one case, the Court then made two things abundantly clear. First, it clarified that acts of persecution as regards to 'religion' cannot be analysed in the context of the legality of religious practices in the country of origin, as sufficiently serious acts can also be carried out under legal pretences. Secondly, the Court also made clear how the wording 'in particular' in Article 10 should be interpreted. This article tells Member States that they "shall take the following elements into account when assessing the reasons for persecution: … (b) the concept of religion shall *in particular* include the holding of theistic, non-theistic and atheistic beliefs, the participation in, or abstention from, formal worship in private or in public, either alone or in a community with others, other religious acts or expression of view, or forms of personal or communal

57 *Fathi* (n 34) para 102.

58 See also Case C-150/15 *Der Bundesbeauftragte für Asylangelegenheiten beim Bundesamt für Migration und Flüchtlinge v N* [2016].

conduct based on or mandated by any religious belief."[59] By using the wording 'in particular', the Court argues, EU legislation provides only a non-exhaustive list of components that may characterise the concept, but the applicant cannot be expected to be able to provide proof of all those concepts as the fact that the applicant is not a member of any religious community cannot be decisive in the assessment of the concept.

Article 9 is also the subject of another case, *EZ*,[60] in which several questions are referred for a preliminary ruling. Namely, the Court is asked, regarding the punishment for 'refusal to perform military service' listed in Article 9(2)(e), if such refusal must take place in a formalised procedure, and if such acts are considered persecutory if they punish the evasion of compulsory conscription. Furthermore, should there be a clear link between the reasons for persecution spelled out in Article 10, and the acts of Article 9, even in the absence of persecution under Article 9(2)(e)? The Court clarified that a formalised refusal of military service is not necessary, while it is necessary for a connection to exist between the reasons stated in Article 10 and the prosecution and punishment mentioned in Article 9(2)(e). Lastly, the Court did emphasise that the existence of a connection between the reasons in the directive and the prosecution for refusal to perform military service cannot be presumed solely based on the connection itself, bit that "there is a strong presumption that refusal to perform military service under the conditions set out in Article 9(2)(e) relates to one of the five reasons set out in Article 10 thereof. It is for the competent national authorities to ascertain whether that connection is plausible."[61]

As the case of *Shephard* has already showed us, persecution in the context of refusing to perform a military service is in itself ambiguous in that there is not enough information either about what 'refusal' means exactly, or what exactly 'military service' entails. Another of the questions in *EZ* asks if Article 9(2)(e) of Directive 2011/95/EU should

> be interpreted as meaning that, for a conscript who does not know what his future field of military operation will be, the performance of military

59 See also: Decision No. 10012810 of the French National Asylum Court, of March 24, 2015, for an example of interpretation of Article 10(1)(d) from a national court, which stated that victims of sexual trafficking share a distinct identity of which they are unable to rid themselves, and as such should be considered as forming a 'social group'. Also, *Ahmedbekova and Ahmedbekov* (n 3), for why taking part in a legal action against a state cannot be considered as belonging to a 'social group,' within the meaning of the same article.

60 Case C-238/19 *EZ v Bundesrepublik Deutschland* [2020].

61 Ibid.

> service would, directly or indirectly, include 'crimes or acts falling within the grounds for exclusion as set out in Article 12(2)' solely because the armed forces of his State of origin repeatedly and systematically commit such crimes or acts using conscripts?

In Shephard, the Court argues that Article 9(2)(e) is intended to protect an applicant from running the risk of committing acts that fall within the grounds of exclusion, e.g., crimes against peace, war crimes, crimes against humanity, etc, an argument it reiterates in the *EZ* judgement. The person can therefore only invoke in their application the likelihood of such acts being committed, and the deciding authorities cannot look only at whether the applicant's unit has already committed such crimes. Previous knowledge that the troops of the country of origin have committed acts as those spelled out in Article 12 serves as an indication that the applicant would be asked to commit the same crimes if he or she serves in that military.

Article 12(1)(a) is also subjected to a preliminary ruling in *Alheto*. According to this clause, applicants are excluded from refugee status if they are receiving assistance from other organs of the United Nations (namely, UNRWA). In essence the main question of interest to a first instance decision is if an application lodged by a person already registered with UNRWA means that an examination is required as to whether that person actually benefits from protection. The Court clarifies that yes, even if the person is registered with another agency, such as UNRWA, an individual assessment is needed as whether said agency can provide effective protection. This view was further clarified in early 2024, when the Advocate General of the Court issued an opinion according to which, considering the conflict in the Gaza Strip, UNRWA could no longer be considered to offer adequate protection to those under its mandate.[62]

Even article 12(1)(c), which spells out exclusion from refugee status on the basis of acts contrary to the general principles of the United Nations, has been subjected to interpretation despite it belonging to the general provisions of national security that are usually highly discretionary to Member States. In *Lounani*,[63] the Court was asked whether a person can only be excluded under Article 12(1)(c) if he or she has been convicted of a terrorist offense or is the participation in terrorist organisations without actually carrying out any acts sufficient grounds for exclusion, the latter being the view that the Court upheld. Further analysis of Court decisions, nevertheless, shows that while not

62 Case C-563/22 *Zamestnik-predsedatel na Darzhavna agentsia za bezhantsite* [2024], Opinion of AG Emiliou.

63 *Lounani* (n 34).

committing a terrorist act does not preclude a Member State from excluding an applicant from refugee status, such participation can be used as grounds for exclusion. In *B&D*,[64] the court ruled that Article 12(2)(b) and (c) must be interpreted as meaning that, even if an applicant has been a member of an organisation that has carried out terrorist acts, this does not automatically constitute a serious enough reason for considering that the applicant has having committed an act contrary to the purposes and principles of the United Nations. Nevertheless, a case-by-case assessment of specific facts should unearth individual responsibility for the acts committed.

The work of the CJEU in interpreting the provisions of Chapter III, a chapter which, from a linguistic assessment would indicate low level of discretion, shows that indeed ambiguity is still present in clauses which do not directly attribute discretionary power. These are often interpretive ambiguities, regarding what should be regarded as 'military service,' 'religion,' or 'serious crimes.' Even though the Directive gives Member States interpretative discretion in these aspects, the Court is still asked to rule on them, showing that Member States do not have all the necessary information to deduce directly from EU law how these provisions should be applied.

3.4 *Chapter IV – Refugee Status (Articles 13–14)*

Article 13 of the Qualifications Directive entitled "Granting of refugee status," calls on Member States to grant the status of refugee to any person who qualifies. Most notably, nevertheless, as Recital 21 of the same Directive makes clear, the granting of refugee status is a declaratory act. This means that while Article 13 calls for the granting of refugee status, this is only meant to serve as a recognition of a status that the applicant has already qualified for. Article 14, on the other hand, lays down the rules according to which a Member State may decide to end or refuse to renew refugee status, in cases when the person in question has ceased to have or has never qualified for receiving refugee status.

In fact, Article 13 is meant to offer little discretion. In *H.T.*, the court makes it clear that, according to this article, interpreted in the context of the aforementioned recital, "member states exercise no discretion in that respect."[65] Non-discretionary, nevertheless, does not mean unambiguous. Returning to the case of *Ahmedbekova & Ahmedbekov,* the referring court is here unsure whether Article 13, while making it clear that refugee status must be given to

64 *B & D* (n 21). See also *Ahmed v. Bevándorlási és Menekültügyi Hivatal* (n 39); Joined Cases C-331/16 and C-366/16 *K. v Staatssecretaris van Veiligheid en Justitie and H.F. v Belgische Staat* [2018].

65 *H. T. v Land Baden-Württemberg* (n 34), para 63.

those that qualify, should also be expanded to apply to the family members of applicants. The Court indeed says that such an extension of Article 13 is permissible, if the family member is not excluded from being a refugee under Article 12.

Article 14 is also the subject of discretionary interpretations in *B&D*.

> In contrast with the ground for revocation laid down in Article 14(1), the ground laid down in Article 14(3)(a) is not subject to transitional arrangements and cannot be limited to applications made or decisions taken after the directive entered into force. Nor is its application discretionary, like the grounds for revocation laid down in Article 14(4).

In other words, the Court says, because 14(1) calls for a revocation of status of a person whose circumstances have changed since the Directive entered force, as it directly refers to the applications that were filed after the entry into force of the 2004 Qualifications Directive. Article 14(3)(a), nevertheless, concerns the revocation of status of a person that should have been excluded under Article 12. Since granting refugee status is a declaratory act, Article 14(3)(a) makes it clear that in cases where refugee status was granted to someone who was not a refugee, exclusion must take place regardless of the time at which the application was filed. Both are vastly different from the provisions of Article 14(4), which clearly use discretionary language (i.e., "Member states *may*") to give discretionary powers in dealing with cases of national security.

Article 14, namely (4), (5), and (6) also provide an example for unclear, or even contradictory, objectives. These provisions of the article allow Member States the discretion of revoking, ending, or refusing to renew status to anyone who constitutes a danger to the security of the Member State, or who has been convicted of a particular serious crime. Nevertheless, as the Recitals discussed in the previous paragraphs state, this Directive must respect and abide by the rules of the Geneva Convention. By including a new ground for exclusion, as defined in Article 14(4), the Directive could be interpreted as introducing more grounds than the Geneva Conventions does, as the exclusion and cessation clauses enumerated in this convention are exhaustive, and they do not contain the acts described in Article 14 of Directive 2011/95/EU.

The case of *M and Others*[66] deals precisely with the predicament of the previous paragraph. It is argued by one of the referring courts that, in essence, Article 14(4) is incompatible with the general requirements of Directive 2011/95/EU,

66 *M and Others* (n 34).

namely of granting a higher level of protection than the Geneva Convention does. If a someone's rights to recognition of refugee status are denied based on Article 14(4), the provisions of the Directive will no longer apply to them. Yet, as the persons cannot be returned to their country of origin, they are "tolerated in the host Member State and have a 'light-refugee' status." This light-refugee status comes from the fact that Member States cannot derogate from the principle of *non-refoulment* enshrined in the Geneva Convention.[67]

The Court answers by relying heavily on the differentiation between 'refugee' and 'refugee status.' While, indeed, a person covered by Article 14(4) would not be able to derive the benefits of 'refugee status' as they are described in the directive, that person would nonetheless not stop being a refugee. Through Article 14(6), which states explicitly that provisions of Geneva must still be observed even in cases such as those described here, the Directive ensures that the principle of *non-refoulment* is observed. This is no way an encouragement to shirk international obligations, the Court argues, as Member States would still be bound by the Charter of Fundamental Rights. Revoking refugee status cannot be confused to someone no longer being a refugee.

The interesting opportunity of Article 14 lies in seeing how discretion itself is interpreted differently at different levels of governance. In *Ahmed,* the governments of the Czech Republic and Hungary argued that since the concept of 'serious crime,' which is found in Article 14 as well as Article 17 (discussed later), is not clearly defined, it is thus left for the legislature of Member States to address. The Court, nevertheless, disagrees with the approach. Any clause that does not specifically reference the national legal order for the purpose of determining purpose and scope should be interpreted in an autonomous and uniform way throughout the entire EU, considering the context of the objectives pursued by European legislation, not national one.[68]

3.5 *Qualification for Subsidiary Protection (Articles 15–19)*

Chapter v of the Qualifications Directive has received most attention in its implementation, likely because they establish a system of protection not covered by the Geneva Convention, namely subsidiary protection. In assessing who might qualify for this protection, attention needs to be given to the definition provided in Article 2(f) for 'person eligible for subsidiary protection':

67 Ibid paras 49 and 95.

68 *Ahmed v. Bevándorlási és Menekültügyi Hivatal* (n 39), paras 35 and 36.

> Third country national who does not qualify as a refugee but in respect of whom substantial grounds have been show for believing that the person concerned, if returned to his or her country of origin ... would face a real risk of suffering serious harm, as defined in Article 15, and whom article 17(1) and (2) does not apply, and is unable, or, owing to such risk, unwilling to avail himself or herself of the protection of the country.

Contrary to the granting of refugee status, where the standard of proof lies in a 'well-founded fear of persecution,' (Article 2(d)), 'real risk,' becomes the standard of proof to which the actions enumerated in Article 15, entitled Serious Harm, are to be held. Nevertheless, the CJEU, as arbiter of correct policy implementation, has not defined exactly what 'real risk' means. What it has made clear, however, is that general situation in a country cannot, in it of itself, be taken as indication of substantial proof of 'real risk.' Here, the sliding-scale concept should be applied: where a person can show that violence directly affects him or herself individually, "the less it will be necessary to show that he faces indiscriminate violence in his country or a part of the territory which is so serious that there is a serious risk that he will be a victim of it himself."[69] Conversely, the less a person can show that he or she is individually affected, the higher the degree of generalized violence needs to be in order for 'real risk' to be considered.

This interpretation of 'real risk' also allows there to be a clear distinction between the three elements of serious harm that Article 15 describes. While (a) and (b) refer to concrete, precise events of serious harm, such as facing the death penalty or facing torture or inhumane treatment, Article 15(c) leaves things broader: "Serious harm consists of ... (c) serious and individual threat to a civilian's life or person by reason of indiscriminate violence in situations of international or internal armed conflict." Coupling this with the interpretation provided by the Advocate General in the case cited in the previous paragraph, then 15(c) allows for far more room of interpretation regarding the balance between the degree of indiscriminate violence and how a person is individually affected by such violence.

Even with this broad approach, the Court still provided in several cases specifics of exactly how the elements of 15(c) should be interpreted. In *Diakité,* the CJEU was directly asked to interpret exactly how 'internal armed conflict' should be defined, in light of the approach from international humanitarian law

69 Case C-465/07 *Meki Elgafaji and Noor Elgafaji v Staatssecretaris van Justitie* [2009], Opinion of AG Maduro, para 37.

which looks at 'armed conflict not of an international character' as depending on the intensity, level of organisation, and duration. It was answered, then, that

> while international humanitarian law is designed, inter alia, to provide protection for civilian populations in a conflict zone by restricting the effects of war on persons and property, it does not provide for international protection to be granted to certain civilians who are outside both the conflict zone and the territory of the conflicting parties. As a consequence, the definitions of 'armed conflict' provided in international humanitarian law are not designed to identify situations in which such international protection would be necessary and would thus have to be granted by the competent authorities of the Member States.[70]

As such, it is impossible to assess whether a person qualifies for subsidiary protection by assessing if the elements of internal conflict as defined by international humanitarian law are met. The existence of armed conflict is necessary but not sufficient for triggering Article 15(c), whereas the level of violence needs to be assessed considering the risk it poses to the individual applying for protection.[71]

Article 15 also creates a differentiation between who can be covered by the different components of 'serious harm.' Unlike points (a) and (b) of the article, (c) refers only to serious and individual threat to a *civilian's life or person*. This, then, makes this generalist approach only applicable to civilians, whereas non-civilian claimants to protection must be processed in light of points (a) and (b). How, then, should a civilian be defined? Some national decisions would point toward use of the definition as it stems from international humanitarian law, namely "persons taking no active part in hostilities, including members of armed forces who have laid down their arms or are otherwise *hors de combat*."[72] As *Diakité* had made clear, the CJEU took the definition of terms from a factual, or contextual, perspective, and less from a perspective strictly

---

70 Case C-285/12 *Aboubacar Diakité v Commissaire général aux réfugiés et aux apatrides* [2014], para 23.

71 See also *RK* (*entitlement to represent: s.84*) [2011] UKUT 00409(IAC) [2011], for an example of interpretation in British national law; CNDA (France), judgment of 11 January 2012, *M. Samadi*, No 11011903 C. and CNDA (France), judgment of 28 March 2013, *M. Mohamed Adan* No 12017575 C for examples of interpretation into French national law; or Judgements I U 498/2012–17 and I U 1327/2013–10 for example of interpretation in Slovenian national law.

72 Article 3 of the Convention (III) relative to the Treatment of Prisoners of War. Geneva, 12 August 1949. For an example of national law using this definition, see United Kingdom Asylum and Immigration Tribunal Judgement *AR* [2006] UKAIT 00048.

grounded in legal definitions. As such, even a member of certain armed forces who has not taken proactive steps toward disengagement, yet who is at least temporarily not engaging in combat roles, could qualify for subsidiary protection under Article 15(c). This would be the case even if the applicant would not qualify under the tenants of international humanitarian law. Furthermore, if recourse is also made to the judgements regarding the exclusion based on serious crimes, mere membership to an armed group is also not automatically pointing to non-civilian status.

The ambiguities of how to approach the issues spelled out in Article 15, particularly at point (c), are best exemplified by the following assessment in the European Asylum Support Office's Judicial Analysis of the Qualification Directive:

> Claims based on specific risk may very often stand to be resolved under the refugee definition or … under Article 15(b) or Article 15(a). It bears repeating that when deciding international protection cases, courts and tribunals must examine first whether a person is eligible for refugee protection and hence application of the 'sliding-scale' under Article 15(c) will only arise if it has been decided an applicant has not established a well-founded fear of being persecuted.[73]

The problem in this case, then, is to determine first under which kind of protection an applicant might best fall, and only afterwards to assess the balance between the effects of violence on the individual concerned, and the degree of indiscriminate violence observed. Legal scholars have argued that the types of threats enumerated and described in these chapters would indicate in most cases a presumption for refugee status to be applied. As such, subsidiary protection status should only be in specific circumstances, and not as an alternative to refugee status.

The other articles in this Chapter deal with cessation and exclusion from subsidiary protection. Firstly, in the *Bilali* judgement, the CJEU clarified that for the cessation clauses of Article 16 to be applied, it is irrelevant whether the change in circumstances that have led to the granting of protection are a result of false statements, change in circumstances in the country of origin, or incorrect assessment made initially by the authorities in the Member State.[74] It has been observed, however, that the standard for exclusion is lower in Article 17,

73 European Asylum Support Office (EASO). *Article 15(c) Qualification Directive (2011/95/EU) – A judicial analysis* (2014).

74 *Bilali* (n 39) para 51.

than the standard for revocation is in Article 14. Whereas Article 14(4)(b) refers to a 'particularly serious crime' as a criterion for revocation of status, the Court has stated that the wording of 'serious crime' signals that the offending conduct referred to is not as serious as in Article 14(4)(b).[75] Nevertheless, in the same judgment the court makes clear that the degree of the penalty provided for a crime cannot be the sole criterion based on which the seriousness of said crime should be judged.

3.6 *Chapter VI – Subsidiary Protection Status (Articles 18–19)*

Article 18 of the Qualifications Directive obliges Member States to grant subsidiary protection status to anyone eligible in accordance with Chapters II and V. Since, as earlier chapters of this work have shown, the Qualifications Directive attempted to patch together different national practices of international protection, subsidiary protection is the mechanism by which different complementary protections were brought together under one umbrella. Article 19, on the other hand, concerns the revocation of, ending of or refusal to renew subsidiary protection status, in accordance with the exclusion and cessation articles in Chapter V. Given that these provisions refer either to the rules regarding the assessment of an application, or to the rules for qualification for and exclusion and cessation of subsidiary protection, rules enumerated in previous chapters of the directive,[76] there is little case law that specifically scrutinizes the demands of these two articles.

One exception comes in the *Bilali* ruling, where the court is asked if

> the provisions of EU law, in particular Article 19(3) of Directive 2011/95 …, preclude a national provision of a Member State concerning the possibility of revocation of subsidiary protection status pursuant to which subsidiary protection status may be revoked without a change in the factual circumstances themselves which are relevant for the purpose of granting that status, but rather only where the state of knowledge of the authority in this regard has undergone a change, and, in that context, without either a misrepresentation or an omission of facts on the part of the third-country national or stateless person having been a determinant factor in the granting of the subsidiary protection status?[77]

75 *Ahmed* (n 39).
76 *Bilali* (n 39) para 56.
77 Ibid para 30.

Otherwise put, the referring court is asking if Article 19 must be interpreted as meaning that Member States cannot revoke subsidiary protection status in a case where, after the granting of the status it was uncovered that the conditions for granting it were not met, yet there is no attempted deceit on behalf of the third-country applicant.

The above question is one of interesting value because it involves incorrect decision making at the bureaucratic level which provides an opportunity for the Court to clarify certain aspects of Directive 2011/95/EU. The applicant in question, who identified as a stateless person, was marked by the Federal Asylum Office of Austria as "probably an Algerian national."[78] Based on this assumption, he was granted subsidiary protection, given the general situation in Algeria. Yet, it eventually became clear that the applicant was eligible for Moroccan and Mauritanian nationality, and as such the subsidiary protection status was revoked. While the decision to assume that the applicant's nationality was Algerian was a mistake on part of the Federal Asylum Office, and while the applicant had never intentionally misled the authorities, this did not change the fact that the status was granted on false grounds. The CJEU, in their answer, agreed with this interpretation, stating that Article 16, which must be followed when implementing Article 19, calls for the removal of subsidiary protection in cases where the circumstances which have led to the granting of status have changed. This, in the Court's interpretation, does not only include a change in circumstances on the ground in the country of origin, but also the emergence of new information which change the perspective upon which the case was originally assessed. As such, while the original decision was based on false information incorrectly provided by the Federal Asylum Office, this has no bearing on the requirement that subsidiary protection be withdrawn in such circumstances.[79]

3.7 *Content of International Protection and Administrative Cooperation (Articles 20–37); Final Provisions*

The final three Chapters of the Directive, while important in managing the asylum regime, are less relevant to the research objectives of the current project, i.e., how the discretionary space of first instance asylum decision makers is constructed. As such, their analysis will be treated in a way that aids

78 Ibid paras 17–29.

79 Nevertheless, the Court also ruled in this case that while withdrawing 'subsidiary protection' includes situations such as the one in the case at hand, this does not immediately imply the withdrawing of residence permits or the ability of the applicant to apply for other forms of protection in accordance with national legislation.

in understanding the general spirit of the clauses, but not with the depth of scrutiny applied in the first six chapters of the directive. Chapter VIII is entitled "Administrative Cooperation," and it compels states to designate contact points with the European Commission and to facilitate the exchange of information (Article 36), and that implementing authorities receive proper training. The "Final Provisions," enumerated in Chapter IX include the responsibility of Member States to draft implementation reports (Article 38), to transpose the present directive (Article 39), or the day in which the provisions of this directive enter into force (Article 41). The provisions are not often the target of preliminary requests or other attempts at interpreting ambiguity.

Chapter VII, on the other hand, applies to refugees and persons eligible for subsidiary protection, and it concerns the rights and benefits that applicants may derive after being granted refugee status or subsidiary protection status, and it provides insight into how certain ambiguous principles of law could be interpreted, even if these are not related to first instance decisions. These include right to being properly informed (Article 22), maintenance of family unity (Article 23), requirement for residence permits to be issued to recipients of one of the two statuses mentioned above (Article 24), and many other benefits such as access to employment, education, welfare, healthcare, accommodation, etc.

One noteworthy aspect is the hierarchy established for ensuring proper protections. The rights of minors, and the obligation to maintain family unity are, as in previous articles, paramount elements of international protection. As Article 23 makes clear, the obligation to keep family unity relates to family members that already existed as a unit in the country of origin, and who are present in the Member State that is awarding refugee or subsidiary protection status. This obligation, nevertheless, does not extend to anyone beyond direct relatives: spouses, minor children, and father, mother or another responsible adult guardian if the applicant is a minor. Discretion is nevertheless given to Member States to decide to apply Article 23 to other family members as well, especially if these are wholly or in large part dependent on the beneficiary to international protection (Article 23(5)).

This is reminiscent of the *Ahmedbekova & Ahmedbekov*[80] case, discussed in previous paragraphs, where the court explicitly states that refugee status can be extended to family members, if Member States wish to do so. Nevertheless, it is worth noting that even in the case in which a Member States does not wish to extend refugee or subsidiary protection status to certain applicants, these

80 *Ahmedbekova and Ahmedbekov* (n 3).

are still entitled to claim the benefits of Chapter VII of the directive, including Article 24, i.e., the issuance of a residence permit. However, while Member States have an obligation to issue residence permits to beneficiaries of refugee status, derogation can occur as usual if there are "compelling reasons of national security or public order."

Case law in this instance shows that there is direct link between the derogation from the principle of *non-refoulement* in Article 21, and the derogation from the obligation to issue residence permits. "A residence permit, once granted to a refugee, may be revoked, either pursuant to Article 24(1) of that directive ... or pursuant to Article 21(3) of that directive, where there are reasons to apply the derogation ... laid down in Article 21(2)."[81] Article 21 further reiterates that *non-refoulment* must be respected, yet, in certain conditions pertaining to national security or public order, a refugee *may be* returned. The Court does clarify that, in this discretionary power given to Member States, a refugee does not need to constitute a *present* danger to the Member State that granted refugee status.[82]

While the case law deriving from Chapter VII of the directive is not relevant directly to first instance decisions, the interpretations of the CJEU can still provide valuable insight into how ambiguities arise and are dealt with. *Ayubi*[83] is an example of why a literal analysis does not serve as a way of understanding the level of ambiguity or discretion given. Article 29, whose scope is the granting of social assistance to recipients of refugee status, uses non-discretionary wording in compelling Members States to give the "necessary" social assistance.[84] While, indeed, the use of the word "shall" indicates a lack of discretion given, there is clear interpretive ambiguity. The Court ruled that the inclusion of the word "necessary" does not mean that Member States are authorized to define and dole out benefits which are sufficient to cover basic needs, but which do not match the benefits given to nationals. A similar consideration is made in *Warendof, Alo & Osso*,[85] where, regarding the issue of freedom of movement (Article 33), the Court states that

81 *H. T. v Land Baden-Württemberg* (n 34).

82 *B & D* (n 21).

83 Case C-713/17 *Ahmad Shah Ayubi v Bezirkshauptmannschaft Linz-Land* [2018].

84 Regarding Article 29 the Court has also ruled in *M'Bodj* (n 43), clarifying that Member States are not required to grant social welfare or health care benefits to a third country national who has been granted leave to reside in Member State, unless the third-country national is intentionally deprived on such care in his or her home country. In other words, the Court establishes that only recipients of refugee status are entitled to the benefits of Chapter VII, since intentional deprivation of health care could constitute grounds for claiming refugee status.

85 *Kreis Warendorf v Ibrahim Alo and Amira Osso v and Region Hannover* (n 34).

> it cannot be determined, from a purely literal reading, whether [Article 33] implies only that beneficiaries of international protection must be able to move freely within the territory of the Member State that has granted such protection or whether it also means that such beneficiaries must be able to choose their place of residence in that territory. [Furthermore], the fact that Article 33 is entitled 'Freedom of Movement' is not sufficient to dispel the ambiguities arising from its wording.[86]

What the Court is essentially arguing, then, is that in cases where the wording of certain provisions are ambiguous, regardless of the language in which the Directive is being interpreted, such provisions should be read in the context of the general 'scheme and purpose' of the rules of which it forms part.[87] As mentioned in this work's introductory chapters, nonetheless, such an approach to interpretation of EU legislation is predicated on the belief that the policy is communicated clearly, and with unambiguous objectives.

4 Judicial and Legislative Analysis of the Procedures Directive

The Asylum Procedures Directive is an integral part of the European asylum acquis, deriving, much as the Qualifications Directive, from Article 78 of the Treaty on the Functioning of the European Union. Through its original iteration (2005/85/EC), this directive established a set of minimum standards for the granting of refugee status. Nevertheless, as these standards did not properly lead to the creation of a truly common asylum procedure, the second phase of the CEAS included a recast Procedures Directive, which no longer uses the wording of 'minimum standards' and instead calls outright for the establishment of common procedures in Article 1. This is further strengthened in the reforms of the Pact on Migration and Asylum, where the Asylum Procedures are spelled out in the forms of a Regulation – removing the flexibility inherent in Directives. For the purposes of this research, however, it is the former legislation that can better inform the type of guidance developed for bureaucratic implementation, as this has had time to build accompanying case law, entrenched operating procedures, guidance reports, etc.

The reasoning behind this version of the directive is explained through several recitals. Recital 7, for instance, acknowledges that disparities remain

86 Ibid paras 24–25.

87 This ruling derives from established case law. See Case C-74/13 GSV *Kft. v Nemzeti Adó- és Vámhivatal Észak-Alföldi Regionális Vám- és Pénzügyőri Főigazgatósága* [2014] para 27.

between the granting of protection from one Member State to the next, while Recital 13 frames the new directive as needed for limiting secondary movements which might occur as a result of divergent legal frameworks. In keeping with the aim of achieving a common procedure, rather than adherence to minimum standards, the context of the EU Charter of Fundamental Rights must always be observed. The Court says as much in *A, B & C,* where it argues that

> the methods used by the competent authorities to assess the statements and documentary or other evidence submitted in support of those applications must be consistent … with the fundamental rights guaranteed by the Charter, such as the right to respect for human dignity, enshrined in Article 1 of the Charter, and the right to respect for private and family life guaranteed by Article 7 thereof.[88]

This is worthy of mention not only because the Charter guarantees the fundamental rights of individuals, but because it also enshrines the principle of good administration for the purpose of delivering said rights. In *H.N.*,[89] the Court upholds this by stating explicitly that while an expectation of good administration is not directly referenced in the Asylum Procedures Directive, article 41 of the Charter, which enshrines this requirement, represents a general principle of EU law. Specifically in that case, the applicant had applied directly for subsidiary protection in Ireland, and was rejected because, according to Irish law, subsidiary protection can only be awarded if refugee status was rejected. This being a case based on the former Procedures Directive, it served as a foreshadowing of the recast version placing greater emphasis on the requirement for a single procedure. The Court said that Irish legislation is not precluded from making subsidiary protection only possible after refusal to grant refugee status. As such, individual applicants have a right, under the Directive, to have their applications processed in the context of good administration. This represents an instance where requirements of procedural implementation are dictated by a mechanism that indirectly regulates asylum procedures in the European Union.

The Asylum Procedures Directive is divided in six chapters, the most notable of which for the current research project is Chapter III: Procedures at First Instance. Nevertheless, as the analysis of the Qualifications Directive exemplified, even provisions unrelated to first instance decisions can help in

---

88 Joined Cases C-148/13, C-149/13 and C-150/13 *A, B and C v Staatssecretaris van Veiligheid en Justitie* [2014] para 53.

89 *H.N.* (n 14) para 50.

identifying difficulties in interpretation of the Directive in general. Chapter I, entitled General Provisions, establishes everything from the Purpose of the Directive (Article 1), to who the responsible authorities are (Article 4), and the permission to adopt more favourable provisions (Article 5). Chapter II: Basic Principles and Guarantees, enumerates several guaranteed rights and responsibilities of applicants and competent authorities, such the right to remain in the Member State while applications are examined (Article 9), the requirements for a decision by the determining authority (Article 11), to the right to legal assistance (Article 22). Chapter IV, on the other hand, enumerates the procedures for the withdrawal of international protection, while Chapter V details in just one article (Article 46) the right to an effective remedy (appeals procedure), another guaranteed right that is directly related to the requirements of the EU Charter. Finally, Chapter VI, General and Final Provisions establishes the requirements of inter-institutional cooperation (Article 49), transposition (Article 51) and the entry into force of the Directive (Article 54). Yet the aspect of procedures that deals only with the examination of an application is indeed the one most relevant here.

Following the Asylum Procedures Directive can lead competent authorities to several types of decisions, from a simple granting of protection to a rejection of such an application. Yet, these represent ends on a spectrum of decisions, not a binary choice. Article 32, for example, allows for Member States to consider applications as unfounded if the applicant does not qualify in accordance with the Qualifications Directive, or the instance in which an individual application can be categorised as inadmissible. Lastly, Article 39 even provides that no examination must be conducted in cases where the applicant is seeking to enter the Member State's territory from a safe-third country. Interestingly, there is no article in the Asylum Procedures Directive that explicitly enumerates how refugee or subsidiary protection status should be issued. If such a status is granted, this is done only in accordance with Articles 13 and 18 of the Qualifications Directive. The Procedures Directive, in turn, details how to properly reject or not examine an application while maintaining the principle of *non-refoulment*.

4.1 *Initiating the Procedures: Rules for Lodging an Application for Asylum*

The Procedures Directive applies "to all applications for international protection made in the territory, including at the border, in the territorial waters or in the transit zones of the Member States … [and] shall not apply to requests for diplomatic or territorial asylum submitted to representations of Member

States."[90] There is definitely a territorial scope involved, as the case of *X and X* before the court of justice has reiterated. While Article 3(2) clearly excludes from the Directive's scope any applications made at diplomatic representations abroad, the referring court in *X and X* asks if, in lieu of the Visa Code, a Member State has an obligation to issue a short-term visa when the reasoning behind the request of such visa is to be able to apply for international protection once the Member State is reached. Such an interpretation of the Visa Code, however, would de-facto allow third-country nationals to submit applications for international protection at diplomatic representations. "Indeed," the Court rules, "whereas the Visa Code [Regulation (EC) No 810/2009] is not intended to harmonise the laws of Member States on international protection, it should be noted that the measures adopted by the European Union on the basis of Article 78 TFEU that govern the procedures for applications for international protection do not impose such an obligation and, on the contrary, exclude from their scope applications made to the representations of Member States."[91] An application for short-term visa based on Article 25 of the Visa Code, i.e., on humanitarian grounds, with the intent of applying for international protection once the Member State is reached, cannot be considered to actually fall within the Visa Code itself. As the end-result of this process is for the individual to stay in the European Union for longer than 90 days in a 180-day period, such an issue is regulated by national law, not the Visa Code. While Article 25 of this Regulation could have been seen as providing a loophole to Article 3 of the Procedures Directive, the Court made sure in *X and X* that such a loophole would be closed.

Article 6 dictates that there are three stages that must be undergone when applying for international protection. First, an applicant makes an application, as the wording of Article 6(1) suggests, meaning that the applicant formally requests international protection. Following this, and no later than three working days after the application is made, competent authorities are requested to register an applicant. This means that said authority must formally acknowledge the making of an application. Finally, lodging an application refers to the formal submittal of a form, or where an official report has reached the designated authority in the Member State. While it is still the applicant that must lodge the application, this is differentiated from simply 'making' an application in that it requires the fulfilment of administrative formalities.

90 Art. 3, Directive 2013/32/EU of the European Parliament and of the Council of 26 June 2013 on common procedures for granting and withdrawing international protection [2013] OJ L180/60.

91 Case C-638/16 PPU *X and X v État belge* [2017].

Article 7 also fits within the scope of initiating asylum procedures, yet it specifically targets the applications made on behalf of dependants or minors. It gives adults the power to make application not only on their own behalf, but also on behalf of any dependent. Interestingly, while Article 2 provides a definition for who should be considered a minor, no such definition exists for who is considered to be a dependent. Minors, according to Article 7(3), should be able to make an application on their own behalf, if they have the legal capacity to do so according to the law of the Member State concerned, or through any adult responsible for him or her. Furthermore, in line with the requirements of Directive 2008/115/EC on common standards for returning illegally staying third country nationals, Member States must ensure that governmental or non-governmental bodies that provide minors with assistance during a returns procedure must also be able to lodge applications on behalf of minors if they are of the opinion that they minor has specific protection needs.

For a completion of all rights guaranteed to minors applying for international protection, most notably unaccompanied minors, Article 25 further develops what guarantees must be in place. These include the appointment of a representative, provision of legal and administrative information, and the general principle that the best interests of the child must always be preserved. Yet, Article 25 also gives several discretionary powers. For instance, 25(2) allows Member States to refrain from appointing a representative for a minor that will likely turn 18 before a first instance decision is taken. Article 25(5) also allows for medical examination to be used to determine the age of minors in cases of uncertainty. It does, however, include certain safeguards, such as respecting individual dignity, restricting the use of this clause to only non-invasive examination, and ensuring that refusal to undergo a medical test does not automatically prevent the determining authority from taking a decision on the application for international protection.

Another important aspect of making an application for international protection refers to the geographic scope of the Directive. As mentioned earlier, diplomatic missions are not covered. Yet, applications made in border areas, territorial waters, or transit zones are. According to Article 8, then, where there are "indications that third-country nationals or stateless persons held in detention facilities or present at border-crossing points, including transit zones, at external borders, may wish to make an application for international protection," Member States must ensure that there is access to information necessary for such application to be made, and arrangements for interpretation must be in place to the extent necessary for granting access to the asylum procedure.

There are several points in Article 8 that bear mentioning. First, the use of the phrase "arrangements for interpretation to the extent necessary," indicates that Member States have a lot of flexibility in implementing what exactly the basic extent of necessity is. Specifically, the use of the word 'arrangement' indicates a wide margin of discretion given. This, however, also comes hand in hand with a loosening of how 'intent to make an application' should be identified. According to Article 2(b), and application for international protection is defined as "a request made by a third-country national or a stateless person for protection from a Member State, who can be understood to seek refugee status or subsidiary protection status." Within this definition, it becomes clear that a formal expression of the wish to apply for protection is a precondition for the applicability of the directive.[92] The wording of Article 8, nevertheless, only asks for 'indications' that an individual may wish to make an application. This shows that there are no formal requirements as to what such a wish should contain or how it should be articulated. Recital 28, in fact, supports an interpretation of this loosening of restrictions: "Basic communication necessary to enable the competent authorities to understand if persons declare their wish to apply for international protection should be ensured through interpretation arrangements." The access to information called for in this article must be read in conjunction with Article 6(1), where it is stated that "if the applications for international protection is made to other authorities which are likely to receive such applications, but not competent for the registration under national law, Member States shall ensure that the registration shall take place no later than six working days after the application is made," not in the three working days called for if the application is made directly to a competent authority.

4.2 *Procedural Guarantees*

Once an application is made, registered, and lodged, Member States are obligated to ensure several basic guarantees, guided principally by *non-refoulment.* Article 9 on the right to remain makes this commitment to *non-refoulment,* by compelling Member States to ensure the right of applicants to stay in the country while an application is examined. Article 9(2) lists the two different situations in which derogation can be made from the right to remain: if the applicant must be extradited pursuant to obligations derived from a European arrest warrant or pursuant to a decision issued by an international criminal court or tribunal, or if the clauses of Article 41 apply. This article addresses exceptions from the right to remain in cases of subsequent applications that are made merely with the intention to "delay or frustrate the enforcement of a

92 European Asylum Support Office (EASO), *Asylum Procedures and the principle of non-refoulment – Judicial Analysis* (2018).

decision which would result in his or her imminent removal from that Member State," (Article 41(1)(a)), but only if relying on such derogation would not lead directly or indirectly violating the principle of *non-refoulment.*[93]

The general principle of Article 9, nevertheless, must be understood in the context of the entire procedure of examining an application for asylum. By 'right to remain,' as the article states, the Directive calls only for a protection from forcible removal from the Member State, but not to the issuance of residence permit. In fact, the CJEU went even further in the *JN* case, to state that the right to remain of Article 9 is in no way affected by the detention of an applicant pursuant to the conditions of the Receptions Conditions Directive.[94] The principle of the right to remain spelled out in Article 9 is also observed in Article 46, whereby applicants must be granted this right until the outcome of any exercise of the right to effective remedy.

Starting with Article 10, which addresses the requirements for the examination of applications, the goal of achieving a mandatory single procedure becomes more explicit. The first step, then, is for Member States to assess if an application qualifies for refugee status, or, if not, if it qualifies for subsidiary protection. These assessments, conducted in this order, are to be made in the context of one procedure. Article 10(3) then goes on to describe what elements must constitute an "appropriate examination" of applications. These include commitments to individual assessment of applications, using precise and up-to-date country of origin information from sources such as the European Asylum Support Office (or later the EUAA) or the United Nations High Commissioner for Refugees, among other "relevant human rights organisations," and ensuring that the personnel examining applications are both well trained in asylum and refugee law and that they have access to seek advice from experts on particular issues.

Procedural guarantees are also spelled out by Article 11, on the requirements for a decision the determining authority. Articles 11(1) and 11(2) both impose the requirement that decisions be given in writing, and that, if refugee and/or subsidiary status is rejected, decisions must include explanations "in fact and in law," accompanied by information on how the decision may be challenged.[95]

93 A preliminary application, according to Article 40 of the Directive, must first undergo a preliminary examination to establish if new facts have arisen which would affect the applicant's claim to international protection status (i.e., decision of admissibility), followed by a further analysis if such new elements have indeed been identified.

94 Directive 2013/33/EU of 26 June 2013 laying down standards for the reception of applicants for international protection [2013] OJ L180/96.

95 Derogation can be made from the requirement of providing information on how to appeal in cases where this information was already given at an earlier stage (Article 11(2)).

This implies that if an applicant is granted subsidiary protection, the decision must not only state this fact, but that it must also explain why refugee status was not granted. Nonetheless, there have been no rulings from the CJEU on any interpretation of the requirement that reasoning must be given in "fact and in law."[96] This is reflected further in the Directive, in Article 12, entitled Guarantees for Applicants, where the guarantees must be informed of the result of the decision in a language they can understand, including information on challenging any negative decision.

Article 12 in fact reiterates many of the guarantees mentioned elsewhere both in this Directive and in the Qualifications Directive. The right to be informed of procedural aspects, rights, and obligations, to receive the services of an interpreter, or benefit of legal counselling from a representative of UNHCR or another organisation that operates in accordance with the laws of the Member States are all guaranteed in Articles 12(a)-(c). Furthermore, 12(d) gives applicants and their representative access to the information supplied by the UNHCR or EASO under the requirements of Article 10. 12(d) and (e) both deal with the right to be informed of a decision, both regarding the content, as mentioned in the previous paragraph, but also to receive such a notice "in reasonable time."

Article 13, which dictates the obligations of the applicant, can be considered as adding an indicator to an otherwise discretionary provision in Article 4(2) of the Qualifications Directive. "Member States shall impose upon applicants the obligation to cooperate with the competent authorities with a view to establishing their identity and other elements referred to in Article 4(2) of Directive 2011/95/EU." This latter article does not impose any requirements on Member States, but only gives them the freedom consider it the duty of the applicant to submit the documents needed for examination. Thus, Article 13 develops a compulsory standard to complement a discretionary clause.

4.3 *The Personal Interview*

Procedural guarantees are also established in the requirements for a personal interview. Article 14(1) guarantees that an opportunity to have the interview itself must part of the procedural safeguards guaranteed by Member States. This guarantee includes any dependents of the applicant, even though, as previously noted, there is no definition of who exactly qualifies as dependent.[97]

96 European Asylum Support Office, *Asylum Procedures and the principle of non-refoulment* (n 92).

97 Member States may establish in national legislation the procedure for examining applications for the only group of the 'dependent' category that is defined in EU legislation: minors.

Several scenarios, nevertheless, do allow a Member State to derogate from the requirement that an opportunity for interview must be awarded. This includes during the preliminary examination conducted in accordance with Article 40 (which regulates the procedures for submitting and examining subsequent applications), if a positive decision on refugee status can be reached based on available evidence, or if the applicant is unfit to undergo an interview. In the case of the latter, efforts must be made for additional information to be provided, in lieu of the lack of information that comes with waving the personal interview. It should be mentioned, as well, that while the interview may be waived if a positive decision on refugee status can be reached, this does not apply similarly for subsidiary protection. In any case, the lack of a personal interview does not mean that a decision cannot be reached (Article 14(3)), nor does it mean that it must be mitigating factor in the reaching of a negative decision (Article 14(4)). In other words, if a Member State does not, or is not able to, conduct an interview, the process of examination cannot be paused, and it does not automatically lead to the refusal of the applicant.

The provisions of Articles 14(3) and (4) are loosened slightly in 14(5). Here, an exception is provided especially to (4), whereby authorities may use the provisions of Article 28(1)(a) and deem an unjustified absence from an interview as an implicit withdrawal of the application for international protection. In fact, while Article 14(1) itself does not require the presence of the applicant at the interview, there are several options in this Directive that give Member States the power to make the interview essentially mandatory. As recalled from Article 13(2)(a), Member States can quire that an applicant appears in person during the process. Furthermore, Article 23(4) allows for national legislation to lay down the rules on the presence of legal advisers during the interview, while Article 25(1) allows Member States to require unaccompanied minors to be present at the time of the personal interview.

Further rules on conducting interviews are found elsewhere in the Directive, showing the importance that the personal interview is given in reaching a decision. Article 34 regulates the rules for the interview during the admissibility examination, whereby an application is judged on merit, not substance, calling on Member States to ensure access to an interview even at this stage of the process. Such focus on the personal interviews can be attributed to Article 4 of the Qualifications Directive, specifically the requirement of an individual assessment of facts and circumstances, since the admissibility procedure should allow applicants to present their "particular circumstances," (Article 34(1)). The only derogation that this article allows is that Member States may allow for personnel from another authority other than the competent asylum authority to conduct admissibility interviews, as long as they are properly trained. This is likely a way for the Directive to allow such interviews to take place in border areas, an issue that will be discussed in greater detail when addressing the requirements for border procedures, and which will likely become more relevant once the reform Regulation enters into force, where border procedures become more and more prominent.

While Article 14 establishes the right to have an interview, Article 15 regulates the inner workings of said interview. Articles 15(1) and (2) safeguard the provisions enumerated in Article 11 by focusing on the right to privacy of the applicant. The former establishes that, unless necessary for the interview, no family members must be present, while the latter stipulates that complete confidentiality must be observed. Article 15(3), on the other hand, can be described as setting the standards for those present at the interview beside the applicant. This includes the requirement that the interviewer must have competences, i.e., proper training, (15(3)(a) and (e)), when possible, it must be of the same gender as the applicant (15(3)(b)), and he or she must not wear military or law enforcement uniforms (15(3)(d)). Article 15(3)(c) also requires that interpreters must be properly trained, especially when it comes to the ability to communicate with the interviewer, and, when possible and requested, the interpreter must be of the same gender as the applicant. Lastly, 15(4) allows Member States to lay down the rules on the presence of third parties at the interviews. As Article 23 makes clear, however, this is not a fully discretionary power; according to the provisions of this Article, the applicant must have access to legal representatives, including those from agencies such as the UNHCR.

Article 16, meanwhile, describes the purpose of the interview, emphasising the requirement of the individual assessment standard of the Qualifications Directive.

> When conducting a personal interview on the substance of an application for international protection, the determining authority shall ensure that the applicant is given an adequate opportunity to present elements needed to substantiate the application in accordance with Article 4 of Directive 2011/95/EU as completely as possible. This shall include the opportunity to give an explanation regarding elements which may be missing and/or any inconsistencies or contradictions in the applicant's statements.

While this article sets the scope of what an interview should achieve, the following article brings to light another common thread found throughout the Directive: the right to be properly informed. A report or transcript of all interviews must be drafted (Article 17(1)), which may include a video or recording (2), and applicants and their representative must have access to these. Interviewees must have the ability to comment and/or provide clarifications on the transcript or report, as a verification step, unless video or audio recording is made ((3) and (4)). Refusal to confirm the contents of the transcript or report shall not in it of itself prevent the reaching of a decision. Once again, this provision is complemented by another article, namely 31(8), whereby in an accelerated or prioritised procedure access to the transcript, report, and/or recording can be given when decision is rendered, but must nevertheless be subject to effective remedy, as is Article 17 in its entirety.

4.4 *Procedural Guarantees for an Individual Assessment*

Another direct reference to the individual assessment is also found in Article 18, which regulates how and when medical examinations must be conducted. This allowance must be made only to identify signs of serious harm, whenever the determining authority deems it relevant (18(1)). The use of the word *relevant* in this Article indicates that such examination can serve a double purpose: not only can they assess whether an applicant has or has not been subject to harm, but it can also serve as a tool for credibility assessment: is the applicant reliable in his or her statements? If, on the other hand, a Member State chooses not to conduct a medical examination, they do have the obligation to inform the applicant that they may choose to have a medical examination conducted on their own. These provisions need to be conducted while keeping Recital 31 of the Directive in mind, whereby it is clearly stated that assessments of this nature must be made within the framework of the Istanbul Protocol on Effective Investigation and Documentation of Torture and Other Inhumane Treatment.

As already mentioned, one of the recurring themes identified in the Directive is that of access to information. Article 19(1) enshrines this guarantee further, especially at first instance and for motivating negative decisions. Information must be made available not only to applicants, but also to any representative they might have. Article 20, on the other hand, guarantees such legal assistance also in appeal procedures, at least the preparation of required documents and participation in any hearings. Legal representation and assistance at other steps of the examination procedure can be limited according to the resources of the applicant, and "only through the services provided by legal advisers or other counsellors specifically designated by national law to assist and represent applicants," (Article 21(2)(a)-(b)). As EASO pointed out in its judicial analysis from 2018,[98] the wording of Article 21 allows for large discretion in how the provisions should be interpreted. Legal assistance can be given by NGOs or government authorities, as designated in national legislation, they need not be specifically lawyers, it can be restricted based on the material needs of the applicant, meaning that applicants who can afford it need not be provided with free assistance. Furthermore, Member States may impose monetary and time limits on said assistance, and in some cases even demand reimbursements for costs (21(4)-(5)). Even more, the wording of Article 20(3) is also worthy of note, whereby representation in cases of appeals can be denied in case the appeal has no "tangible prospect of success." As the right to information is ever present, so is the discretionary freedom given based on reasons of security and public order. We see this in Article 23(1). Legal representatives, indeed, must have access to the information present in the application file, yet an exception is given where security could be threatened, the safety of those providing information could be put in jeopardy, or it could compromise the investigative interest or international relations of the Member State.

As the literary analysis showed, there is little formal discretion given to the guarantees that must be observed when dealing with vulnerable groups. Article 24 of the Procedures Directives, for instance, compels competent authorities to assess whether an applicant is in need of special procedural guarantees, specifying that such an assessment can be integrated into the assessment referred to in Article 22 of the Receptions Conditions Directive. This would indicate that special *reception* needs take precedent over special *procedural* needs. To understand this case, a short detour into the Reception Conditions Directive is needed.

Article 21 of this Directive, which opens the chapter on Provisions for Vulnerable Groups, provides a delineation of who a member of a vulnerable group is:

> Member States shall take into account the specific situation of vulnerable persons such as minors, unaccompanied minors, elderly people, pregnant women, single parents with minor children, victims of human trafficking, persons with serious illness, persons with mental disorders, and persons who have been subjected to torture, rape, or other serious forms of psychological, physical or sexual violence, such as victims of female genital mutilation, in the national law implementing the Directive.

---

98 European Asylum Support Office, *Asylum Procedures and the principle of non-refoulment* (n 92).

Furthermore, Article 22 states that Member States must assess if an applicant might have special reception needs arising from the above definition. Article 22(2), then, states clearly that such an assessment "need not take the form of an administrative procedure." This, in fact, is an approach to vulnerable groups which is not included in the Asylum Procedures Directives, but only in Article 31(7), which allows for the prioritisation of applications from those who fall under the definition of Article 22 of the Receptions Conditions Directive. Returning nevertheless to applicants in need of special procedural guarantees, by referencing the special assessment for vulnerability in Article 24, the Asylum Procedure Directive is drawing an equivalence between vulnerability and the need for special procedural guarantees.[99] Yet, by giving precedence to the examination of special reception needs, the Directive also allows for this assessment to take place outside of an administrative procedure. That being said, if special needs are identified, Member States shall cease to apply accelerated or border procedures.

Article 24 of the Procedures Directive also establishes a balance between certain temporal demands placed on decision making. The assessment of needs must be done within a "reasonable time," the interpretation of what is reasonable not being provided. Yet, according to Recital 29, applicants with special procedural needs must be "provided with adequate support, including sufficient time, in order to create the conditions necessary for their effective access to procedures." An equilibrium must be struck between what qualifies as "reasonable" in accordance with Article 24, and what is "sufficient" according to Recital 29.

Perhaps the most well defined and protected vulnerable group is that of unaccompanied minors, covered by Article 25. Member States must ensure that these minors have access to a representative (Article 25(1)(a)), and that such access is given free of charge throughout the entire procedure – including withdrawal of protection. Such a representative must be observant of principle of the best interests of the child, a concept reinforced in Article 23(3)(a)-(b), whereby those conducting interviews or preparing decisions must observe the

99 This is reinforced by Recital 29: "Certain applicants may be in need of special procedural guarantees due, inter alia, to their age, gender, sexual orientation, gender identity, disability, serious illness, mental disorders or as a consequence of torture, rape or other serious form of psychological, physical or sexual violence." The Directive, however, never directly makes an explicit link between special procedural needs and vulnerable groups. This is likely because of the requirement for individual assessment of facts. If the Directive would have tied administrative procedures to group characteristics, this could have hampered the application of Article 4 of the Qualifications Directive.

same principle, Article 25(6), whereby "the best interests of the child shall be a primary consideration for Member States when implementing this Directive," and Recital 33, which explicitly defines the principle as being linked to the provisions of the Charter of Fundamental Rights of the European Union and the 1989 United Nations Convention on the Rights of the Child.

The only possibility for derogation granted in this directive comes from allowing Member States to refrain from appointing a representative when the unaccompanied minor will likely turn 18 before a decision at first instance is rendered. Furthermore, where the age of a minor cannot be determined with certainty, a medical examination may be requested, as long as the right to dignity, information and representation are respected, and the refusal to undergo a medical examination is not the sole consideration when rejecting an application. We also see in Articles 25(6)(a)&(b) an example of applicants with special procedural guarantees, where the discretion of Member States to an accelerated procedure (Article 31(8)) is restrained. This can only be applied if the applicant comes from a safe country of origin, has introduced an admissible subsequent application, or once again, if there are security reasons invoked by the Member State. Similarly, border procedures (Article 43) can only be applied if the applicant comes from a safe country of origin, a subsequent application has been introduced, there are security considerations, there is a safe third country that the applicant could go to, or if the applicant has misled authorities in any way. Lastly and similarly, a Member State can only declare an application to be inadmissible, based on the safe third country consideration of Article 33(2)(c), if and only if to do so is consistent with the previously espoused rights of children.

While also advocating for the needs for certain procedural guarantees, the articles which regulate the procedure in the event of withdrawal of application deal with a very specific aspect of the application process: the one where, either explicitly or implicitly, an applicant abandons his or her application for protection. Article 27 requires Member States to make a decision, either to discontinue or reject, in the event of explicit withdrawal, insofar as national legislation allows for such a possibility. Article 28 makes a similar demand, but this only in the context of an 'implicit' withdrawal. A rejection, in this case, can only happen if the application is categorised as unfounded after an adequate examination has occurred. For an application to be able to be considered implicitly withdrawn, it must be ascertained that the applicant has failed to respond to requests for information or, without proper justification, did not show up to the interview, or he or she has absconded. In the event of a discontinued application, Article 28(2) clearly states that an applicant must have the right to request that an application be reopened, without being subject to the provisions of a subsequent application (Articles 40 and 41). This may be subjected to a time limit of at least nine months. After this time has elapsed, Member States may stipulate that a case cannot be reopened and must thus be treated as a subsequent application.

Last of the procedural guarantees made in this Directive is that of the role that UNHCR must be allowed to play in the application process. Article 29 reiterates many of the already mentioned guarantees that must be made for UNHCR. They must have access to applicants, including those in detention and/or border areas, as well as access to information on individual applications for protection, subject, of course, to the approval of the applicant (29(1)(a)-(b)). Representatives of the organisation must also be afforded the opportunity to present their views, even if another organisation which is working on behalf of the UNHCR in the Member State.

4.5 *Guarantees for the Examination Procedure at First Instance*

Perhaps the most relevant section of the Directive, Chapter III (and other related instruments) regulate the procedures for examining application at first instance. Article 31 lays down the process for the examination procedure, specific that basic guarantees listed in previous sections must be observed, and as soon as possible a decision must be reached, but within six months of the lodging of application, or from the moment the responsible Member State has taken charge of the applicant, pursuant to the Dublin regulation. This time frame, however, is quite flexible. If the application presents a complex issue in fact and/or law, if there is an event of mass arrivals, or if there is a failure of the applicant to fulfil their obligations, the six-months' time limit can be extended for a further nine months, and an extra three months may be added in duly justified and necessary cases. In any case, the article finally states that "Member States shall conclude the examination procedure within a maximum time limit of 21 months from the lodging of the application," (Article 31(5)). In such a case, one may wonder, what is the relevance of the shorter period established?

There may also be a postponement of concluding an examination if the danger in the country of origin shows indications that it might be temporary. In this sense, Member States shall ensure regular review of the situation in the country, at least every six months (31(4)(a)), must provide information on the reason for the postponement (b), and must inform the European Commission of such postponements (c). Opposite postponement, Member States may in certain cases prioritise an application (Article 31(7)) if it is likely to be well founded, or if the applicant is vulnerable in accordance with Article 22 of the Reception Conditions Directive or has need for special procedural guarantees.

Article 31(8) allows for accelerated procedures to take place at border and/or transit zones, if the applicant has raised facts that are inconsistent, contradictory, false, or not relevant to the application, if he or she comes from a safe country of origin, has likely disposed of or destroyed relevant documents, has introduced subsequent applications, has entered the territory illegally and has not presented him or herself to the relevant authorities as soon as possible, or if they are a danger to security or public order. These provisions must be read in conjunction with Article 43 on border procedures, whereby it is clearly stated that if a decision on admissibility cannot be taken within 4 weeks, the applicant must be granted entry. Lastly, in cases of mass arrivals of asylum seekers, these procedures may be implemented at special locations close to the border which may accommodate the large number of arrivals (Article 43(3)).

An application can also be categorised as unfounded if the qualifications for protection from Directive 95/2011/EU are not met, or if any of the conditions from Article 31(8) are met. On the other hand, an application is inadmissible (Article 33) in several cases: if protection has been granted by another Member State (Article 39), if a non-EU country can be considered a first country of asylum, if there is a safe third country for the applicant (Article 35), or if this is a subsequent application with no relevant new information. A country can be considered first country of asylum if the applicant has been recognised in said country as a refugee, or if she or he enjoys sufficient protection, especially from *refoulment*. Similarly, a third country can also be categorised as safe country of origin, according to Article 36, if the applicant has nationality there, or residency as a stateless person, and no claim has been submitted on behalf of the applicant arguing that the country is not safe. This description is only a starting point for identifying the safe country of origin concept, as Member States "shall lay down in national legislation further rules and modalities for the application," (Article 36(2)). In all events, the Directive does include, in Annex I, and directly referenced in Article 37, rules on the national designation of the safe country of origin concept:

> A country is considered a safe country of origin where, on the basis of the legal situation, the application of the law within a democratic system and the general political circumstances, it can be shown that there is generally and consistently no persecution ... no torture or inhuman or degrading treatment or punishment and no threat by reason of indiscriminate violence is situations of international or internal armed conflict.

This final phrasing, referring to indiscriminate violence in situation of international or internal conflict does refer us back to the case-law interpreting these provisions in the Qualifications Directive. Now, in this Annex, the Directive also gives certain indicators that must be assessed when making this decision: the relevant laws and regulations in the country, observance of basic freedoms, respect for the principle of *non-refoulment*, and the existence of a system for effective remedies. Article 37(2), however, does provide that a regular review of the situation in the country of origin must be undertaken for those countries designated as safe third countries, information from UNHCR, EASO/EUAA, or other actors must be taken into account when such decision is made (3), and the Commission must be notified of any such designation.

Finally, the concept of safe third country is elaborated upon in Article 38. This concept can be applied when there is no threat to life or liberty, no risk of serious harm as defined in the Qualifications Directive, the principle of *non-refoulment* is respected, and the freedom from torture, cruel, or inhuman treatment is guaranteed. For a country to be considered a safe-third country, there must exist the possibility to request refugee status and be entitled to the guarantees of the Geneva Convention. Nevertheless, Member States are open to some discretion. They may require that the applicant have a direct connection to the third country based on which it could be expected that he or she can go to said country. Member States may also establish in national legislation the rules and methodologies by which competent authorities determine if a country is a safe third country. Effective remedy is seen again as a cornerstone of the provisions, as applicants must be able to challenge the designation of a third country as a safe.

There are, nonetheless, still certain obligations that must be observed. If a decision is based solely on the consideration that a country is a safe third country, Member States must inform the applicant and draft a letter to the authorities of the third country, informing them that the application has not been examined in substance. If the applicant is not allowed to return to the third country, Member States must grant him or her access to the procedure detailed in the Directive. A second type of safe third country is the European safe third country, covered by Article 39. Any country which observes the provisions of the Geneva Convention, has established an asylum procedure, and observes the European Convention for the Protection of Human Rights and Fundamental Freedoms can be categorised as such. In this case, if the applicant is seeking to enter, or has already done so, illegally, from a safe third country, no examination of the applications needs to take place.

The provisions regarding European safe third countries must be read considering the clauses found in Article 33(2)(a), whereby an application can be considered as inadmissible if another Member State has granted international protection. The Court has made this link themselves, in *Ibrahim et al.*[100] A Member State may declare an application as inadmissible, the Court argues, even if the material conditions that the asylum seeker would enjoy in the other Member State would be substantially lower, as long as these would not amount to abject poverty. Links in reasoning for interpreting these provisions may be found nevertheless with the interpretation that the Court offers in other cases that deal with different, yet not completely unrelated, concepts. *Aranyosi and Căldăraru,*[101] for example, is a case which deals with the execution of a European Arrest Warrant in cases where the requesting country suffers from systematic deficiencies in detention facilities. In fact, in Paragraph 5 of the Advocate General's opinion for this case, he states that "the Court will have to ask itself whether the principles which it has identified in other areas of EU law, such as those ... concerning the Common European Asylum System, can be transposed to the specific mechanism of the European arrest warrant at the risk of blocking that mechanism." There are, of course, limits to drawing the comparison between the two systems: although they both have to do with the creation of an area of freedom, security and justice, they fulfil different obligations. The CEAS is based on a "comprehensive body of rules harmonised at the Union level," while the European arrest warrant is intendent to ensure prosecution and punishment as opposed to protection from persecution. That being said, "in circumstances ... characterised by a systemic deficiency of detention conditions in the issuing Member State, the executing judicial authority may legitimately ask the issuing judicial authority for any information necessary to enable it to assess ... whether surrender of the requested person is likely to expose him to detention conditions that are disproportionate."[102]

Finally, as it has already been mentioned, Article 40 establishes the rules of subsequent applications. Namely, and something that has not been addressed hitherto in this project, this article calls for the examination of a subsequent

100 Joined Cases C-297/17, C-318/17 and C-319/17 *Bashar Ibrahim, Mahmud Ibrahim and Others, Nisreen Sharqawi, Yazan Fattayrji, Hosam Fattayrji v Bundesrepublik Deutschland and Bundesrepublik Deutschland v Taus Magamadov* [2019].

101 Joined Cases C-404/15 and C-659/15 PPU *Pál Aranyosi and Robert Căldăraru v Generalstaatsanwaltschaft Bremen* [2016].

102 Ibid. We may think back to previous chapters where it was shown that in some cases the provisions of Dublin were suspended, and asylum seekers were not returned to Greece due to what was perceived as serious deficiencies in the asylum system there. See also Joined Cases C-540/17 and C-541/17 *Bundesrepublik Deutschland v Adel Hamed and Amar Omar* [2019], and Case C-517/17 *Milkiyas Addis v Bundesrepublik Deutschland* [2020], all cases which ask similar questions about the level of support received for asylum seekers if they were to be sent from Germany to Italy.

application on its substance, only if a preliminary examination indeed establishes that new facts have risen. If such new facts are identified, the examination has to re-enter the procedure described in this Directive. This is enshrined in Article 42, which states that "Member Sates shall ensure that applicants whose application is subject to preliminary examination pursuant to Article 40 enjoy the guarantees provided for in Article 12(1)." Nevertheless, it may be established in national legislation that the applicant is obliged to justify with facts and evidence a new procedure.

One interesting result of the provisions listed until now is that they seem to allow, not entirely in line with the requirement of individual examination of applications, group-level categorisations of applicants. Indeed, it is not provided that final decisions on cases should be based on these categorisations, and individual assessment of facts and of context needs to be studied. Yet, in *H.I.D. and B.A.*,[103] the court made this principle clear: categories of asylum applications can be made based on nationality or safe country of origin information, and this can inform the decision to place an application in accelerated or prioritised procedure.

4.6 *Withdrawal of International Protection and Effective Remedy*

The final guarantees covered by the Asylum Procedures Directive are in case of withdrawing international protection, although this does not directly relate to a first instance decision. Article 44 allows for withdrawal to take place if new facts show that there are serious reasons to reconsider the protection granted. Article 45 complements this with a description of procedural rules, and these follow the lines already observed in other guarantees at other stages of the procedure: the right of the applicant to be informed (45(1)(a)), and the right for the applicant to defend his or her status, in a personal interview or written statement (45(1)(b)). Member States may not, however, when seeking information for the purposes of reconsidering applications, request it from actors of persecution or serious harm (45(2)(b)). Finally, Member States may also withdraw protection is the applicant has renounced such status, or if he or she has acquired the nationality of the Member State.

Article 46, on the other hand, establishes concretely the right to an effective remedy. This must be granted against decisions of categorising applications as unfounded, inadmissible, taken at border or in transit zones, of not examining or refusing to reopen an application, or against a decision to withdraw international protection all together. Similarly, it is important, a decision to grant

103 Case C-175/11 *H.I.D. and B.A. v Refugee Applications Commissioner and Others* [2013].

subsidiary protection instead of refugee status must also be subject to effective remedy, pursuant to Article 46(2). Again, a balance on the requirement of time limits is called for: Article 46(4) calls for reasonable time limits, but not so that they render an exercise in effective remedy impossible or excessively difficult.

In *Diouf*,[104] the CJEU was faced with a question regarding an application which was deemed to be unfounded during an accelerated procedure. This ruling was on the first version of the Procedures Directive, which did not include, as the recast version does, "unfounded" applications as being subjected to effective remedy. The referring court also argued that, since accelerated procedures examine an application on merit, not substance, these should not be subject to effective remedy. The Court agreed that "the decisions against which an applicant for asylum must have a remedy are those which entail rejection of the application for asylum for substantive reasons or, as the case may be, for formal or procedural reasons which preclude any decision on the substance. It follows that decisions that are preparatory to the decision on the substance or decisions pertaining to the organisation of the procedure are not covered by that provision."[105] Interpreting the access to effective remedy as something that covers the procedure for preparing a final decision would therefore not be consistent with the requirement of expediency of decision-making. Therefore, the Court argued, deciding in an accelerated procedure cannot be challenged, if the motivation for examining the application in such a way is well-founded. In other words, the outcome of a procedure may be challenged, but not the motivation for entering the specific type of procedure. Presumably, this is because the final decision will reflect not only the substance of the application, but also the preparatory examination undertaken, thus still being subject to effective remedy.

Since effective remedy is one of the cornerstones of the Directive, it follows that the CJEU has interpreted these provisions in several ways. In *Sacko*,[106] it has made clear that, if procedures such as personal interview have been followed, national courts or tribunals can dismiss an appeal altogether without hearing the applicant, if there is no doubt that the appeal is unfounded. There have also been several questions on the power of national tribunals in the appeal process. In *QJ*[107] the referring court asks if, in the case where a tribunal

104 Case C-69/10 *Brahim Samba Diouf v Ministre du Travail, de l'Emploi et de l'Immigration* [2011] I-07151.

105 Ibid paras 41–44.

106 Case C-348/16 *Moussa Sacko v Commissione Territoriale per il riconoscimento della Protezione internazionale di Milano* [2017].

107 Case C-113/17 *QJ v Ministerstvo vnútra SR Migračný úrad* [2018].

grants an appeal, yet the competent authorities consistently reject the application, can the tribunal grant protection even if it does not have such competences under national law? Similar questions were raised in *Torubarov*[108] and in *D&I*.[109] In the latter case, the referring court asks specifically if the tribunal hearing an appeal may take into account information which was not presented during the examination procedure, and if not, if they are allowed or not to refer the new information back to the competent authorities. In the case of *Belastingdienst v Toeslagen*[110] we see a mix of themes from the Procedures Directive converging. Aside from effective remedy, the questions asked here have to do with the suspensory effect of withdrawal in case an appeal is made against an effective remedy. The court says explicitly that there is no need for a two-level jurisdiction: the right to remain, and all rights deriving from the procedures in the Directive, must be ensured up to the process of effective remedy. There cannot be, however, an appeal of an appeal.

The Procedures Directive, while establishing complex sets of procedural rules and guarantees, does open avenues for interpretation, and use of discretionary powers. Interestingly, however, are the recent developments of using political solutions to any of the legislative ambiguities described in this chapter. Take, for instance, the EU-Turkey Agreement, which while having no legal basis, was seen as a way to deal with the failures of Dublin and of border procedures in dealing with a large number of asylum seekers coming at one time. Considering this agreement, Greece amended its asylum law, restricting the access of applicants on islands close to Turkey, thus allowing for an easy return. Leaving aside the political decision to classify Tukey as a safe third country, this presented further problems when it came to access granted to basic receptions conditions and proper effective remedy. The agreement, basically, altered border procedures by making, de facto, Turkey a safe third country. It is, in fact, as many of the cases before the Court of Justice have shown, after the issuance of these rulings that CJEU began employing less and less judicial activism, and started relying more and more on judicial passivism, leaving thus many provisions in an ambiguous state of interpretation.

---

108 Case C-556/17 *Alekszij Torubarov v Bevándorlási és Menekültügyi Hivatal* [2019].

109 Case C-586/17 *Staatssecretaris van Veiligheid en Justitie and I. v D* [2019].

110 Case C-175/17 *X v Belastingdienst/Toeslagen* [2018].

5 Conclusions

Taken together, the last two chapters sought to add to the understanding of how the implementation of asylum policy happens by providing an extensive analysis of the ambiguities found in the Qualifications Directive and the Asylum Procedures Directive. By looking specifically at their provisions regulating first instance decisions, we can identify what ambiguities are being passed down in the policy process, eventually making their way to the street-level. The literal analysis of the Directives, coupled with the interpretation provided by the CJEU, shows why it is important to move the understanding of asylum policy implementation, and harmonisation, beyond the limiting perspective centred around transposition.

Despite varying numbers of discretionary provisions found in the directives, it is evident that interpretive ambiguities often emerge. For example, while access to effective remedy has no literal discretion provisions, it makes up a great deal of preliminary ruling requests before the CJEU. What is crucial is the difference between the ambiguities identified in a black-letter analysis, and the interpretive ambiguities identified through case law analysis. Through the work of the Court, the tensions between the objectives of the CEAS, become more evident. In *Alheto*,[111] for instance, the Court clarifies that the approximation of rules under the Qualifications and Asylum Procedures Directives aims to limit movements, while many other cases underline the importance of the individual assessment of a claim to international protection in the context of protecting rights.

Many cases also involve clarifications that would seem straightforward by means of a literal reading of the directives. Such is the case in *B&D*,[112] where the court must explain what the meaning of refugee is, or in *Ahmedbekova & Ahmedbekov*, were it clarifies that the concept of family unity means that refugee status must also mean that family members are entitled to protection.[113] In other instances, nonetheless, ambiguities may be observed because of incomplete information or conflicting goals. Referring to *Alheto* again, we have an example where it is unclear if some who has already been recognised as a refugee by another actor – therefore meeting the requirements for protection – must still have their application assessed, since already benefiting from protection is ground for exclusion. Other interpretations include, for instance, what

111 *Alheto* (n 38).
112 *B & D* (n 21).
113 *Ahmedbekova and Ahmedbekov* (n 3).

'real risk' is, or how to assess whether a conflict constitutes 'internal armed conflict' in the context of the two directives.

Even cases that deal with provisions often thought to be entirely discretionary – i.e., national security, have been scrutinised. In *Lounani*,[114] the court is asked to interpret if being convicted for a terrorist offense is enough to exclude someone from refugee status. It shows that not even questions of national security, for which states often have discretion in implementation, are straightforward. The analysis of discretionary clauses and the examples presented in this chapter show the importance of moving beyond transposition. We should not only care about how the asylum acquis is transposed, but also how it is implemented in practice. Even when directives are transposed correctly, interpretive ambiguities arise. This demonstrates that the importance placed on bureaucratic norms of implementation is crucial, since it is through these norms that any ambiguities passed down are settled. The following part of this book will look specifically at how this happens in Romania and the Netherlands.

114 *Lounani* (n 34).

CHAPTER 5

National Implementation of the CEAS: The Case of Romania

Romania is governed by a civil law system, meaning that judicial precedent is not a source of legal rules, and that only the Constitution and other statutory legislation are sources of legislative procedures. When a statute is silent, legal textbooks and treaties are often used for guidance. Legislation is enacted by a bicameral parliament, while the executive branch, led by the Prime Minister, oversees the ruling bodies that are charged with implementing policies and administering the county and local levels of governance.[1] The executive is also charged with the implementation of international treaties or agreements.

While the legislative branch issues the statutory legislation of Romania, the Government relies on decisions and ordinances. Decisions are issued to regulate areas of law enforcement, and ordinances are passed only based on a facilitating law, and within the restrictions and conditions enumerated in said law. Individual ministers in the governmental cabinet can also issues their own rules in the forms of ministerial orders and decisions, and agencies subordinated to the government can formulate rules and guidelines as well. The judicial branch, on the other hand, operates its civilian courts organised at the county and municipal level, under the principle of double jurisdiction. Any decision from a first instance court can be challenged and subject to a *de novo* trial on the law and the procedure by a higher court or a court of appeal. While before 1989 the administration of the judicial system fell under the Ministry of Justice, post-1989 saw this responsibility fall upon the High Court of Cassation and Justice, as well as lower courts, pursuant to Article 126 of the Romanian Constitution. Unlike in other systems, however, the Romanian High Court for Cassation and Justice cannot rule on the constitutionality of acts, as this function is reserved for the Constitutional Court.

There are several pieces of legislation, aside from those that directly influence asylum, that are relevant for the present work. For understanding the general role of bureaucrats in the administration of the state, with the Administrative Code, being one of the most relevant. Before understanding

1 The Presidency of Romania is also a part of the executive, but its powers and responsibilities are not relevant to this analysis.

 | DOI:10.1163/9789004700826_006

how the laws governing asylum are written, we must understand the architecture of the laws governing the state's administration.

1 Constitution, Human Rights, and Good Governance

Today's constitution is a result of an update done to the 1991 Constitution drafted after the fall of Romania's communist regime. As stated, the Constitution is the fundamental law of Romania since rulings of courts do not constitute law. The document establishes the structure of government and relations between the branches, the mechanism by which laws are passed, and the rights and responsibilities of citizens.

The first post-communist constitution, approved in November 1991 and adopted through a national referendum in December 1991, contained 152 articles spread over 7 chapters, or Titles (*Titluri* in Romanian). None of these were altered with the later revision in 2003. These Titles are (I) General Principles, (II) Rights, freedoms and fundamental duties, (III) Public Authorities, (IV) Economy and public finances, (V) the Constitutional Court, (VI) Revising the Constitution, and (VII) Final and transitory provisions. In 2003, however, a new Title was introduced into the constitution, entitled "Euro-Atlantic Integration." This Title includes a new Article 148, regarding integration into the European Union, and Article 149 regarding accession to the North Atlantic Treaty.

Article 148, which is of particular interest here, states that "as a result of accession, the provisions of the constitutive treaties of the European Union as well as other community regulations of an obligatory nature, have priority over contrary dispositions in internal law," and "Parliament, the President of Romania, the government, and the judicial authority shall guarantee the fulfilment of the obligations emerging from the accession act." But even before this amendment was brought about, there are several instances in the Romanian constitution where reference to international structures is referenced.[2]

Article 11 obliges the Romanian state to fulfil all obligations arising from international treaties, and that all such treaties that are ratified by parliament become internal law. Article 18 guarantees that foreign citizens and stateless persons enjoy the general protections enshrined in the constitution, specifically mentioning that the right to asylum is awarded and withdrawn in accordance with the law and with respect for the international treaties and conventions

2 Romania's previous constitution, the 1966 Constitution of the Socialist Republic of Romania, made no reference to the role of international treaties or agreements on national law.

to which Romania is a part. Art. 19(3) sates that foreign citizens and stateless persons can only be extradited if there is an international convention based on which to do so, or in conditions of reciprocity. Both expulsion and extradition, according to Art. 19(4), can only be done based on a judicial decision. Article 20, on the other hand, directly deals with issues of human rights, claiming that "constitutional provisions regarding the rights and freedoms of citizens will be interpreted and applied according to the Universal Declaration for Human Rights, with the all other pacts and treaties to which Romania is a part [...] If there are any inconsistencies between the pacts and treaties regarding fundamental human rights to which Romania is a part, international regulations have priority, with the exception of cases where the Constitution or internal laws include more favourable provisions." From a black-on-white perspective, this indicates that even if a reform of the Common European Asylum System would see a race to the bottom for offering and withdrawing international protection, the Romanian legislation should maintain the more favourable standards already existing in the national law.

Despite the thoroughness of the Romanian constitution in addressing the organisation of the state, and the observance of international standards for human rights, several critics have labelled this document a "façade constitution,"[3] widely used for political reasons. According to Paul Blokker, an analysis shows that "legal Romania" and "real Romania" stand at a distance, with constitutional language far removed from societal interaction. Venelin Ganev builds on this view to claim that, in the run-up to EU accession, Romania was showing signs of a consolidated democratic governance, including cross-party conflicts that did not affect the overarching constitutional structure,[4] this being one of the reasons Romania was deemed ready for accession. These progresses, however, have been reversed in the years following Romania's entrance into the EU, with corruption being the main driving factor.

What some might consider even more distinguishing, however, is the inability of Romania to adequately adapt to the process of Europeanisation, particularly as a result of incomplete social, political, and economic reforms carried out pre-accession.[5] While trends similar to those seen in the 2004 enlargement wave are also apparent in the 2007 enlargement countries, namely the rise

3 Paul Blokker, 'Romanian Constitutionalism: Form without Content?' [2012] *SSRN Electronic Journal* 1.

4 Venelin I. Ganev, 'Post-Accession Hooliganism: Democratic Governance in Bulgaria and Romania after 2007' (2013) 27 *East European Politics and Societies: and Cultures* 26.

5 Svetlozar A. Andreev, 'The Unbearable Lightness of Membership: Bulgaria and Romania after the 2007 EU' (2009) 42 *Communist and Post-Communist Studies* 375.

populist messages, sharp increase in political competition, and widespread perception of social dissatisfaction, "EU institutions have been much more sensitive to signals about sleaze and administrative ineptitude in the two [2007 enlargement] member states than they used to be in the case of the previous entries from East-Central Europe."[6] As a result, Romania is considered to be among the laggards of proper European integration.

These macro-level developments, far removed from the street-level where the bureaucrats at the centre of this study conduct their work, bear significance because they point to the nature of governance in Romania. This book previously argued that the rules prescribed by the Asylum Procedures Directive and the Qualifications Directive are based on the principles of good governance,[7] namely transparency, accountability, effectiveness, and the rule of law. These are, in fact, benchmarks important for the overall process of integration that Romania must undergo.[8] By November 2017, a report from the Commission stated that none of the benchmarks could be considered fulfilled,[9] and one year later, in 2018, specifically stated that "the entry into force of the amended Justice laws, the pressure on judicial independence in general and on the National Anti-Corruption Directorate in particular, and other steps undermining the fight against corruption have reversed or called into question the irreversibility of progress."[10]

But the lack of progress generally on good governance has also led to a continued lowering level of political participation. Of course, here some of the blame must also be attributed to the influence of former authoritarian regimes, since it is in Central and Eastern Europe that we see this trend in post-accession years.[11] Another perspective points not necessarily to the democratic

6 Ibid 390.

7 Torben Beck Jørgensen and Ditte-Lene Sørensen, 'Codes of Good Governance. National or Global Public Values?' (2012) 15 *Public Integrity* 71.

8 See Decision of 13/XII/2006 establishing a mechanism for cooperation and verification of progress in Romania to address specific benchmarks in the areas of judicial reform of and the fight against corruption.

9 Commission, 'Report from the Commission to the European Parliament and the Council on Progress in Romania under the Cooperation and Verifications Mechanism' (2017).

10 Commission, 'Report from the Commission to the European Parliament and the Council on Progress in Romania under the Cooperation and Verifications Mechanism' (2018).

11 See Steven E. Finkel, Stan Humphries, and Karl-Dieter Opp, 'Socialist Values and the Development of Democratic Support in the Former East Germany' (2001) 22 *International Political Science Review* 339; Natalia Letki and Geoffrey Evans, 'Endogenizing Social Trust: Democratization in East-Central Europe' (2005) 35 *British Journal of Political Science* 515; Pia Horvat and Geoffrey Evans, 'Age, Inequality, and Reactions to Marketization in Post-Communist Central and Eastern Europe' (2011) 27 *European Sociological Review* 708; Marc Hooghe and Ellen Quintelier, 'Political Participation in European Countries: The Effect

legacy of the member state in particular, but rather to the idea that citizens in these countries, including Romania, are faced with a regime that deviates from the ideal more and more each day.[12] Whichever the case, it still holds true that while institutionally all elements of a democratic regime are written in black and white, political elites still abuse their power, discriminate, and supress. Combine this with a very limited economic growth, and countries in the post-Communist sphere are more likely to see diminished levels of political involvement.[13] As Lipsky argued, public opinion can often serve as a deterrent for abuse of power on behalf of implementing officials; lower political participation may also translate into lower levels of societal pressures made by those charged with policy implementation. How, then, is the work of implementing officials managed, monitored, and evaluated? The following sections will dive into the specifics that regulate the activity of Romanian bureaucracies and bureaucrats. Following this, an image of the formal discretionary space that each bureaucrat in Romania must navigate will start to emerge, within which the specifics of asylum bureaucracies will be applied.

2 OUG 57/2019 – The Administrative Code

Government Emergency Ordinance (*Ordonanță de Urgență a Guvernului*, or *OUG*, in Romanian) regarding the administrative code is an ordinance issued by the Romanian Government in July 2019 with the scope of regulating the organisation and functioning of the "public administration authorities and institutions, the statute of personnel in these organisations, administrative accountability, [and] public services."[14] For the purposes of this legislation, Article 2 defines central public administration authorities as "the Government, its ministries, other specialised central organisations subordinate to the Government or its ministries, administrative autonomous authorities," and Article 4 states

of Authoritarian Rule, Corruption, Lack of Good Governance and Economic Downturn' (2013) 12 *Comparative European Politics* 209.

12 Margit Tavits, 'Representation, Corruption, and Subjective Well-Being' (2008) 41 *Comparative Political Studies* 1607; Danielle N. Lussier, 'Contacting and Complaining: Political Participation and the Failure of Democracy in Russia' (2011) 27 *Post-Soviet Affairs* 289.

13 Marc Hooghe and Ellen Quintelier, 'Political Participation in European Countries: The Effect of Authoritarian Rule, Corruption, Lack of Good Governance and Economic Downturn' (2013) 12 *Comparative European Politics* 209, 211.

14 Article 1, OUG 57/2019 regarding the Administrative Code [Administrative Code].

that the code must be applied within the activity of public administration authorities and institutions.[15]

It is in this legislative document that we see how the Government, institutionally, perceives the role of the bureaucratic institutions charged with implementation. 'Public Administration' is defined in Article 5(b) as "the totality of activities undertaken, under a regime of public authority, to organise and enforce the law and the deliverance of public service, with the scope of satisfying the public interest." Central public authority, meanwhile, is differentiated as being "the totality of activities undertaken, under a regime of public authority, to organise and enforce the law and the deliverance of public service, with the scope of satisfying the *national/general* interest," (emphasis added). The small difference between the two definitions indicates that the focus of interest must be taken as relevant from a regulatory point of view. Indeed, the ambiguities regarding which must be pursued, the *public interest* or the *national/ general* interest are visibly present.

Nowhere is this more evident than in Article 5(kk), where a 'public service' is one undertaken by public authorities "with the purpose of satisfying a general need or a public interest." Meanwhile, a 'public authority' is defined as "an organisation belonging to the state or to the territorial-administrative unit which acts with public authority for satisfying a *public interest"* (Article 5(k), emphasis added); and a 'functional compartment,' is "a functional structure within public authorities of central public administration, public institutions with *national interest* [...] made up of people with relatively stable tasks and responsibilities, subordinated to an unique authority," (Article 5(q), emphasis added). A definition or differentiation between the national/general interest and the public interest is only marginally addressed in Article 10, whereby it is stated that the "public national interest takes precedence of the local public interest."

When defining the role of organisations, the Code often refers to their activity as being withing a 'regime of public authority.' Here, in Article 5(jj), we see a definition which focuses on the ensemble of prerogatives and restrictions found in law regarding the exercise of attributes by public authorities and institutions and which confer the possibility for their imposition by "judicial force [...] for the defence of the public interest." Moreover, 'standards of quality,' and

15 Asylum in Romania is regulated by the Directorate for Asylum and Integration, which is subordinate to the Ministry of Internal Affairs, meaning that the provisions of the Administrative Code directly apply their work. More on this specific organisation is dealt with further in this chapter.

'standards of costs,' are both measured, according to Article 5(nn) and (oo), based on their ability to deliver a public service.

The Code focuses on the decentralisation of responsibilities and resources away from the central authorities. Defined in Article 5(o), administrative capacity is the ensemble of financial, material, institutional, and human resources that an administrative-territorial unit has at its disposal, the legal framework under which it operates, and the way these resources are valued in its activities, meaning that there is a need to pay attention to local authorities and their capacity for implementing policies. De-concentration (Article 5(u)) also shows a tendency of moving away from the central authority, while maintaining strong bonds of supervision, as it calls for the distribution of responsibilities and financial resources to organisations that operate in the administrative-territorial units but are still subordinated to the central authority.[16]

The Code calls on public authorities and institutions to uphold not only the legal provisions of Romania, but also adhering to the treaties and international conventions to which Romania is a part. Articles 7, 8, 9, 11, and 12 reflect these requirements of adherence to law and international conventions and treaties: they ensure that administrations must act based on principles of equality, transparency, proportionality in respect to the public interest, impartiality, and continuity. Most interesting, however, is Article 13, under the tile "The Principle of Adaptability," whereby "authorities and institutions of public administration face the obligation to satisfy the needs of society." Given the content of this article, and its title, it one might assume that 'discretion' is considered a general principle of public administration according to OUG 57/2019.

Specific mechanics of managing bureaucracies are first dealt with in Article 26. Here, it is stipulated that the government exercises direct control of its ministries and subordinate organisations, and that it can request that administrative acts be withdrawn if they are illegal, without basis, against the public interest, and if they have not yet produced any judicial effects. Article 53 similarly calls that all ministries (and structures subordinated to them), must regulate their policy area with respect to the hierarchy of legal acts. For this, ministers must issue orders and instructions meant to build the norms for implementing laws, with the ministers being the ones who must consider such an act important enough to be issued.

Asylum specifically falls within a special legal category and is considered a de-concentrated service. Article 277 allows ministries to have local structures

16 'Decentralisation,' which allows from transferring responsibilities and resources to local public authorities is also defined, in Article 5(x).

that deliver public services – a central point of command, with a subordinate structured physically removed from the centre. While these de-concentrated departments are geographically removed from the central authorities, the ministries decide on the organisational structure, number of staff, mandatory norms and work instructions, and the only cooperation called for is between the ministries and the prefects in each county (Art. 279).[17] The heads of these organisations are named and removed from office by order of the minister. Article 281, on the other hand, allows for the heads of de-concentrated organisations to name or dismiss personnel within their own office, and draft the budget for the organisations they lead.

The section entitled the "Public Official's Statute" enumerates the governing principles of a public official's conduit, such as the supremacy of the Constitution and law, priority of public interest, equality of treatment, professionalism, moral integrity, etc. A 'public official' is defined as any person lawfully named into a public office, and that make decisions and/or undertake technical activities that ensure the functioning of public authorities and institutions. While Article 371 states that public officials must act objectively, professionally, legally, and impartially, article 373 titled "Principles that guide the exercise of a public function," lists a total of 11 principles that officials must be guided by: (a) legality, (b) competence, (c) performance, (d) efficiency, (e) impartiality and objectivity, (f) transparency, (g) responsibility, in accordance with legal provisions, (h) orientation toward the citizen, (i) stability in exercising public function, (j) good-faith, and (k) hierarchic subordination. These show the constraints placed on public officials, not only from a legal perspective, but also from a hierarchical one.

The law also differentiates between different prerogatives for public power, namely general and special. A special prerogative is of particular interest here, since it involves "activities of ensuring the necessary support for defending fundamental freedoms" (Article 370(3)(e)) and activities that "refer to the exercise of public authority in areas where the state has exclusive competency, with the purpose of implementing laws and other normative acts." A general prerogative, on the other hand, has to do with drafting normative acts, proposing public policies and strategies, public audits, managing public funds, etc. Undertaking these activities and being a member of an institution of public order (such as the Ministry of Internal Affairs), qualifies public officials for

17 Emergency Ordinance 30/2007 regarding the organisation and functioning of the Ministry of Internal Affairs specifically calls on the Ministry to "monitor the cooperation between de-concentrated structures of public administration with local public authorities (Art.3(1)(a)(3)).

'special statute' according to Article 380. This entails that special laws may be passed to regulate specific duties, rights, and incompatibilities other than those mentioned in the present law.

Moreover, Article 380(4) states that "special statutes applicable to … institutions of public order … the special provisions may also regulate (a) the special legal framework for the work rapport, (b) career management, and (c) administrative accountability and the specific mechanisms for its implementation." This means that, despite the fact that the Annexes of this legal document include a rulebook for professional evaluation, institutions such as the Ministry of Internal Affairs, where asylum decisions are taken, have large discretionary powers in drafting the special statute of their public officials. The Ploiești Court of Appeal gives a similar interpretation when stating that special statutes can indeed regulate corrective measures, including withholding career advancement as a form of disciplinary action. The Court then goes on to argue that in the case before it at the time, which had to do with a police officer employed by the MAI, the legal instrument with the applicable provisions is an Order of the MAI, and not the public official's statute.[18] Article 382 of OUG 57 specifically allows for derogations from the present code to be made in cases where a special statute of public officials is concerned.

OUG 57/2019 also enumerates the rights and duties of public officials. Notably among duties included, we see requirements not be influenced by personal opinions (Art. 432(4)), or not to express opinions that do not conform to the reality of working in their specific institution (Art. 434(4)). Furthermore, Article 437 establishes an obligation for public officials to obey the instructions of their superiors, except in circumstances where they believe these to be illegal and motivate such beliefs in writing, once again giving weight to hierarchical considerations. Article 441 references resources again, obliging public officials to use public goods efficiently, while we see in Article 447, titled "Relations with citizens," that interactions must be respectful, in good faith, correct, and guided by moral integrity. Given the special statute, we should expect similar requirements in the legislation that specifically deals with interactions with asylum seekers.

An interesting aspect of this legislation is Article 449, which for the first time defines some sort of discretionary powers for public officials. Under the heading of "Objectivity and responsibility in decision making," this Articles calls for public officials to follow legal provisions, but also to use their 'capacity for judgement' (*capacitatea de apreciere* in Romanian) objectively and impartially.

18 *Decision nr. 1067* Ploiești Court of Appeal, June 16, 2010.

This reference to a capacity for judgement does not have a definition in the legislation, but it is the closest that it comes to allowing for decisions made based on the judgement of how legal provisions should be applied in specific contexts. This same article also states that superiors must consider the proposals of subordinates when these might lead to improved working conditions. They are also tasked with ensuring that all duties are distributed evenly and fairly, and that performance is measured correctly. As we will see in further paragraphs, much of the power within institutions is held by head of said institution, especially when it comes to the evaluation and career advancement of subordinates.

Before seeing how these superiors yield tremendous power in their institutions, it is important to point out that this Ordinance calls for one public official in each institution to be charged with providing ethical counselling and correct monitoring of behavioural rules – in other words, a compliance officer. The roles and attributes of this officer as described in Articles 451 – 454 show that their presence is largely for corrective intervention. Nonetheless, according to Article 454, they can point out procedures that may lead to breaking the proper rules of conduit of public officials. At least on paper, there is an awareness that certain institutional norms may deviate from policy ideal and/or goals.

Returning, however, to the large power concentration at the top of institutions in the Romanian public administration system, one needs only look at the system of evaluation, rewards, and accountability devised in OUG 57/2019. To be promoted to a higher position, Article 479 says that a public official must have occupied the current post for at least three years, must have participated in professional development activities, must have received at least a 'good' in performance evaluations, and must have no disciplinary measures taken against him or her. All these requirements are at the mercy of those charged with running an institution. Any punishments for misbehaviour, which includes firing, can be applied for any action with serious consequences.

Nonetheless, the basis for taking any of the disciplinary actions lies in large part with the head of the institution. Annex VI to this law, which enumerates the methodology for evaluating the profession performance of public officials states that the report is drafted by the immediate supervisor and approved by the head of the institution. The entire evaluation process is, in fact, very much internal to the institution in which the public official conducts his or her duties. Even if the head of the institution wishes to delegate these powers away, they could only do so to "to the person that occupies the next leadership post," (Annex VI, Article 11(7)). Other than the possibility that public officials will defer decisions to the leadership under such a structure of oversight and accountability, this also means that professional evaluations are done by members of the institution in which the rules, written or unwritten, have been accepted as matter of fact.

3 Managing Asylum in Romania

First instance asylum decisions in Romania are made by workers from the Directorate for Asylum and Integration of the General Inspectorate for Migration (IGI-DAI). These are departments within the Ministry of Internal Affairs (MAI). According to Emergency Ordinance 30/2007 regarding the organisation and functioning of the MAI, this ministry is the public authority charged with defending the rights and fundamental freedoms of people (Article 1(2)(a)), fulfilling the obligations that befall Romania as a Member State of the European Union (Article 1(2)(c)), and regulating the legal regime of aliens, of asylum seekers, and of people that have acquired some sort of protection in Romania (Article 1(2)(u)). In order to achieve these goals, the Ministry must, among others, "fulfil regulatory functions which ensure the elaboration of the normative and institutional framework needed to achieve the strategic objectives and transposing the *acquis Communautaire,"* (Article 2(b)). Moreover, in Article 3(1)(b)(14), the MAI is charged with implementing Romania's policies regarding asylum, an action categorised under the heading of "order, public safety and national security."

The minister can issue orders that directly impact its areas of competence. In September 2016, for instance, Ordinance nr. 130/2016 entered into force, which approved the internal regulations for regional centres of processing and housing asylum seekers.[19] The rules state that the centres are open to all asylum seekers who do not have the resources to maintain themselves until their right to reside in Romania expires, asylum seekers who are undergoing the assessment of their application, beneficiaries of international protection, or those whose movements have been restrained according to Law 122/2006 regarding asylum, a law which will be discussed in further detail below.

A great of effort was put in place by the EU to ensure that the right of the asylum seeker to be properly informed is paramount. Article 5 of Order 130/2016 states that from the moment of his or her lodging, those seeking

19 Ordinance 130/2016 and the regulations approved are in fact two separate documents. Ordinance 130/2016 only has two articles: one which approves the set of regulations, and one which establishes the entry into force of said regulations. The regulations themselves, however, are comprised of 78 articles and 15 annexes.

international protection must be properly informed of their rights, obligations, interdictions, and disciplinary sanctions applicable during their stay in one of the centres. Annex 2 to the regulations describes this information, which range from rights such as freedom of correspondence, freedom to roam about the reception centre and outside, to formulate requests or complaints, or to participate in religious activities. Meanwhile, obligations include respecting the program hours of the centre, have a considerate attitude towards authorities, to respect the rights of others, to inform centre staff of any diseases or infections of which he or she might suffer, etc. Several interdictions are also listed, such as inciting violence, leaving the centre without informing the staff, publicly using obscene words or gestures, etc. Possible disciplinary actions range from a verbal or written warning to interdiction from receiving the daily allowance for a period of one to three months, or temporary or permanent removal from the centre.

There is little in these rules that deals directly with first instance decisions. Article 6 demands that as soon as an asylum seeker becomes a resident of one of these centres, they must be subjected to a through searching of their body and belongings and undergo a medical examination. These are done, according to Article 6(2)(b-c), in order to ascertain if the personal has any identity documents, and if the asylum seekers show any signs of physical violence, something that hints towards an assessment of torture or persecution. But these are not done out of consideration for examining the claims of the asylum seekers. In fact, this Minister's order is clear in what the purpose is, enumerating these in Article 7: to find and dispose of any dangerous objects or materials, to find documents that may help to ascertain the identity of the asylum seekers, or any other documents that can be considered when determining the member state responsible for examining an application. In fact, the only reason the Romanian legislation can make this requirement for a medical examination is because it is not technically carried out as part of the assessment of facts, but rather as a part of conditions for reception. And while the Procedures Directive of the EU calls for Member States to allow asylum seekers to opt out of medical examination during the process of examining an application, the Receptions Conditions Directive, in its Article 13, allows Member States to mandate that a medical screening to be done for the 'purposes of public health.'

This act does end, with Article 78, by showing an overview of the geographical spread of asylum centres, both for processing and reception, in Romania. There are six centres, located in Bucharest, Timișoara, Rădăuți, Galați, Maramureș, and Giurgiu. These are the six centres where asylum seekers are received and housed while they undergo the asylum procedure. According to information from the Ministry of Interior, as of September 2020 there were 6 officers employed in the Bucharest regional centres that are tasked with assessing applications for international protection, 5 in Galați, and 3 in Giurgiu, Rădăuți, Maramureș and in Timișoara, making the total around all regional centres 23.[20] An ordinance of similar nature, Ordinance nr. 84/2016, was also issued to deal with food security, housing, and hygiene of asylum seekers in case of emergency.[21]

The Minister also issues ordinances that directly regulate bureaucratic asylum procedures. The 2019 Methodology for Using the National Eurodac System is an example, which determined the competent authority charged with managing the EURODAC system, how the information gathered must be kept, and what kind of data can be collected.[22] Another order, passed in 2016 in collaboration with 12 other institutions of the Government, established an integrated action plan for managing a crisis situation in the area of migration, and called for coordination among actors such as the MAI, Ministry of Health, Ministry of Labour and Social Protection, Romanian Secret Service, and many others.[23]

Nonetheless, not all ministerial orders must directly address the issue of asylum for them to have an impact on the job of those making first instance decisions. Take, for example, Ordinance nr. 82/2018 regarding the rules for wearing police uniforms. Passed in 2018, this Minister's order states that "police officers that undergo activities with the public are obliged to wear, during working hours, the institutional uniform [of] … the general inspectorate for immigration (IGI) [among others]," the appropriate uniform in this case being police garb and all related equipment. As such, Order 82/2018 contradicts Article 15(3)(e) of the Asylum Procedures Directive, which calls on Member States to "ensure that the person who conducts a personal interview on the substance of an application for international protection does not wear a military or law enforcement uniform," and the Norms of Implementation developed by MAI

20 Information obtained from the Ministry of Interior's Office of Information and Public Relations, September 2020, through information requested according to Law 544/2001 regarding the freedom to access information for the public interest.

21 Order nr. 84/2016 regarding the feeding and provision of resources to reception centres, as well as providing personal hygiene products to foreigners falling under the scope of activities in the integrated centres mentioned at Art. 4 of the Government Emergency Ordinance nr. 53/2015 for establishing measures to be applied in case of an increase of massive influx of immigrants at Romania's frontiers.

22 Methodology Regarding the usage of the national management system of EURODAC transactions, published in the Official Gazette, Part I, nr. 931, November 19, 2019.

23 Order Nr. 161/2.276/1.412/2.872/9.311/512/854/2.233/6.073/144/46.684/253/5.186 regarding the approval of the Integrated Action Plan for Managing a Crisis Situation in the field of Migration. Published in the Official Gazette, Part I, nr. 1051, December 27, 2016.

for Law 122 regarding asylum, which state that no uniforms can be worn by public officials conducting interviews.[24]

As previous sections have shown, there are many Orders that can come from the Minister of Internal Affairs that can have an impact on how asylum applications are managed. The entire administrative structure, from Constitutional Provisions to the demands of the Administrative Code, to specific ministerial orders, show the vast amounts of regulations that shape the work of bureaucrats in the Ministry of Internal Affairs. Nonetheless, given the special statute of that immigration bureaucracies hold, it is time to delve into two specific sets of legal documents to clarify our understanding of the discretionary space in which street-level bureaucrats at the Directorate of Asylum and Integration work. Firstly, Government Decision 639/2007 and the Regulation for Organisation and Functioning of the General Inspectorate for Immigration will provide the architectural set-up of the IGI and the Directorate for Asylum and Integration which is a part of it. Secondly, Law 122/2006 regarding asylum in Romania, and the Methodological Norms for the Implementation of Law 122/2006 will provide the specifics not of how asylum bureaucracies are built architecturally, but also how the inner workings of this system aid or hamper proper first-instance decision making, and how the specific provisions of Directive 2011/95/EU and Directive 2013/32/EU are transposed in national law.

3.1 *The Structure and Role of The General Inspectorate for Immigration (IGI)*

The General Inspectorate for Immigration was established in 2012, replacing its predecessor, the Romanian Immigration Office.[25] As such, Government Decision 639 from 2007 which establishes the organisational structure and responsibilities of IGI is a piece of legislative act that has been amended throughout the years: in 2008, 2010, 2012, and finally in 2016.[26] It was in 2012, in fact, that the title of the legislation changed to fit with the newly formed institution. For example, Article 2 currently states that the General Inspectorate is "led by an inspector general [...] aided by two deputy inspectors general." Until the 2012 amendments, however, the Decision only called for one deputy.

24 Art. 23 Methodological Norms for implementing Law nr. 122/2006 regarding asylum in Romania from 13.09.2006. Official Gazette, Part I, Nr. 805 from 25 September 2006.

25 Article II of Emergency Ordinance 18/2012 for modifying emergency ordinance 30/2007 regarding the organisation and functioning of the Ministry of Administration and Internal Affairs and for modifying some normative acts.

26 Government Decisions 212/2008, 1368/2010, 838/2012, and 467/2016.

Article 3 describes the very architecture of IGI. It is organised centrally and in the territory, (i.e., de-concentration), and it is further subdivided in directorates, services, and other "functional structures." Meanwhile, Article 5 establishes the general competences of the IGI, divided in three categories: migration, asylum, and general. For the purposes of this study, only its competences in the field of asylum are relevant. Table 6 below enumerates exactly the attributes that IGI has, as listed in Article 3(b). It is worth noting that since the original drafting of this Decision in 2007, Article 3(b) has not been subject to any amendment.

TABLE 6 Attributes of the IGI in the field of asylum, according to Article 5(b)(1–12) of HG 639/2007

1.	Receives, lodges, and resolves, in an administrative stage, asylum claims made to its territorial structures or other organs of the Ministry.
2.	Receives and relays to judicial institutional all complaints received from asylum seekers
3.	In cases of an effective remedy, makes available to judicial institutions copies of all documents used when reaching a decision.
4.	Is a party in the trials that have to do with asylum claims
5.	Initiates the procedures required to appoints a legal representative in the case of unaccompanied minors, and they ensure proper safety for said minor until a representative is appointed.
6.	Decides on allowing access to Romanian territory to asylum seekers that have lodged an application at border crossings
7.	Can decide on sending asylum seekers to a safe-third country
8.	Send and analyses requests to take back or tack charge of asylum seekers and, in collaboration with the General Inspectorate for Border Police, completes the transfer of asylum seekers to other Member States.
9.	Ensures access to medical care for asylum seekers.
10.	Drafts and sends to the Ministry of Labour the documents necessary for the transfer of material means given to those who have obtained a form of protection in Romania.
11.	In consultation with the Ministry of Foreign Affairs, establishes the list of safe third countries.
12.	Receive, analyses, and manages information referring to the situation in the countries of origin of asylum seekers.

Chapter III, which begins with article 6, starts to dive a little deeper into the attributes of public officials working at the IGI. According to Article 8, these can conduct searches in public or private enterprises frequented by foreigners when there are suspicions that laws are being broken by said foreigners. They are also allowed to work alongside law enforcement to investigate and/or accompany foreigners who are suspected or proven to have broken the law, or to "take any necessary measure to figure out and validate the real identity of asylum seekers." 'Any necessary measure,' without any other context, provides a great deal of interpretative ambiguity.

In Article 4, however, we start to get a hint of where one must look if the task at hand is to understand the rule book by which bureaucrats operate: "The attributes and concrete tasks of the personnel, as well as the internal circuit of documents, are decided through the regulation for organisation and functioning," which must be approved by the minister. In this case, this such regulation was published in the Official Gazette nr. 123 on February 15, 2017. This particular regulation is meant to define the entire scope of activity, beginning with the mission of the IGI, which is to implement Romania's policy in the field of migration, asylum, and the integration of foreigners (Art. 1), and that in order to achieve this it must cooperate with other institutions of the Ministry of Internal Affairs, similar institutions in other countries, NGOs or other international organisations, and diplomatic/consular missions in Romania (Art. 2).

We see in this document also a detailed organisational structure, which is drawn out in Annex 2. The Inspector General has in its direct coordination 7 offices or compartments: Control, Judicial, Human Resources, Financial, Secretariat, Psychological Assistance, and Information and Public Relations. As mentioned in the current version of OUG 639/2007, there are two deputy inspectors general, each with several subordinates. For the purposes of this work, we are particularly interested in the Directorate for Asylum and Integration, led by a chief commissioner, and overseeing the Office for International Protection, the Office for Integration and Relocation, and the Dublin Office.

Stemming from here, we also see a strict adherence to hierarchical structures within the organisation: "hierarchic relations of authority are kept between the IGI leadership and all IGI structures with the purpose of keeping and perfecting the state of functionality of the internal relational system … and between the heads of IGI structures and the heads of subordinate structures, as well as between the heads and personnel of these structures," (Art. 5(1)(a-b)). The emphasis on hierarchic authority does not end there. Further, in Article 5(2), it is specified in even more detail that functional authority relationships are established in compartments without a leadership position between the personnel with the highest ranking and those with lower positions. All this, of course, "with a view of guiding and binding unitarily, according with the established purpose and objectives." Thinking back to the discussion earlier in this chapter, whereby it was shown that the current set up of the Romanian administrative system is already guided by a strong deference to leadership in decision making, the regulation for the organisation and function of the IGI surely reinforces this point.[27]

As already pointed out, the specific structure within the IGI that deals with asylum seekers and international protection is the Directorate for Asylum and Integration (DAI). Section 13 of this act deals entirely with attributes of this Directorate. It is the structure charged with ensuring access to the asylum procedures, to update the country-of-origin information, and to assess requests from other Member States to readmit beneficiaries of international protection in Romania. Article 47 lists 22 main attributes of the DAI, ranging from coordinating and sustaining access to procedure, including activities that are related to assessments, to implementing the Dublin procedure, or communicating and cooperating with EU institutions or NGOs in the field of asylum.

Article 48 goes on to list the attributes of the Office for International Protection, which is the office charged with the activity of the regional centres where asylum procedures are lodged, where a new procedure can be undertaken, where international protection is granted, identity is checked, and where temporary documents are issued (Art. 48(1)(a)). They are tasked also with solving cases where the issues of first country of asylum, safe third country, or safe European country play a role, or to coordinate all activities related to detained asylum seekers or those who have restrictions imposed on their movement. This office also deals with requests for family reunification, revocation of protection, defends the institution when effective remedy is undertaken, relationship with consular offices, holds trainings for other officials and magistrates that deal with cases of asylum, and oversees projects funded from the EU's Asylum, Migration, and Integration Fund (AMIF). But most importantly, at Article 48(1)(g), we see that the DAI is also charged with "evaluation and assuring the quality of the asylum procedure and of the degree of valuation and utilisation of the country-of-origin information." In other words, the

27 As a final point on this matter, articles 20, 21, and 22 deal with the leadership of the IGI subordinate offices, such as the Directorate for Asylum and Integration (DAI), but also the three offices mentioned above that work under the umbrella of the DAI. Each one of these articles only calls for the person in question (deputy general inspector, general director, director, etc.) to be "unhindered" in its subordination to their hierarchical supervisor.

DAI, which is charged with coordinating and taking an active part in the asylum procedure, is also tasked with evaluating its own participation in it.

We see this self-regulatory aspect quite often. Article 48(3)(d), which deals specifically (and rather redundantly) with the coordination of asylum procedures, states almost verbatim the same provision: The Office for International Protection is charged with assuring the quality of asylum procedure. Letter j), meanwhile calls on this Office to also draft and present proposals for measure to be taken, to have a "strict application of laws and other normative acts." Letters k) and l) furthermore call on the Office to organise the "thorough studying of laws and other normative acts, after publication … and to follow the mode of application of judicial rules in the field of asylum and to make proposals for the perfection of said norms."

Other attributes are also listed which bear special consideration. Article 48(3)(h), for instance, gives the DAI the responsibility for drafting opinions toward the Constitutional Court, the European Court of Human Rights, or the Court of Justice of the European Union in all cases regarding asylum. That being said, it is important to note that while several times the DAI generally and the Office for International Protection specifically have called on to monitor all laws and normative acts passed at the national level, nowhere in this regulation is the DAI required to keep updated on any rulings from the Court of Justice, and to adjust procedures accordingly.

3.2 *Law 122/2006 regarding Asylum in Romania and Its Norms of Implementation*

Law 122/2006 is the national legislation regulating the issuance of international protection. Since passed in May 2006, the law has been amended 14 times. The following pages will explain the provisions of this law and, where relevant, information regarding previous amendments or implementation reports will be provided. The legal act, as approved by the legislative branch, is supplemented by the procedural requirements laid out in the Methodological Norms of Implementation, drafted and adopted by the Romanian Government, and which provide the procedural rules by which the provisions of Romania's asylum law must be implemented. As such, when appropriate, the provisions of Law 122/2006 will also be contextualised by the norms of implementation.

The fact that the Government drafts the law's methodological norms of implementation is nothing unusual. It is always the case that the executive branch, being the one charged with implementation, is charged to draft the procedures by which a law becomes policy. It is worth noting, nonetheless, that in this case it was also the Romanian Government, not a Member of Parliament, that initiated the law, as it is its prerogative to do. On November 16, 2005, the minister at the time charged with the management of the Government's General Secretariat sent a letter to the Secretary General of the Senate asking to for the upper house of Parliament to examine, in an emergency procedure, the bill submitted regarding asylum in Romania. This letter had as a legal basis a government decision, Nr. E372/10.11.2005, whose single article made the same request of the Senate.

One advantage provided by the legislative procedure in Romania is that all bills submitted for consideration in Parliament must be accompanied by an Exposition of Motives (*Expunere de Motive,* in Romanian) drafted by the initiator. In it, the initiator must show the needs that require normative intervention, the essence and finality of proposed regulations, political, economic, social, or cultural effects desired, any new effects that the proposed regulation has on existing measures (i.e., amendments brought, derogations made, or abrogation of), implications on national legislation, in case of ratification or approval of treaties or international agreements, a list of stages through which the project went during its drafting, including research, studies, pilot programs, etc., and, in case of emergency ordinances, the needs for immediate regulation.[28]

In this case, the Motives presented by the Prime Minister make it clear from the opening statement that the intended purpose of this bill is to align the procedures of Romania's asylum institutions to those spelled out in the Community acquis, given the context of Romania's efforts for accession at the time, and the "significative modifications in the community legislation determined by the necessity of adopting a common asylum policy."[29] At the same time, the document goes on, the bill proposed by the Government also regulates aspects of the Romanian asylum system with provisions that "reflect the practice developed in this field at the national level."

The specific aspects of community law that motivated the development of this bill are divided in two separate categories by the drafters: those whose transposition is needed to fulfil the commitments made for accession, and those that must be implemented the moment that Romania officially becomes a member of the EU. The former of the two categories includes Directive 2001/55/EC (Temporary Protection Directive), Directive 2003/9/EC (Receptions Conditions Directive), Directive 2003/86/EC (Family Reunification Directive), and Directive 2004/83/EC (Qualifications Directive).[30] Meanwhile, the

28 Art. 28–29 of Law 24/2000 regarding the technical legislative norms for drafting normative acts. Official Gazette, Part I, nr. 139 of March 31, 2000.

29 Expunere de Motive, Law 122/2006 regarding Asylum in Romania.

30 The first iteration of the Asylum Procedures directive did not appear until December 2005, one month after the bill was submitted to the Senate for approval.

Government also establishes that it is necessary to create the necessary legal framework so that the obligations of Regulations 2725/2000 and 207/2002 (EURODAC), and Regulation 343/2003 (Dublin Regulation) may be implemented starting on January 1, 2007, Romania's day of accession to the Union.

The new law brought several major changes to the existing legal framework in Romania, and these are worth mentioning before analysing the provisions of the law that are in force today. These are, however, the changes enumerated and described in the Exposition of Motives. Later sections will also address more detailed changes made to asylum policy throughout the years. It is at this instant, however, that we see for the first-time what changes Romania's authorities deemed essential to make to harmonise the country's policies with the provisions of the Community acquis. Table 7 lists these changes:

The bill itself had little opposition during Parliamentary procedure. The first step in the procedure, following the registration of the bill in the Permanent Bureau of each house of parliament, is for the Legislative Council to issue a favourable or unfavourable notice on the bill in question. This notice must be in line with the institutional goal of the Legislative Council, which is to ensure the systematisation, unification, and coordination of all legislation.[31] As such, the Council issues a favourable decision on the bill, with several observations and proposals.[32] Curiously, the Legislative Council's notice begins by reiterating the need for this legislation given the context of Romania's upcoming EU accession:

> The legislative initiative takes place in the context of Romania's accession to the European Union, when national legislation must align with the community acquis, considering the Council's Directives in this area ... The proposed regulation is based on the judicial statutes of the European Union, subsumed to the third community pillar – Justice and Home Affairs ... and is justified by the need of complete harmonisation of Romanian legislation to the community acquis.[33]

As for the rest of the Notice, the Council's proposals are all technical in nature, none addressing the substance of the law itself. For instance, several proposals are made to encapsulate the judicial terminology needed, or discrepancies

31 Law 73/1993 regulates the role and scope of the Legislative Council, as an advisory body to Parliament. Its scope is spelled out in Article 1.

32 Notice Nr. 1664/4.11.2005 of the Legislative Council.

33 Ibid 1.

TABLE 7 Main changes to asylum legislation brought about by Law 122/2006, according to the Government's Exposition of Motives

Family Reunification	The meaning of family reunification was extended to include the possibility for refugee status to be awarded to minors resulting from marriages that took place after the applicant's entry on Romanian territory, of minors that were born out of wedlock, or of minors adopted by the main beneficiaries of refugee status.
Exclusion	Exclusion clauses were extended to cover the EU's temporary and subsidiary protection mechanisms.
Administrative Procedure	New provisions on how asylum interviews should be conducted. A provision was included to allow asylum seekers who lodge a subsequent application to remain in Romania while the request is processed.
Effective Remedy	In cases of border and accelerated procedures, the law took away from the courts the option to send a file back for re-examination to the National Office for Refugees [the predecessor of IGI-DAI] New regulations were introduced regarding the choice to make use of an effective remedy, or the conditions for filing a petition. The new law also calls for cases brought before a judge to be held in secret sessions, in line with the principle of confidentiality.
Unaccompanied Minors	New regulations regarding the effects of refusing to undergo an age assessment. New provisions also introduced regarding reunification of unaccompanied minors with family members.
Cessation or Revocation	Separate procedures were introduced for the cessation or revocation of subsidiary protection.
Dublin	New regulations for dealing with the transfer of responsibilities for analysing an application for international protection, and for identifying the Member State responsible.
Definitions	A set of definitions specific to asylum were introduced, and existing terms redefined.

in formulations between different articles are pointed out.[34] In a sense, this addresses ambiguities in terminology in the process of transposition.

By January 2006, four senate committees had issued favourable notices on the bill, namely the Committee for equality of opportunities, Committee for labour, family and social protection, the Committee for human rights, cults, and minorities, and the Judicial Committee. The latter, in its report Nr. XVII/1691/2005, also proposed several amendments. The first part of the report, it should be mentioned, uses almost identical wording as the Exposition of Motives or the Legislative Council's notice when it references the need for harmonisation with EU acquis, and the changes that this proposed legislation brings to the current institution of asylum. One of the amendments proposed was brought forth by a representative from the Ministry of Internal Affairs and accepted by the members of the Committee, but this only had to do with changing the wording of Article 1 to make clear that the law determines the *legal* regime of foreigners that request international protection (previous version did not include the word *legal*). Other substantive amendments brought by the Committee include:

- The mention that, in the context of a Dublin procedure, the right to remain ends when the decision is issued that Romania is not the Member State responsible for examining an application. Right to remain is also addressed again in Article 19, where the initial wording of "must leave the Romanian state" is amended to "must leave the territory of the Romanian state."
- Ensuring that asylum seekers with special needs receive unrestricted adequate medical attention. The wording in the initial draft, which was deleted through an amendment, stated that those with special needs have the right to receive "following the recommendation of a medical specialist, prothesis and medical devices that ensure a minimal functioning of affected organs."
- Article 64 initially called for judicial authorities to motivate decisions within 10 days; this was amended to 5. A provision was also eliminated which stated that "if the appellant gives up a case, the conclusion becomes irrevocable."

The Senate approved the bill with only these amendments on February 6, 2006, with 73 votes in favour, 2 against, and one abstention. We do notice, nonetheless, that part of Parliamentary procedure has already ensured that certain provisions that were non-compliant to the European acquis were addressed in the stage of transposition. The elimination of any predetermined restrictions on medical attention and of the consequences initially envisioned for giving up

34 The exact wording of the original bill analysed by the Council is unknown. The only version available publicly is the one from November 16, 2005, which had already included all changes proposed.

an appeal case were both decisions that more closely resemble the ideals of the Common European Asylum System.

The Bill was sent to the Chamber of Deputies who in this case served as the deciding chamber, and it was registered in the Permanent Bureau on February 08, 2006. All committees that analysed the bill – the Committee for Budget and Finance, the Committee for Health and Family, the Committee for Labour and Social Protection, the Judicial Committee and the Defence and Public Order Committee – issued favourable notices, without proposing any amendments to the Senate's version.[35] The bill was eventually voted upon on April 04, 2006, with 230 votes for, 2 against, and 2 abstentions.[36]

3.3 *Scope and Definitions in the Law*

The modifications listed above, which were made through Parliamentary procedure to the initial draft presented by the Government, are not the only changes that this law has suffered. Since it was adopted, many more amendments have been made, most notably to transpose the new requirements of the CEAS provisions from 2011 and 2013. In the following sections the provisions of the law that are currently applicable will be analysed. Where certain institutional changes have been made that are worth mentioning in the context of first instance decisions, these will be highlighted. As such, a clear line will be drawn from the institutional past of asylum in Romania, to the changes brought about by EU legislation, to the current manifestation of asylum policy.

Article 1 of Law 122 sets the scope of the law as establishing the "legal regime of foreigners who request international protection in Romania, the legal regime of beneficiaries of international protection in Romania, the procedure of granting, ceasing, and revoking international protection in Romania, the procedure for establishing the Member State responsible with analysing a request for asylum, as well as the conditions for granting, excluding, and ceasing temporary protection." In Article 2(a) the phrase "type of protection" is defined as international protection or temporary protection, awarded by the Romanian state. This specific point was amended in 2013 and in 2014. Up until 2013, "humanitarian protection" was also listed as a type of international protection offered by the Romanian state, and until 2014 international protection was subdivided in refugee status or subsidiary protection status. This was also

35 See report Nr. 32/84/08/02/2006 on PL-X 44/2006 from the Chamber of Deputies.

36 During the floor debate, no substantial modifications were brought to the bill, and no vocal opposition was raised. The complete transcript of the session can be found (in Romanian) at http://www.cdep.ro/pls/steno/steno2015.stenograma?ids=6071&idm=7.

evident in the wording of Article 1, which until 2014 stated that this law establishes the legal regime of foreigners who request *a type of* legal protection of in Romania.

Several definitions were introduced in 2014 and 2015 with amendments meant to transpose the requirements of the Qualifications Directive and the Procedures Directive. Through Ordinance 1/2014,[37] which transposed the new Qualifications Directive, the definition of "refugee" (Article 2(f^1)) was introduced for the first time, as someone who fulfils the conditions of the Geneva Convention. The definitions of 'father' and 'mother' were also introduced in the list of family members of asylum seekers with this ordinance. Until then, the law did not envision a scenario where the beneficiary of international protection could be minor.[38] Law 331/2015,[39] on the other hand, transposed the provisions of the Asylum Procedures Directive and of the Reception Conditions Directive. As such, it introduced in Romania's asylum legislation definitions for "applicant with special procedural guarantees" (Art. 2(b^1)), "applicant with special reception needs" (Art. 2(b^2)), "reception conditions" (Art. 2(p)), and "material reception conditions" (Art. 2(q)).

Another point worth noting is the definition for "application for international protection," in Article 2(d). This is listed as a "a request made by a foreign national or a stateless person for international protection from the Romanian state, as long as he or she is not requesting explicitly another type of protection." The definition from the Directive 2013/32/EU, however, states that such an application is a request made by a foreign national or stateless person, but also adds the wording "who can be *understood* to seek refugee status or subsidiary protection status." This wording, not present in the Romanian version, allows for an application for international protection to be made implicitly, and for the need for protection to be deduced by public officials without an explicit request being made.

3.4 *Procedural Guarantees*

Procedurally, Article 3 allows for the use of interpreters from other institutions where these are available, but also states that, in cases where no interpreters or translators are available, "trustworthy persons" that speak the needed language can be used. This often, in practice, translates to using other asylum seekers for

37 Government Ordinance nr. 1/2014. Official Gazette, Part I, nr. 63 of 24 January 2014.

38 The law did envision, however, that unaccompanied minors could be beneficiaries of international protection.

39 Law nr. 331/2015 for amending and completing some normative acts regarding foreigners. Official Gazette, Part I nr. 944 from 21 December 2015.

purposes of interpreting and translating interviews and/or other interactions. According to a 2018 report by the European Council on Refugees and Exiles (ECRE),

> In Timișoara asylum seekers complain about the lack of interpreters at the stage of registration and lodging of the asylum application. The same issue was reported in Giurgiu and Rădăuţi with the mention that IGI-DAI turns to asylum seekers or refugees accommodated in the centre for interpretation. In Rădăuţi, asylum seekers still complain about the fact that the Border Police does not use interpreters who speak their native language at the border and, as a consequence, their names, date of birth and reasons for their asylum application are not recorded correctly. Therefore potential errors in the recording of personal information may arise during the assessment of their asylum application by IGI-DAI and contradictions may appear between the statements made at the border and those made during the personal interview.[40]

Similarly, Article 45(2) of the Asylum Law also calls for the use of interpreters during the personal interview. Still, in most reception centres these are not enough: in Galați the few interpreters available are also used by the courts; in Rădăuți, it was often reported that people used for interpretation had no experience doing so; Timișoara and Giurigu have also reported a shortage of interpreters.[41] The most illustrative example of how interpretation happens in practice during the phase of first-instance decision making can be seen in Rădăuți. Here, asylum authorities often use double interpretation, such as from Kurdish to Arabic and then from Arabic to Romanian. This inefficient arrangement was invoked in one particular appeal before a court, however the Rădăuți Regional Court dismissed the appeal by stating that "the asylum seeker was expressly asked by the case officer if he agrees with the interpreters [...] The applicant's criticisms regarding the double interpretation were found to be 'exaggerated and taken out of context, given that the applicant said he understood well the Kurdish asylum seeker used as interpreter, insisting on bringing him at the interview.'"[42]

40 Felicia Nica, 'Country Report: Romania' [2018] *Asylum Information Database* (*AIDA*), 22.

41 Ibid., 26.

42 Ibid. See also Decisions 2201/2018 and 3595/2018 of the Rădăuţi Regional Court, and Decision 5170/2018 of the Giurgiu Regional Court for other examples of appeals where it was alleged that inadequate interpreters were used during the interview phase of analysis of an application for international protection.

In terms of procedurals guarantees, first and foremost the DAI is charged with ensuring that all foreign citizens and/or stateless persons on Romanian territory or at a border crossing have access to the asylum procedure, excepting only those who fall under an exclusion clause (Article 4), and that such access is granted without any sort of discrimination (Article 5). Article 5^1, on the other hand, enumerates non-exhaustively the categories that make up vulnerable people: minors, unaccompanied minors, people with disabilities, the elderly, pregnant women, single parents with minor children, victims of human trafficking, people suffering from grave illness, people with mental illness, people who have been subjected to torture, rape, or other type of psychological, physical or sexual violence. Whether or not an applicant falls within one or more of these categories is determined following the lodging of the application for international protection, by public officials from the IGI, and under an individual examination of each situation. It is these same officials, then, that must call for the proper measures to be taken in cases where vulnerabilities are identified. This article was originally introduced by Ordinance 1/2014 and amended with Law 331/2015 to make clearer the need for timely evaluations, and for constant evaluation of the situation of asylum seekers with special reception needs.

Article 6, meanwhile, enshrines in law the principle of *non-refoulment*, by forbidding the expulsion, extradition or return of any asylum seeker or recipient of international protection, except for cases involving national security or public order. A threat to public order is defined as having been convicted of any crime committed intentionally and for which the foreseeable maximum punishment is above 5 years (Article 6(4)). This article, however, is supplemented with instruction from the Norms of Methodological Implementation. Here, it is mentioned, exception from the principle of *non-refoulment* must be made in cases where proof exists that asylum seekers intend to commit acts of terrorism or if they favour terrorist activities. In such a case, the temporary identity document issued must be withdrawn, and expulsion, extradition, or forced return must be carried out as soon as the application for international protection has been denied.

Other procedural guarantees are also spelled out: respect for family unity (Article 7), the supremacy of the best interests of the child (Article 8), and confidentiality (Article 10). Article 9 makes clear that both refugee status and subsidiary protection status are issued for undetermined time periods. Article 11 guarantees that the illegal entry or residence of people who have received international protection cannot be punished. Article 19^{14} does allow for detention in cases where an asylum seeker has made an illegal entry in Romania.

This is because, the article argues, illegal entry in Romania represents evidence of a risk of absconding.

3.5 *Street-Level Bureaucrats in Law 122*

Starting with Article 12, we also see a focus on the personnel charged with receiving and examining an application for international protection. Article 12 itself states that competent authorities must investigate all matters in law and fact that can lead to an informed decision, even if such matters were not invoked in the initial claim. This is referred to as the 'active role' of the authorities, and the Methodological Norms of Implementation specify what elements must be taken into account: documents that the asylum seeker possess that can elucidate his or her identity, age, or nationality, information given by the asylum seekers regarding his or her personal situation, but also regarding the country or region where they or their relatives held previous residence, previous lodged asylum applications, travel itinerary and documents, as well as justifications invoked in the application for asylum. This is a non-exhaustive list, indicated by the fact that any assessment must 'at least' include these elements.[43] The specific wording of this article in the Norms of Implementation have been subject to amendment in January 2016.[44] Until then, competent authorities were obliged to collaborate with an asylum seeker only if it was needed for the assessment, or if the asylum seeker requested to do so.

Returning to Law 122, Article 12[1] calls for all personnel to be adequately trained, including through interactions with institutions at the EU level, in all aspects referring to: international and EU human rights and asylum legislation, how applications for international protection from vulnerable people must be assessed and how this category of people must be identified, interview techniques, country of origin information, and the procedure for determining a member state responsible. The specifics of what training needs to cover were only introduced in the law in 2015, and once again knowledge of developments at the CJEU or ECtHR are not part of the required training of asylum public officials. The Ministry of Interior states that compliance with these requirements is verified by means of "annual professional evaluations, and [...] targeted inspections."[45] It should be noted that, in 2020 alone, in coordination

43 Art. 13. Methodological Norms for implementing Law nr. 122/2006 regarding asylum in Romania from 13.09.2006. Official Gazette, Part I, Nr. 805 from 25 September 2006.

44 Government Decision nr. 14/2016 for amending and completing the Methodological Norms for implementing Law nr. 122/2006 regarding asylum in Romania.

45 Information obtained from the Ministry of Interior's Office of Information and Public Relations, September 2020, through information requested according to Law 544/2001 regarding the freedom to access information for the public interest.

with EASO, 250 "practitioners" in the field of asylum were trained in Romania in 10 different modules: inclusion, interviewing techniques, evidence assessment, interviewing vulnerable populations, interviewing minors, country of origin information, cessation, Dublin Regulation, Reception, as well as a manager's module.[46]

Public officials must individually examine each asylum request and make an objective and impartial decision, consulting country of origin information needed to reach a decision. Once again, the Norms of Implementation give room for manoeuvre when it comes to country-of-origin information:

> In applying article 13 of the law, public officials who must consult country of origin information of asylum seekers must search any existing information in public sources on the internet, libraries, expert opinions, reports and materials of institution, centre, or specialised organisation, and materials published by the Romanian Ministry of Foreign Affairs, as well as any other source that can contribute to enhanced knowledge in the country of origin, and if necessary, the countries of transit.[47]

The requirement of countries of transit to be included in this analysis was not added to the law until 2015.[48] The same Article 13 also establishes a single procedure of examining an application, by specifying that any application is first analysed from the perspective of refugee status, and then from the perspective of subsidiary protection. Furthermore,

> at an institutional level there is a mechanism for evaluating and assuring the quality of the asylum procedure that consists of a sample of interviews and decision made in the regional centre, and reports are drafted with the observations and recommendations of the evaluators to ensure a unitary practice and to improve the way in which asylum applications are analysed.[49]

46 Ibid.

47 Art. 16. Methodological Norms for implementing Law nr. 122/2006 regarding asylum in Romania from 13.09.2006. Official Gazette, Part I, Nr. 805 from 25 September 2006.

48 Law nr. 331/2015 for amending and completing some normative acts regarding foreigners. Official Gazette, Part I nr. 944 from 21 December 2015.

49 Information obtained from the Ministry of Interior's Office of Information and Public Relations, September 2020, through information requested according to Law 544/2001 regarding the freedom to access information for the public interest.

The article in the Norms of Implementation that describes how the examination of an application must be carried out provides a checklist for evidence that implementers need to look for individually in each case. There are (a) all relevant country of origin information at the time a decision is made, (b) statements and documents provided by the asylum seeker, including information regarding alleged persecution, or threat thereof, or exposure to serious risk, (c) individual circumstances, such as the person's past, gender, age, all with the purpose of evaluating the possibility of persecution or serious threat, (d) if the actions of the asylum seeker have been carried out with the sole purpose of creating the conditions necessary for applying for asylum, and (e) if the possibility exists for another state to offer protection. If the asylum seeker has been previously subjected to persecution or direct threat or risk, a well-founded fear is assumed, unless there are reasons to believe to such persecution or risk will not repeat itself.[50]

Other procedural guarantees enshrined in the law are that decisions issued must obligatorily include the situation in fact and law, information regarding effective remedy and the time limits applicable (Article 14), and that those elements which cannot be proved must be taken in good-faith if the applicant has made all efforts to substantiate the application, missing elements are justified, all statements are consistent with the known situation in the country of origin, and the credibility of the applicant has been established (Article 15). Finally, asylum applications made by unaccompanied minors must be analysed with priority, and IGI-DAI must immediately take the measures necessary to appoint a legal representative for the applicant (Article 16).

Article 17 begins the chapter of the law which enumerates the rights and obligations of asylum seekers. The rights enumerated are in line with those found in the European asylum acquis: the rights to legal counsel and interpreters, to contact and be assisted by UNHCR representatives or other NGOs, to be informed of all aspects of the asylum process, and to confidentiality, are all found in this article. The right for both asylum seekers and UHCR representatives to have access to the information enclosed in their files was included in 2015. But this article also serves as an example of conflicting provisions that must be at times reconciled (in this case, by a court). In a case before the Bucharest Court of Appeals,[51] the predecessor of IGI, the Romanian Office for Immigration (ORI) asked the court to grant it permission to detain Z.E.,

50 Art. 16. Methodological Norms for implementing Law nr. 122/2006.

51 Civil Sentence Nr. 549 of the Bucharest Court of Appeal, Section VIII Administrative and Fiscal Conflicts.

a Chinese citizen, until an order for expulsion could be carried out. Z.E. had been charged with attempted murder, being sentenced to 5 years in prison and immediate expulsion upon release. Following an early parole, the ORI made the request of the Court.[52] Z.E., however, also had an application for international protection in progress, particularly at the stage of appealing a negative decision. As such, the order that he be expulsed from Romania within 24 hours of his release from prison was in direct contradiction to Article 17(1)(a) of Law 122, which says that a foreigner may remain in Romania for 15 days after a negative decision has been issued, the only exceptions allowed being those whose application was rejected in an accelerated or border procedure. The court eventually allowed the ORI to detain Z.E. until the asylum process was resolved and the provisions of 17(1)(a) no longer applied, but not for more than 2 years.

Several rules are also spelled out in the Norms of Implementation, particularly about how the right to be informed should be handled by public functionaries. The general right to be informed of the asylum procedure, the rights and obligations and the consequences of not following these, as well as the consequences of withdrawal of an application must be presented in writing by the public official charged with receiving the application, and only according to a pre-determined model established by the general director of the IGI. In certain cases, where it may be needed, the information may also be presented orally during the interview.[53] Similar rules are also spelled out for securing the rights of asylum seekers with special needs (Article 17(1)(l)). Workers in IGI must collaborate with the UNHCR and other NGOs to identify asylum seekers with special needs, and the evaluation of what those special needs entail must be done by the same workers in collaboration with other state institutions, "according to need."[54]

There are several obligations that the law requires of asylum seekers during the asylum procedure. Moreover, a new section was introduced in 2015, titled "Limiting certain rights of applicants for international protection." All the articles in this new section, from Article 19^1 to Article 19^{16}, are subsets of the Article 19 that was originally introduced. This Article 19 listed all obligations that foreigners have during the entire asylum procedure. These include

52 According to Emergency Ordinance 194/2002 regarding foreigners in Romania, if a tribunal that has ordered an expulsion has not explicitly granted permission for detention, the ORI may ask the Bucharest Court of Appeals to take this action.

53 Art. 2. Methodological Norms for implementing Law nr. 122/2006.

54 Ibid Art. 5.

the requirement to submit a written application to one of the MAI's territorial offices, to present complete and accurate information, to submit all available documents relevant to the applicant's situation, or to submit their travel document to the authorities in exchange for a temporary ID attesting the fact that the applicant is in the process of applying for international protection. Several obligations also include notifying IGI-DAI officials of changes in residence, or to obtain written permission to leave the locality of residency for any reason. The Methodological Norms do not provide a clear definition of what might qualify an applicant to be allowed or not to leave the area of residence, but only that such a request must be resolved "at once."[55] Applicants are also obligated to submit themselves to any medical examinations, as well as vaccinations necessary for public health. This is supplemented by Art. 8 of the Norms of Implementation, by clarifying that an applicant has the "obligation to present him or herself *only* at those medical examinations that are scheduled for public health reasons."

Articles 19^1–^{16} are not the only 'obligations' introduced by Law 331/2015. Article $19(h^1)$ was also introduced that year to oblige applicants to submit to corporal and material controls. Article 19(j), on the other hand, was modified in the same law not to add another obligation, but to ensure that certain procedural guarantees are respected. Specifically, this article compels applicants whose applications are rejected to leave Romanian territory within 15 days, unless the application was rejected as unfounded in accelerated procedure, in which case the applicant must leave Romania "at once." Another clause was also added in 2015 to clarify that this "obligation does not subsist if the foreigner has a right to residency regulated according to the legislation regarding the regime of foreigners in Romania." This modification is in line with the case law of the CJEU discussed in the previous chapter, whereby it is clarified that rejecting an application for international protection does not immediately lead to an obligation to leave the territory of a Member State. Nonetheless, more obligations than rights were introduced in 2015. Articles 19^1–^{2} and, 19^4, 19^6 deserve special mention.

Art. 19^1 lays down the right of the IGI-DAI to limit the material reception conditions in certain cases, with Article 55^1 of the Norms of Implementation listing the three instances where this can be done: if the applicant changes residences without notifying the authorities, the applicant does not respect

55 Art. 7. Methodological Norms for Implementing Law nr. 122/2006. The article does mention that such a request to leave the area of residence is not necessary in cases where the presence of the applicant in another locality is requested by national authorities or the courts.

his or her application to provide necessary information or fails to show up to the established meetings, or if the applicant repeatedly breaks the rules of the regional centres for housing applicants. Article 19^2 also gives authorities the power to implement restrictive measures, including the establish an applicant's residence in a regional reception centre, or in "especially designed interior spaces". While it is specified that no restrictive measures can be implemented for the simple fact that an application is made, these can be adopted "for the purpose of completing the necessary formalities, for limiting abuses of the asylum procedure, as well as in cases where the applicant presents a danger to national security." The procedural guarantee that restrictive measures cannot be arbitrarily adopted becomes less clear, however, considering that Article 19^4 allows the IGI-DAI to house applicants in regional reception centres, even if they have material means with which they could support themselves, for the entire Dublin procedure and/or the stage of identification and establishing the elements of the application.

Finally, Article 19^6 deserves consideration because it provides a level of procedural specificity unusual to asylum law in Romania. Here, the article resembles more something out of the Norms for Implementation. It establishes that for checking identities, the case officer must check all relevant databases, must fingerprint and photograph the applicant, conduct a preliminary interview, and, if necessary, request information from institutions specialised in national security. This is also the article that defines as a risk of absconding all applicants that have attempted to illegally cross the border after making an application for protection, that have made an application only after being detected illegally crossing the border, or in relation to whom there are reasons to believe that they might leave the Romanian territory after making their application.

Chapter IV of the law entitled "Forms of Protection," describes exactly the types of international protection available in Romania. Foreigners can be conferred refugee status (declaratory), granted subsidiary protection (non-declaratory), or given temporary protection (Art. 22).[56] Refugee status is defined in Article 23 verbatim in line with the definitions of the Qualifications Directive, but the corresponding section in the Norms of Implementation provide a rulebook for case officers to follow when establishing the motives for persecution. For each of the elements in the definition for refugee, Art. 10 of

56 Until 2013, 'humanitarian protection' was also an option. According to Articles 29 and 30, which were eliminated by Law 19/2013, Romania could accord humanitarian protection to persons who come from areas engulfed in conflicts, if Romania is not involved in said conflict.

the Norms of Implementation provides the following elements that must be considered:

- Art. 10(a): Regarding the concept of race, this article asks case officers to "particularly consider colour, descendance, or belonging to a particular social group."
- Art. 10(b) Regarding the concept or religion, case officers must consider theist or atheist beliefs, participation or lack of it in public or private rituals, either alone or together with others, or other forms of expressing beliefs.
- Art. 10(c) Nationality is defined as belonging to a group defined by its cultural, ethnic, or linguistic identity, common political or geographic origins, or through the relation it has with the population of another state, regardless of citizenship.
- Art. 10(d) A social group is defined by the common and unchangeable characteristics or history of its members, its distinctiveness from most of a country's population. Article 11(d)(iii) reads: "A social group can include a group based on a common sexual orientation. Sexual orientation cannot be invoked in the sense of this article if the acts specific to the sexual orientation are criminal offenses according to Romanian legislation. Gender aspects can be included in the notion of sexual orientation, with the condition that these are not the only reason invoked in the application of this article."
- Art. 10(e) Political opinion means having any political opinion, especially regarding a specific problem or agents of persecution, regardless of whether such opinion is openly expressed.

Several other articles in the Norms are meant to guide public officials in applying articles 22 and 23 of Law 122. In assessing a well-founded fear and serious risk, authorities must consider whether these are due to events that have taken place before or after the applicant has left the country of origin, or similarly if such fears or risks are due to actions taken by the applicant following his or her departure from the country of origin, especially if these represent a continuation of beliefs and actions held previously. It is also mentioned, nonetheless, that there must exist a link between motives invoked and the acts of persecution, leaving out the possibility for officials to apply the sliding-scale model of assessing the risk an applicant is exposed to as a result of indiscriminate violence. In fact, of the 7 appeals filed in Romanian courts in 2020, two were supported by the respective court because of the threat of indiscriminate violence in Iraq,[57] and five were rejected. Four of those 5 appeals also involved applicants from Iraq or Afghanistan whose claims were rejected.

57 Decisions nr. 553/2020 and nr. 554/2020, Rădăuți Regional Court.

3.6 *First Instance Decisions – Architecture, Rights, and Obligations*

The description of the architecture of Romania's procedure begins in Chapter V. A person is considered an asylum seeker from the moment he or she has expressed their will to the competent authorities, in writing or verbally, from which it can be understood that they request protection from the Romanian state (Art. 34(1)). While the law does not outright allow for an application to be inferred by the authorities without an explicit request, Article 35^1 does come close by stating that "if there are elements that lead to the idea foreigners in holding centres, preventive arrest, penitentiaries, border crossings, or international transit areas intend to request protection, the personnel of the relevant authorities must provide information regarding the possibility of making a request." This article, introduced in the law in 2015, is the only one that requires authorities to screen for possible applicants without an explicit request being made.

Applications must be made in border crossings or on the Romanian territory (Art. 36(1)(a-b)), and, where applicable, an application can also be made for protection needs arising *sur place* (Art. 36(1)(c)). Applications must be registered within 3 working days if made directly to the IGI, or within 6 days if made to another authority (such as border police). In extenuating situations, i.e., mass influx, registration can take up to 10 days (Art. 36^1). Asylum seekers can make their own application, or it can be made by their legal representative, in a language that the applicant understands (Art. 37). The Norms of Implementation specify that once indication is made that an request for protection will be made, a form must be filled, either by the applicant or by the IGI-DAI worker if the applicant cannot read and/or write.[58] Annex I to the Norms specifies that the form must mention the applicant's name, parents' names, date and place of birth, civil status, spouse's name, date and place of birth, details regarding family members accompanying the applicant, country of origin or residence, travel document, reason for requesting asylum, date and way of leaving country of origin, transited countries and time spent in each, date and way of entering Romania, place of residence in Romania, and spoken languages. The form must also include a disclaimer that all the rights and obligations enumerated in Articles 17 and 19 of Law 122 have been described. Finally, for the copy issued to the applicant, they are also informed of the date and time at which they must present themselves for the interview "for determining a form of protection." While collective applications are not allowed according to Article 37(3) of Law 122, the Norms mention that in such cases it

58 Art. 19. Methodological Norms for implementing Law nr. 122/2006.

is the duty of the IGI-DAI officer to inform applicants of the requirement that applications be made individually.

The rights of minors are very prominent in the Law, reflecting the priority given to the well-being of children in legislative documents from all levels of governance. The law itself requires that the legal representatives of minors be charged with defending their rights, including making applications for protection on their behalf. Children over the age of 14, however, can make their own application (Art. 39(1–2)). Unaccompanied minors who make an application are registered as such, but the application is lodged only when a legal representative is appointed. Case officers must in this case draft a legal statement explaining that the unaccompanied minor is an asylum seeker, record the identification data, and "immediately" notify the child protection agencies. Officially, what this means, is that the asylum procedure for unaccompanied minors is suspended from the moment an application is made until a legal representative is appointed (Art. 40). Furthermore, interviewing minors can only happen in front of the legal representative, and if the case officers consider the minor to be mature enough; otherwise, interviewing the parents suffices (Art. 47).

Since the rights of minors are prominent, there is also mention of age assessment procedures, as well as guidance for credibility assessments. The given age is believed only if there are no "serious doubts" (Art. 41(1)). If serious doubts exist, medical expertise can be requested (Art. 41(2)). If the applicant refuses to undergo the medical examination, he or she will be considered an adult, with the assumption that they turned 18 on the day the application is made – for bureaucratic form-completion purposes (Art. 41(3–4)). In any case, this cannot be the case if there are justified reasons for the refusal, and the refusal itself cannot be invoked as a reason to deny protection (Art. 41(5) & (7)).

There are also procedural guarantees built into the asylum procedure for applicants whose cognitive abilities are limited. In these cases, a legal guardian must be appointed, but it was not until 2015 that a point was introduced that also allowed the guardian to participate in the interview (Art. 42). Other clauses introduced at different points altered the dynamics of the interviews. Until 2014, for instance, the preliminary interview did not exist, and was only a time when the asylum seeker would fill out the form described in previous sections. As of now, however, Article 43 calls for a preliminary interview during which the form is discussed, but also when an assessment is made if the Dublin procedure is appropriate. Another amendment was brought in 2015 to Article 44, which calls for fingerprinting applicants, to also include a photograph of the asylum seeker.

Article 45 lays down the rules for the second interview of the procedure, namely the interview for determining international protection. This needs to be done by an employee of IGI-DAI, and it is up to them if the family of the applicant needs to be present. The asylum seekers must have access to an interpreter they can reasonably be expected to understand, while no interview is required if authorities decide they can confer refugee status based on existing evidence, or in cases of applicants with reduced cognitive abilities. Asylum seekers cannot refuse to undergo an interview if their legal representative is absent, and rescheduling in such cases can only happen once, and only if the representative's absence is justified. An interview report is drafted by the interviewer, including identification of applicant, interviewer, interpreter, and representative, reasons invoked for protection, and the statement from which it should be understood that all information presented during the interview is real. If it is the case, the report also includes clarifications made by the applicant. A new interview may be requested only if needed.

Here the norms of implementation mention specifically that, for the duration of the interview, no police uniforms may be worn, conflicting with the previously mentioned Ordinance 82/2018 of the Minister of Internal Affairs which required all ministry workers except those in undercover operations to wear police uniforms. The same article of the Norms, Article 23, also specifies that legal representatives are not allowed to intervene during the interview, only at its conclusion. Article 17 of the same act, meanwhile, establishes that all who conduct interviews, and indeed who assess application for protection, must have higher education, and must have specific expertise in the field of asylum. The same requirement is not made for managers of asylum institutions who are not involved directly in assessing applications, but who must oversee the activity of entire bureaucracies.

In assessing an application, authorities can seek information from several sources. Any public institution, agency, or organisation that operates in Romania may be contacted for documents necessary to reach a decision in a case, while the Ministry of External Affairs (MAE) is charged to draft country of origin information report. IGI and MAE are together responsible for drafting the list of safe third countries (Art. 49). Similarly, when necessary and with the consent of the applicant, medical expertise may also be requested (Art. 49^1). Finally, the application must be decided based on the documents existing in an applicant's file and the motives invoked, which must be analysed considering the country-of-origin information and the applicant's credibility (Art. 50).

Reaching a decision must happen within 30 days, unless more time is needed, in which case 30-day extensions may be used. In any case, this cannot surpass 6 months, or 9 months if the case is overly complex or if Romania is experiencing a mass-influx (Art. 52). The decision may confer refugee status, offer subsidiary protection, or reject altogether the application (Art. 53). In any case, this must be communicated in writing, in Romanian or in a language understood by the applicant, and it was not until 2014 that information regarding effective remedy also had to be communicated in case of negative decisions (Art. 54). If communication is not possible, a notice is posted publicly at the IGI office, and the day of posting is considered the day of delivery of decision for purposes of effective remedy time limits. It is in Articles 55–70 that the rules for effective remedy are presented. Interestingly, and in contrast to the findings that will be presented in the next chapter, there is no legal review conducted by the IGI-DAI of any cases that are taken to court for appeal. A complaint is immediately sent to the competent tribunal, and the IGI-DAI's lawyers always defend the decision issued by the case workers. Table 8 below shows the number of appeals lodged against a decision issued by IGI-DAI between 2015–2019, and how many of those appeals were upheld by the court.

Family reunification also takes noteworthy importance in the asylum procedure. A request for protection can be made by a beneficiary of protection on behalf of his or her family (Art. 71), and in this case the worker must request birth or marriage certificates that attest to family ties. An extra interview may also be requested with the beneficiary in Romania in such cases, and if any documents relevant to the decision are with the family members in the country of origin, IGI-DAI officers may contact the consular officers and MAE to assist with securing any evidence. In case of a positive decision, the case officer must request the issuance of a visa for the family members.[59] Finally, according to Article 72 of Law 122 family reunification procedures are done *ex-officio* in case of unaccompanied minors.

The final aspects of Law 122 that are relevant to first instance decisions are accelerated and border procedures. Accelerated procedures are for all manifestly unfounded applications, applications from people who represent a threat to public order or national security, or applications of people who come from a safe country of origin (Art. 75(1)(a)). Unfounded applications are those of which there is no basis for invoking fear of persecution or serious risk in the country of origin. This means that either no fear is invoked by the applicant, no data or information is offered to substantiate claim, or there is an "evident lack of credibility" as evidenced by incoherent, contradictory, or flagrantly untrue statements (Art. 76). It is worth noting that when OUG 1/2014 was passed, a point was removed from the law which categorised as unfounded applications

59 Art. 30. Methodological Norms for implementing Law nr. 122/2006.

TABLE 8 Number of appeals and number of successful appeals, 2015–2019[a]

Year	Number of appeals	Appeals upheld
2015	306	55
2016	381	21
2017	791	44
2018	650	54
2019	598	68

a Information obtained from the Ministry of Interior's Office of Information and Public Relations, September 2020, through information requested according to Law 544/2001 regarding the freedom to access information for the public interest.

all those from asylum seekers that could have benefitted from internal refuge as recognised by the UNHCR. The accelerated procedure can be triggered at any time, including during the regular procedure (Art. 78), and the decision must be issued within 3 days of its triggering (Art. 79). Effective remedy must be sought within 7 days from the moment that a decision is issued that an application is unfounded, although this time limit was only 2 days until an amendment in 2015 (Art. 80).

A second reasoning for considering an application as manifestly unfounded is if the application is being deceitful, or in bad faith abuses the asylum procedure. According to the Norms of Implementation, this is measured by how often and seriously an asylum seeker evades their obligations as spelled out in Article 19. In fact, a list is provided of cases where such deceit is present: using false documents, presenting false elements to substantiate the application, the applicant destroyed or deteriorated documents relevant to the application, deliberately withheld the fact that he or she submitted another application for protection in another country, made an application with the purpose of frustrating authorities in their efforts to remove them from the country, or entered illegally and has no justifiable reason for delaying making an application (Arts. 76(3)(a)-(f)). Until 2015 if a safe third country rejected an asylum seeker's application, this made the application unfounded in Romania as well. The list of safe countries is drafted by order of the minister of internal affairs, following a recommendation from the IGI. In 2019, 315 applications were rejected in an accelerated procedure, therefore including manifestly unfounded applications. 167 were rejected in 2018, 382 in 2017, 105 in 2016 and 99 in 2015.

Article 82, which deals with making an application in a border zone, specifies that authorities are obligated to issue a decision within three days. The possible decisions in this case are: (1) positive, (2) to allow access to the territory and to the ordinary procedure, or (3) to declare the application manifestly unfounded and deny access. Emergency Ordinance 53/2015, however, gives the opportunity to derogate from the requirements of Article 83. In an effort to pass legislation that could deal with a mass influx of asylum seekers at the borders, the Government clarified in this ordinance that the IGI may grant access to the ordinary procedure without an interview in cases where the applicant comes from a country origin for which the rate of admissibility in an administrative phase is, nationally, at least 30%, or if the applicant belongs to a vulnerable group.[60] This last reason for derogation is in line with the guarantees offered by Law 122 broadly, as Article 84 also states that applications from those with special procedural guarantees are not subject to border procedures and must be given immediate access to the ordinary procedure, unless they are deemed a threat to national security or public order. Until 2015, this guarantee was only extended to unaccompanied minors.

The concepts of first country of asylum, safe European country, or safe third country are defined and discussed in articles 95–97. If an applicant has transited a third country where he or she received protection, this is considered the first country of asylum as long as basic freedoms are respected, there is no exposure to serious risks, and *non-refoulment* is respected (Art. 95). If these conditions are met, IGI may declare the application as inadmissible. Until 2015, this was the case not only for applicants that received protection in the third country, but also for those that had the opportunity to request protection but did not. A safe European country, similarity, is a non-EU country which has ratified the Geneva convention, has an asylum procedure in its internal legislation, and abides by the European Convention on Human Rights.

The difference between a safe European and a safe-third country is that the IGI has no discretion in awarding protection if the safe European country expresses their willingness to the take the applicant that transited through their territory before entering Romania. Similarly, a safe third country is a country that respects the same guarantees as a safe country of origin, is willing

60 Information obtained from the Ministry of Interior's Office of Information and Public Relations, September 2020, through information requested according to Law 544/2001 regarding the freedom to access information for the public interest.

to take the applicant back, and clear link exists with the asylum seekers. If these conditions are met, the IGI must declare the application as inadmissible. Only when it comes to a first country of asylum, then, does the IGI have discretion as to declaring the application as inadmissible or not. The decision to apply the provisions can only be taken if the applicant has been given the opportunity to sustain an interview to establish the facts regarding these cases (Art. 97^1). The IGI is also charged with drafting a list of safe European countries and safe third countries (Art. 97^2), however the Romanian government supports the adoption of a list of safe third countries at the EU level, as a way to facilitate national bureaucratic implementation of the CEAS.[61]

4 Conclusion

The information in this chapter shows Romania's asylum governance as one categorized by de-concentration, and at the same time by a deference to hierarchy in decision making. Previous literature would indicate that the bonds of supervisions are more likely to break down in systems where the workers are removed from the central authority. However, the work of street-level bureaucrats tasked with making first instance decisions is defined largely by the black-on white guidelines, with little indication that they have much to say about the creation of said guidelines, or indeed much flexibility in the interpretation of ambiguous provisions. Instructions given to bureaucrats leave little room for manoeuvre, and a lack of proper reviews of the quality of decisions removes collaborative decision-making between caseworkers. Some hints are given that the development of CJEU case law is followed, but no formal mechanisms exist for guarantee timely adherence to of rulings.

The verticality in quality assessment is also indication of the working conditions of street-level bureaucrats at the IGI-DAI. The lack of any mechanism for a horizontal peer review of work, one that can quickly respond and adjust to the needs of each case officer's current work assignments, shows that the method of evaluating bureaucratic processes is not about ensuring access of the bureaucratic clientele to the benefits given by the institution. Annual randomised evaluations of a sample of cases do little to respond the quickly

61 Information obtained from the Ministry of Interior's Office of Information and Public Relations, September 2020, through information requested according to Law 544/2001 regarding the freedom to access information for the public interest.

changing conditions on the ground, and even less to ensure the quality of a decision before it is issued.

If public administration in central and eastern Europe is characterised by informal patterns of behaviour,[62] the values and norms that persisted post-1989 in the region should be, to some extent, seen throughout. In such case, the deference to hierarchy model of implementation from Romania could potentially be observed in other countries in the region as well. The way street-level bureaucrats make decisions is highly influenced by managerial relationships, and the case of asylum policy in Romania shows that the little influence they have over the creation of the guidelines they must strictly adhere to makes adaption to changing world conditions slow and rigid. This has implications for an entire region that can, at any time, face unexpected influx in asylum seekers, as it was shown in the case of those fleeing the war in Ukraine starting in 2022.

This is not to say that discretion is not present in the work of bureaucrats. Some examples were highlighted in this chapter. The sources that should be checked for information on country of origin, or the need for family members to be present during interviews – or indeed, if interviews are even necessary – are some examples of decision left to the bureaucrat. By and large, however, discretion is more likely to be absent, or discouraged, then present. In the case of asylum governance, Romania has been able to avoid a system collapse largely because it remains at the bottom of destination countries in the EU. In fact, IGI-DAI reported less applications lodged in Romania in 2015, at the height of Europe's 'refugee crisis' than one-year prior in 2014.

62 Jan-Hinrik Meyer-Sahling and Kutsal Yesilkagit, 'Differential Legacy Effects: Three Propositions on the Impact of Administrative Traditions on Public Administration Reform in Europe East and West' (2011) 18 *Journal of European Public Policy* 311.

CHAPTER 6

National Implementation of the CEAS: The Case of the Netherlands

The description of Romania's governance apparatus should not immediately lead to any conclusions of how the provisions of Europe's asylum acquis are implemented across the entire Union. As the opening chapters showed, one of the discrepancies in literature that tries to assess the effectiveness of governance structures is that there are two conversations: one which focuses on institutional efficiency and performance, and another which sees value in shying away from any form of generalised standards.[1] Focus needs to be not on comparing structures of governance, but rather the communalities in strategy formulation, building national institutions, and attempts to reform the system to adapt to changing conditions. Like the problem of relying exclusively on a black on white, hard law analysis,[2] using one-size-fits-all metrics such as acceptance rates of asylum applications allows for very little to be inferred about the procedural compliance to the CEAS mechanisms. Previous chapters have elaborated on and exemplified how deficiencies in Europe's asylum systems can manifest themselves in implementation, by paying attention to the discretionary space of those charged with implementing asylum policy. If attention is truly to be shifted toward a focus on communalities in strategy formulation, the street-level bureaucrat is a good place to start.

As in the previous chapter, it is taken that the most complete understanding of a street-level bureaucrat's working conditions can only come from analysing their role within the entire system of governance. In the Dutch context, division of power among levels of authority is fundamental. The political system is built on the idea that while the central government is a key administrative player, its power is balanced by the authority given to municipalities or other competent administrative institutions.[3]

---

1 Brint Milward et al., 'Is Public Management Neglecting the State?' (2016) 29 *Governance* 311.

2 Hrafn Asgeirsson, *The Nature and Value of Vagueness in the Law* (*Law and Practical Reason*) (Hart Publishing 2020).

3 Netherlands Institute for Multiparty Democracy & Instuut voor Publiek en Politiek. 'The Dutch Political System in a Nutshell' (2008).

 | DOI:10.1163/9789004700826_007

1 The Principles of Governance: The Dutch Constitution

The current Dutch Constitution can be traced back to the one issued by King Willem I in 1815, making it one of the oldest in the world. That document included several provisions which were imposed by international convention, leading to the addition of – even if limited – clauses on freedom of religion, habeas corpus, and freedom of the press. The London Protocol of 1814, agreed upon by the great powers of Europe at the time, allowed Willem I to become sovereign King in the Netherlands only if those rights were respected constitutionally. This showed "international law and constitutional law working as a system of communicating vessels,"[4] to ease the integration of the diverse newly established kingdom. These communicating vessels, this chapter will argue, fits the description of many interactions between domestic and international law. Indeed, when in the 1950s the Constitution was being amended to "include provisions making it possible for supranational sources of law to take effect in the Dutch legal system [...] the point at issue was not really whether direct effect should be possible or indeed permissible in the existing system, but whether the Constitution should say so in so many words."[5] The intertwined role of international and domestic law was taken as a foregone conclusion. The problem rested only on how – and in how many words – to give effect to such principles, eventually creating a system so open to influence form international law that the EU is often referred to as the "fourth tier of government."[6]

Yet, despite being through the Constitution that the principles of governance are enumerated, there is no direct reference to EU law or European integration anywhere in the document. One likely reason, as it will later be described in greater detail, might be because government and governance procedures should be set forth through other legislative acts, such as the Aliens Act 2000. The constitution serves to enumerate the principles upon which the Dutch system should rest, and the tone is set from the very first article, which states that "all persons in the Netherlands shall be treated equally in equal circumstances." The specific phrasing indicates that the fundamental rights

---

4 Stephan Wendehorst, 'Religious Rights between International Law and Constitutional Law: A System of Communicating Vessels – From Premodern Historical Evidence to a Reassessment of Doctrine' in Robert Uerpmann-Wittzack Evelyne Lagrange, and Stefan Oeter (eds.) *Religion and International Law: Living Together*, (Brill Nijhoff, 2018), 28.

5 Jit Peters, 'The Dutch Constitution and Dutch Constitutional Values' in Alfred Kellermann (ed.) *EU Enlargement* (TMC Asser Press 2001).

6 Ibid 60.

enshrined in this document are valid to everyone in the Netherlands, without specifically referencing citizenship or residency.

If one is not convinced that the wording in Article 1 is meant to alleviate any of the ambiguities that could have emerged regarding who these fundamentals rights apply to, the very choice of words throughout Chapter 1 ('Fundamental Rights') makes this clear. Only 4 provisions of this first chapter are specifically reserved for "Dutch Nationals": the right to be eligible for appointment to public service (Art. 3), the right to elect members of representative bodies and stand for elections (Art. 4), the right to a free choice of work (Art. 19(3)), and the right to receive aid, for those who cannot provide for themselves (Art. 20(3)). In all other cases, rights are either reserved for 'everyone,' or they can be restricted for 'no one.' Issues of migration and citizenship are brought up early. Article 2(1) states that Parliament must regulate Dutch nationality, as it must do with admission and expulsion of foreigners (Art. 2(2)), extradition (Art. 2(3)), and restrictions on the right to leave the country (Art. 2(4)).

The second chapter of the Constitution begins listing the attributes and architecture of the country's government, establishing in Art. 42 that Ministers are responsible for acts of government, and that the Cabinet, which is comprised of the Prime Minister and other Minsters, "shall consider and decide upon overall government policy and shall promote the coherence thereof," (Art. 45(3)). Chapter 3, on the other hand, describes the responsibilities and composition of the States General, which represent the country's population and consist of a Lower House (*Tweede Kamer*) and an Upper House (*Eerste Kamer*).

It is noteworthy that many of the constitutional principles, maybe not unexpectedly, lay down institutional principles of transparency, cooperation, and balance of power, but it leaves most procedural matters to be laid down by Acts of Parliament. All in all, the Dutch Constitution requires or allows acts of parliament to regulate or draft rules on matters in 153 different provisions, ranging from royal succession and funding for education, to the power and methods of the ombudsman, taxation, military service, rules relating to the state's finances, civil, criminal, and administrative law and procedures, legal status of public servants and their employment protection, public access to information, delegating responsibility for handling disputes not arising from civil law, organisation, composition and powers of the judiciary, regulations for issuing of pardons, granting amnesty, composition and power of the administrative organs of provinces and municipalities, and many other areas of policy.

There are however, two articles that clearly highlight the importance of understanding Acts of Parliament. Article 132(5) states that "provisions in the event of non-compliance in matters of regulation and administration required under Article 124, paragraph 2,[7] shall be regulated by Act of Parliament. Provisions may be made by Act of Parliament [...] in cases of gross neglect of duty by the administrative organs of a province or municipality." But Acts of Parliament are more than just the legal text comprising regulatory provisions. They represent the will and political composition of the political elites at the point in time when they are passed. The cementing of this will, which is very much dependent on temporal contexts, is given by Article 120, which states that "the constitutionality of Acts of Parliament and treaties shall not be reviewed by the courts."

Parliament, then, is crucial. In the Dutch context, Parliament – or the States General – has three main duties: to draft laws alongside the government, check government's implementation of laws and other activities, and forming the bridge between the electorate and government when it comes to policy. The Lower House approves bills proposed the government and may amend them, or it may initiate its own legislation – powers that the Upper House does not possess. The *Eerste Kamer* can only approve or reject a bill in its entirety, without amending it. Both chambers have power over the acceptance of ministerial budgets, crucial for implementing policies. Furthermore, the States General holds the right to inquiry, allowing an appointed parliamentary committee to summon anyone it wishes – from politicians and civil servants to citizens.

2 Public Service in the Netherlands

There are four levels of administration in the Dutch political system: the central government, the provincial authorities, the municipal authorities, and, less relevant to this research, the water management boards. Each of these has a distinct set of functions and responsibilities. Provincial authorities regulate housing and planning, environmental policies, welfare, public transport, and economic and agricultural policies, among other policy areas. Municipal authorities, on the other hand, regulate local land usage, maintain local infrastructure, waste management, fire, and police departments, and perform other administrative duties. The relationship between these levels, however, is better described as organic, rather than rigid.

7 Art. 124(2): Provincial and municipal administrative organs may be required by or pursuant to Act of Parliament to provide regulation and administration.

> The central government, the 12 provincial authorities and the 393 [in 2023: 342] municipal authorities [...] decide for themselves which tasks they address within their own territories and the limits of higher regulations. The government's package of tasks changes continually as a result of changing social conditions. Central government, the provincial authorities and the municipal authorities are free to take policy initiatives, which enables them to take up new tasks and discontinue others.[8]

As a result, it can be expected that overlap in attributes happens. Housing and welfare policies, for example, can be found in the governance wheelhouse of both the provincial and municipal governments. It is in this large intertwined system of multilevel governance that civil servants find themselves. When it comes to supporting the work done by Ministers, civil servants working in the Hague provide the support necessary for ministers to answer questions in front of parliament or in the media, and the preparation of legislative or policy proposals. Nevertheless, most central government civil servants perform operational tasks, supervision, or support processes (such as accommodation, human resources, or procurement).

The leadership in Dutch ministries can be clearly separated in two categories: political and official.[9] The most senior official in a ministry is the Secretary General, responsible for the policy and management of the institution, and immediately subordinate are Directors General responsible for specific policy areas. "If the Minister or State Secretary primarily consults the Directors General, the Secretary General focuses primarily on the management of the Ministry and the coordination of policy. This partly depends on the preferences of the Minister or State Secretary, the Secretary General's perception of his tasks and the agreements reached between the senior civil servants concerned, including the Directors General."[10] This would indicate that, at least theoretically, changes of the political landscape, as well as changes in 'official' leadership could greatly alter both the policy focus and working conditions of ministries.

Dutch civil service is one best categorised as fluid, in a constant flux of change, often as a reaction to large societal trends such as increased globalisation, changing economic order, or the "erosion of the automatic authority of

8 Ministry of the Interior and Kingdom Relations (BZK), 'The Dutch Public Service: Organisation and functioning of the government in the Netherlands, the position of civil servants and the main developments' (2016), 19.

9 The wording 'political' and 'official' is used in *The Dutch Public Service* (n 70) report.

10 Ibid 21–22.

institutions and professions," among others.[11] These trends have created two major shifts in recent years. The first is horizontal, from government to governance, with less steering done by central government authorities, and more within a framework of cooperation between different types of organisations each with monitoring and evaluation mechanisms. Naturally, a vertical shift has also occurred, best described as one that acknowledges the new realities of multilevel systems of governance, including relationships of cooperation and interdependence not only at the domestic level, but also within the European sphere.[12]

The shift toward a system that includes the dynamics of European policy is seen by the Dutch government as having direct implications in the way discretionary space is constructed and navigated.

> The increasingly broad and deep involvement of national civil servants in Europe raises questions about the extent to which their activities can still be steered and monitored just as effectively by their Ministers and State Secretaries in The Hague [...] the greater physical distance from their Minister or State Secretary and the complexity of the decision-making in international organisations can be expected to increase the discretionary freedom of civil servants.[13]

Moreover, recent research has also shown that "global megatrends" are seen as directly impacting the work of public actors. New stakeholder dynamics which lead to ambiguous interests that need accounting for, new collaborative arrangements in work environments, power shifts to new authorities, new working practices, and increased demands for ethical considerations are all listed as direct consequences of trends that develop outside of the Netherlands but impact the work of public actors.[14]

---

11 Ibid 66.

12 The Ministry of Interior and Kingdom Relations measures the manifestation of "Europeanisation of national public administration" by the percentage of new laws and regulations that originate in Brussels (approx. 60–80%), or the number of civil servants that reported an active involvement in EU-related work (90% of senior civil service officials in 2007).

13 Ibid 66.

14 Philip Marcel Karré, Martijn van der Steen, Zeger van der Wal and Thomas Schillemans, 'Public Administration in the Netherlands: State of the Field' in Geert Bouckaert and Werner Jann (eds), *European Perspectives for Public Administration* (Leuven Univeristy Press 2020).

Even in this environment, there is little belief that bureaucrats will take differing positions than those adopted by the organisations for which they work. Even more, not only does the Dutch government not consider that Europeanisation leads to negative outcomes of discretionary powers, but rather that it helps standardise the definition of the key tasks of government and the core of civil service. This is attributed to the rules drawn up for the implementation of the internal market, whereby any EU citizens can apply for any vacant position in another Member State, excepting only specific areas such as defence or public order. The central state is not retreating from all aspects of governance, however. Security and justice, domains under which asylum management falls, are being brought even deeper under the responsibility of central authorities, meaning that there is an increase not only in the level of intervention, but also in the size of the administrative machinery.[15]

When talking about workers at the front line of bureaucracy, one should not assume however that there is a large integrated machinery that spans across all levels of governance. Because of what the government self-describes as a "decentralised unified state," a complicating factor of trying to assess the machinery of civil service officials as a unitary organisation is the fact that "many tasks […] form part of the area in between government and society,"[16] indicating a special status for the work that street-level bureaucracies do.

The decentralisation is evident in the way the work in civil service is shaped, beginning from the very process of recruitment. Turning once again to the self-assessment conducted by the Ministry of Interior and Kingdom Relations, we learn that

> recruitment takes place for a specific job, not for a career, [but] there are three important exceptions to this rule. Firstly, career systems exist for specific sectors […]. This concerns the police, the judiciary, the Defence department and the diplomatic service. Secondly, in the early 1990s a general (management-oriented) career system for senior civil servants, in particular those in central government, was introduced: the General Administrative Service (ABD), including another tier for senior civil servants, the senior management group. Finally, a management traineeship was introduced for high potentials in the central government and at a number of municipal authorities.[17]

15 Ibid 66–67.
16 Ibid 34.
17 Ibid.

This means that, with a few exceptions, recruitment is job-oriented, thus being guided by the rules and expectations of the institution doing the recruiting.

An effect of this type of decentralisation is an uncertainty about the total number of workers employed in civil service. While certain trends in the total number of government personnel can be observed over periods of time, such as an overall 5% reduction from 1982 to 2015, the changing nature of civil service and of who falls within the definition of this type of worker make irrelevant any conclusions drawn based on absolute numbers alone. Even when it comes to assessing specifically the total number of workers employed that deal directly with asylum seekers, much uncertainty exists about what the exact number might be.[18] This implies an assumption that knowing this total number is irrelevant. If we simply interpret a worker being 'in public service' as being 'in the service of a public employer,' the only consideration that matters is that the employer be created pursuant to public law.[19] By this reasoning, the number of employees that have been or are being recruited to do specific jobs, and any resulting fluctuations and uncertainty in the number government employees, are related to the current priorities as laid down in legislation.

When comparing this decentralisation of civil service with the working conditions described by Lipsky,[20] one cannot be faulted for assuming that a great deal of power is given to senior managers of each tier of governance. Government personnel become such based on an appointment, not a contract in the sense a private sector employee is used to, meaning not only that decisions of recruitment are made from a starting point of decentralisation, but also that the rules of the jobs are established unilaterally by the government – the party doing the appointing. "In a certain sense," the Ministry of Interior acknowledges, "this construction reflects the fundamental legal inequality between the government, with public authority, and those who work for it."[21]

This description should not immediately provide the image of an overly asymmetrical power relationship. While civil servants are appointed, consensus must still be reached with those doing the appointing. The status of all civil servants in laid down in the Civil Servants Act 1929, where they are defined

18 Angelina van Kampen, 'Country Report: Netherlands' *Asylum Information Database* (*AIDA*), (2019), 15. Furthermore, none of the IND officials interviewed for this research in March 2020 had any knowledge of the total number of employees working on the assessment of asylum applications.

19 Ministry of the Interior and Kingdom Relations (BZK) (n 8), 41.

20 Michael Lipsky, *Street-Level Bureaucracy: Dilemmas of the Individual in Public Service* (Russel Sage Foundation 2010).

21 Ministry of the Interior and Kingdom Relations (BZK) (n 8), 40.

as those appointed to work in the service of the public. To be a civil servant two criteria must be met: a decision of appointment, and the public law foundation upon which the employer is based.[22] It is also in this Act, in Article 125, that employers are empowered to impose rules on the legal position of their subordinates. They must issue rules regarding dismissal, salaries, working conditions, and employee participation, and must ensure the pursuance of an 'integrity policy.' Very little about the management of each government department is spelled out in the Civil Servants Act, showing the need for ambiguity when it comes to maintaining a 'decentralised unified state.' Even in their own reporting, the government acknowledges that the 1929 Civil Servants Act is a law devoid of much substance, as the main rules are established elsewhere. The only vague standard found in this Act refers to the obligation of employers and civil servants conducting themselves as it benefits proper government representatives. It is on this vagueness that the mutually conflictual relationship between managers and street-level bureaucrats is based, as it forms "the basis for more concrete requirements that civil servants and their employers can impose on each other."[23]

The relationship between managers and workers, and specifically the role of hierarchy in managing discretion, can be somewhat seen in Article 125 of the Civil Servants Acts. This article forbids civil servants form expressing public opinions that might negatively impact the work of the office for which they work, having their freedom of expression limited by the concept of a "functioning standard" – an assessment of whether confidential information is involved, the damage that the opinions create to the colleagues or managers, the seniority of the civil servant, and the degree of involvement in the matter upon which a comment is publicly made.[24] In other words, a civil servant may not speak up against an official measure taken within their own domain of work, but they may do so about a measure in which they were not involved.

To generalise between the rights and obligations of civil servants may prove difficult, as each sector of government is subject to its own regulations. While this means that the governance structures of each sector are charged with drawing up these rights and obligations of their own workers, any changes to these rules can only be done with the consent of the civil service trade unions. Some standardisation does exist, nonetheless, as the rules regarding dismissal

22 Certain groups of civil servants, such as judges and military personnel, have their own legal regimes. The main differences, however, have to do with issues such as the appointment for life of judges, or rules regarding military discipline for military personnel.

23 Ministry of the Interior and Kingdom Relations (BZK) (n 8), 42.

24 Ibid.

show, where basic common principles still stand. The conditions for dismissal must be shown to have been met, and the employer must ensure that it made all efforts to reassign the worker in question to a more suitable position. Other bases for dismissal are a lack of suitability, inability to function for a longer period, or serious dysfunctions. The employee must have explicitly been given a chance to improve their performance or long-term incapacity and finding a new job for the worker must be proven to be impossible. Two elements are worth highlighting: dereliction of duty, in it of itself, does not constitute a right to dismiss a worker, and a civil servant cannot resign. Bureaucrats must request dismissal, thus fulfilling one of the general conditions for lawful dismissal.

2.1 *The General Administrative Law Act*

Civil service law constitutes a part of the country's legal administrative body of law, meaning that the General Administrative Law Act encompasses every decision from appointment to dismissal of civil servants. The requirements imposed by this act for government decisions – e.g., providing adequate justification and consideration of interests – must also be considered in all decisions regarding civil servants, and several possibilities for appealing managerial decisions are available.[25] The provisions of this act are in fact very relevant in this case, because they spell out the type of work conducted by official authorities.

An official authority is either an organisation established by public law, or any other person or body invested with public authority (Art. 1.1), while an interested party is one affected by an order (Art. 1.2). An order is defined as any written decision of an administrative authority, which constitutes a public law act. An administrative decision is a specific type of order that is not general in nature, including within this definition rejections of applications for orders – or a request made by an interested party. Lastly, a policy rule is another type of order which is not a generally binding regulation, but that rather lays down the general rule for weighing interests, determining facts or interpreting statutory regulations in the exercise of a power granted to an administrative authority (Art. 1.3). Especially for the purposes of filing appeals, refusals to issue an order and failure to make an order in due time shall be equated to an order in it of themselves (Art. 6.2).

By specifying the power of authorities to issue policy rules necessary for enacting their powers, it provides the general mechanism by which interpretative ambiguities should be dealt with. Art. 3.2 calls for order to be issued based

25 According to the 2016 report of the Ministry of Interior and Kingdom Relations, "this may involve very serious decisions (punitive dismissal), but also, for example, a refusal to grant remuneration for a snack bought during a short service trip."

on "adequate information" of the issues that "match the purpose of the authority." Art. 3.46, on the other hand, states that "proper reasons" must be used when issuing an order. To achieve this, Art. 4.81 gives authorities the powers to establish the policy rules relating to a power conferred to it, while Art. 4.82 states that "to explain the reasons for an order, it shall only be sufficient to refer to a fixed practice insofar as this practice is contained in a policy rule." Ambiguities, then, can be settled through usual work practices so long as these practices are contained in a policy rule.

Sometimes the interpretation of such ambiguities is constrained. Art. 4.13 allows for a 'reasonable time' to be taken to respond to an application, but no longer than 8 weeks – 57 days are thus defined as the upper limit of "reasonable time," unless another statutory law states otherwise. The act also makes several other references that are of interest for this research. First, Article 1.6(b) clarifies that the General Administrative Law Act does not apply to the execution of measures depriving persons of their liberty under the Aliens Act. Furthermore, Article 1.7, which falls under Title 1.2 – Implementing Binding Decisions of authorities of the European Communities (now the European Union), specifies that no opinions or outside consultations are required for orders implementing binding decisions of the Communities, requirements that are otherwise made for regular orders.

Most interestingly is the similarity between the process of filing an application for an order and the process of lodging an application described in the Asylum Procedures Directive. First, after noting and confirming receipt of the application (Art. 3.17), public servants must determine if the application is complete. If the application is incomplete, it may be discarded only if the applicant has been given the opportunity to rectify any omissions (Art. 3.18 and Art. 4.5) – a process descried in the act as "admissibility." Art. 4.1 states that applications for administrative decisions must be lodged in writing with the competent authority, and Art. 4.2 requires that all relevant documents and information be supplied. In line with some of the reasonings of the CJEU, however, Art. 4.3 allows for privacy considerations to be weighted when certain information is requested, such as medical or psychological examinations. Only in cases where such documents are required in provisions of statutory law must they be supplied. Subsequent applications are also regulated in this section, clearly stating that they must be motivated with new facts, or they may be rejected outright (Art. 4.6). This shows an almost natural harmony existing between general decision-making in the public sector, and asylum procedures.

Several provisions regarding the enforcement and evaluation of the Administrative Law Act are similarly relevant. A supervisor, for instance, is someone who, pursuant to statutory regulations, oversees the observance of provisions (Art. 5.11), but may only exercise powers in a manner that is 'reasonably' needed for the performance of duties (Art. 5.13). Regarding the ability of administrative authority to enforce provisions derived from statutory regulations, an 'enforcement action' is defined in article 5.21 as a "physical act taken by or on behalf of an administrative authority against what has been or is being done, kept, or omitted in breach of obligations laid down by or pursuant to any statutory regulation." Orders can nonetheless be rescinded, even if an appeal against said order is currently underway (Art. 6.18), while Article 6.23 allows the option for a two-tier appeal process to take place – i.e., appealing the appeal.[26]

A glimpse of how a discretionary space should be navigated in the Dutch administrative process can be seen in the way the concept of 'mandate,' or the power to make orders in the name of an administrative authority (Art. 10.1), is dealt with. An order made by an official *within the limits of power* is deemed to be an order by the administrative authority. The limits placed on – and inversely the enhancement of – the powers conferred by statutory regulations are crucial in understanding the factors that influence how decisions are reached, not only what those specific decisions should be. Mandates can be issued generally, or for specific cases (Art. 10.5), but the mandatory must always be prepared to account for the use of mandated power (Art. 10.6). Alternatively, powers may also be 'delegated' to other authorities, but this type of transfer never takes places between manager and subordinates (Arts. 10.13 and 10.14). Finally, Art. 10.43 states that an order may be stayed pending any investigations whether an annulment of said order is necessary.

The structure and development of Dutch public administration shows a system in which little outright discretion is held by actors of implementation, but not necessarily in a way that hinders flexibility and adaptability. While a strong reliance on statutory regulations and managerial supervision is described, many specifics are left up to administrative authorities to implement. The ability for orders to be rescinded without a conclusion of an appeal process shows the flexibility needed to review decisions based on self-evaluation, rather than imposed by a different authority, such as a court.

Discussions surrounding discretionary powers granted to public authorities have been specifically discussed in the Netherlands, most notably in the context of a 2017 report from the Council of State which no longer allowed the use of terms such as "discretionary freedom" or "policy freedom," opting instead for

---

26 Articles 7.2 – 7.28 describe the appeal process for different kinds of orders, underlying the obligations and roles of administrative authorities whose order are appealed, and the interested parties making the appeal.

"discretionary space" and "policy space," both under the larger terminological umbrella of "decision space."[27] While the former were the terms used for many years, the decision centred around the use of the word "freedom" as "no use of public law power is entirely free, but always bound by the rules of law."[28] The separation of the two terms – discretionary space and policy space – implies that differences exist that must be taken into account. Discretionary space refers to the interpretation of vague terms to grant powers for interpretation. When an applicant for asylum must submit the elements *necessary* to support his or her application, it is within the discretionary space of the bureaucrat assessing the application to interpret what may be deemed necessary. On the other hand, policy space does not have to do with the power to interpret provisions, but with the choice of whether to take certain actions – e.g., the case of a *may* clause. While the distinction between the two terms is important, however, both represent a type of ambiguity within the scope of this research: both are incomplete sets of information, which public actors must act upon to make decisions – either by interpreting or choosing whether to implement a provision or not.

3 Entering the Asylum Procedure

The Dutch package regulating asylum procedures lies in three main legislative and regulatory acts: The Aliens Act 2000, the Aliens Decree 2000 implementing the Act, and the Aliens Act Implementation Guidelines 2000(C). To best understand the legal basis on which public servants operate, the provisions of these acts should be analysed in tandem. The system created here is one that does not identically match the architecture of the asylum process as spelled out in the Common European Asylum System. This is not to say that the process of asylum is non-compliant to EU requirements, but rather provisions form the European acquis have been (at least in theory) re-arranged in a system unique to the Netherlands.

An asylum seeker may apply for international protection at a border crossing or on the territory of the Netherlands. The first steps in the procedure are carried out by either the Royal Military Police (*Koninklijke Marechaussee*, in case of border registration), or the Aliens Police (*Vreemdelingenpolitie*, in case of registration on the territory). The application, Dublin assessment, and refugee

27 Raad van State. "Jaarverslag 2017," (April 2018), 61.
28 Ibid.

TABLE 9 The 5-track system of the Dutch asylum system

Track 1 – Asylum seekers who enter the Dublin procedure.
Track 2 – For applicants coming from safe country of origin or who benefit from another mechanism for international protection.
Track 3 – Prima facie determination that there is a likelihood of granting protection status
Track 4 – General Procedure. Should last 8 days, but may be extended by 6, 8 or 14 days.
Track 5 – Similar to track 3, but ID and/or other documents still need to be submitted.

status determination are all done by the Immigration and Naturalisation Service (IND) of the Ministry of Security and Justice.[29] The majority of applications happen after the applicant is already present on the territory, and the initial registration process lasts approximately 3 days. Furthermore, no legal aid is provided during the registration and identification process.[30]

A 5-track system for assessing asylum claims has been used in the Netherlands since the beginning of 2016. Each of the tracks described in Table 9 determine the type of assessment that an application will be placed under, and the placement in each track is a declaratory action.[31]

The implementation of this system is described in Decision of the State Secretary for Security and Justice of 26 February 2016 amending the Aliens Act Implementation Guidelines 2000, the document where this policy architecture is first presented.[32] Here it is stipulated that

29 Angelina van Kampen (n 18), 15.

30 Information resulting from interviews conducted with IND officials, for the purposes of this research, in March 2020.

31 Information resulting from interviews conducted with IND officials, for the purposes of this research, in March 2020. Of note, those interviews also clarified that applicants that enjoy protection from UNRWA do not immediately get placed in Track 2. See the analysis of Case C-585/16, *Serin Alheto v Zamestnik-predsedatel na Darzhavna agentsia za bezhantsite* [2018], in Chapter 4.

32 WBV 2016.4. 'Besluit van de Staatssecretaris van Veiligheid en Justitie van 26 februari 2016, houdende wijziging van de Vreemdelingencirculaire 2000' [*Decision of the State Secretary for Security and Justice of 26 February 2016 amending the Aliens Act Implementation Guidelines 2000*].

> as soon as the application for a temporary asylum residence permit has been submitted, the IND will provide the foreign national with the information brochure 'Part A: Information about the Dublin Regulation for persons applying for international protection', in accordance with Article 4 of Regulation (EU) No. 604 / 2013.

And that for the purposes of a Dublin assessment,

> IND conducts an interview within the meaning of Article 5, first paragraph of Regulation (EU) 604/2013. During this interview, the IND offers the foreign national the opportunity to correctly understand the information provided to him/her in accordance with Article 4 of Regulation (EU) 604/2013; in any case, the IND will ask questions in the context of Regulation (EU) 604/2013; and the IND will inform the foreign national about the results of the examination of the fingerprints of the foreign national.

This is the description of the 'Dublin registration interview' called for during the procedure, meant to establish identity, nationality, and travel route to the Netherlands, but also to examine if another Member State is responsible for processing an application, as determined by the mechanism laid down in the Dublin procedure.[33]

If no other country is deemed to be responsible for taking charge of the applicant, and therefore the IND foresees the applicant entering the general asylum procedure, a Rest and Preparation (R&P) period begins which allows the asylum seeker 6 days of rest while preliminary investigations may start. The R&P lasts much longer than 6 days in practice, often as long as 12 months.[34] This is attributed to a general lack of capacity at the Immigration and Naturalisation Service (IND). Motion No. 2431 of the Lower Chamber of the States General, from November 7, 2018, calls on the government to "ensure sufficient capacity at the IND, so that the legal deadlines are not exceeded, the waiting times are reduced and asylum seekers quickly obtain clarity."[35] On the other hand, IND officials have also clarified that, while uncommon, the R&P is also sometimes reduced, especially in cases where there are medical reasons to do so.[36]

33 Aliens Decree 2000, Article 3.109ca.
34 Angelina van Kampen (n 18), 11.
35 Parliamentary Paper 19637–2431 of Nov. 7, 2018.
36 Interviews conducted with IND officials, for the purposes of this research, in March 2020.

Aside from giving the asylum seeker time to prepare for the asylum process, the R&P period is also used to carry investigations into any documents belonging to the applicants, medical conditions that may impact the ability of the applicant to stand for interview or indicate special procedural guarantees, and to give the Dutch Council for Refugees access to offer counselling.[37] A lawyer should also be appointed during this time, although during discussions in the Upper Chamber of the States General on the adoption of the 2019 budget of the Ministry of Security and Justice, a motion was adopted whereby it was called on the government to carry out an ex ante implementation test of a proposal to "phase out legal aid" until day 5 of the application process.[38]

The extensive guidance given also in the Aliens Act Implementation Guidelines 2000 (from here on referred to as "Implementation Guidelines") shows the level of detail in the expected ways of behaviour during administrative procedures. Specifics are given, for example, on how to handle documents taken during the registration period, when to give them back in case of positive decisions being issued (after the investigation is complete, and only if documents are authentic), when to keep the documents permanently (if forged), or when to return the documents in case of negative decision (at Schiphol Airport if departing by plane, at the border crossing if there is evidence that the applicant will depart from another airport). On the other hand, when it comes to an age assessment, it "will not be offered to the foreign national if, in the opinion of the officer charged with border control or with the supervision of foreign national and the IND, the foreign national is clearly of age or clearly a minor." While this wording does indicate a high level of discretion when deciding the need of an age assessment, a deeper analysis shows this is not as straight froward. Indeed, such a determination is made by the bureaucrats tasked with making the assessment, but the space within which decisions can be made is highly regulated.

The age assessment is made in two sessions, by either one official charged with border security or the supervision of foreign nationals and two employees of the IND, or two officials charged with border security or supervision of foreign nationals and one employee of the IND.[39] The purpose of these sessions is to assess:

37 Aliens Decree 2000, Article 3.109.

38 Parliamentary Paper 35000-VI No. D, December 18, 2018. See Also Angelina van Kampen (n 18), 12.

39 Implementation Guidelines, Ch. 2 'Application Procedures', Subchapter 2.2 Rest and Preparation Period.

- whether the applicant is obviously not a minor based on external characteristics and/or statements of the foreign national who claims to be a minor, and
- whether the applicant is obviously a minor based on external characteristics and/or statements of the foreign national who claims to be of age.[40]

This wording would indicate that age assessment is a tool for verifying the veracity of claim. Moreover, in the age assessment section of the Implementation Guidelines we observe a process of internal reviews conducted not through a hierarchical control measure, but rather horizontally among employees handling the same case. For each session described above, the officials make their own independent evaluations, yet both sessions must reach the same conclusions for a decision to be made. For this purpose, one of the reasons for which a medical examination can be requested is that the "age assessment does not show that the foreign national is clearly an adult or a minor."[41] Appearance, behaviour, statements, and "any other relevant circumstances" are all part of the assessment made by the IND and border officials.

3.1 *General Procedure*

If following the investigations done during the R&P period it is determined that no special action is necessary, the asylum procedure may start. Alternatively, it may be decided that special guarantees are necessary, or that the start of the asylum procedure should be postponed. "The IND processes an application for a temporary asylum residence permit in the general asylum procedure if no time-consuming investigation is necessary for the assessment of the application," with time consuming research being defined as investigations where the results are not expected during the general asylum procedure.[42] It may also be decided that to assess credibility an applicant, there is a need to place him or her in an extended procedure. This can happen at any time during the assessment, and it is at the discretion of the case worker. For example, after the second interview a case worker may realise that to assess the credibility of

40 WBV 2016.4. (n 32).

41 The Implementation Guidelines specifically say that "X-rays are made of the growth plates in the hand/wrist area and of the collarbones. A doctor then determines whether the degree of maturation of these growth plates matches the age specified by the foreign national."

42 WBV 2016.4. (n 32).

TABLE 10 Information sought during registration interview in the Netherlands

Information sought during registration interview, as detailed in implementation guidelines
Personal Details
Place and Date of Birth
Nationality, Religion and Ethnic Origin
Date of his departure from the country of origin
Date of arrival in the Netherlands
Possible residence in third country
Possession of identity documents
As deemed necessary: travel itinerary, history of training and military service, life, and work in country of origin

each element, more time would be needed. This may also happen if additional information regarding the country of origin is needed.[43]

The Aliens Decree is very detailed in the steps to be taken during the General Asylum Procedure, which should be conducted within 8 days of lodging an application (Art. 3.110). Article 3.112 states that an initial interview will be conducted on the first day, and the Decree and Implementation Guidelines both make clear that this interview must not ask any question regarding the motives for requesting asylum. In fact, a simplification was carried out in January 2019, likely to streamline the time taken in the asylum procedure.[44]

The second day of the procedure is reserved for giving the asylum seeker an opportunity to prepare for the second interview, which takes place on the third day and allows the applicant "the opportunity to provide as completely as possible the elements necessary to support the application." Following this interview, the applicant must submit any comments or clarifications on "incorrectly translated passages or misconceptions in the [interview] report," by the fourth day, at the latest.[45] This interview will not take place, however, if the applicant cannot be subjected to it for medical reasons or if they are unaccompanied minors below the age of 12.

43 Information obtained from interviews conducted with IND officials, for the purposes of this research, in March 2020.

44 Angelina van Kampen (n 18), 11.

45 Art. 3.113, Aliens Decree 2000.

The fourth day of the process is crucial in determining the timeline in which a decision will be made. If, on this day, the intention to reject the application within the prescribed 8 days becomes apparent, the applicants shall be notified by the sixth day, at the latest, and a decision shall be announced by the eight day, at the latest.[46] Article 3.115, on the other hand, provides a very rigid understanding of how extensions to the 8 day time limit may be applied, for which reasons, and the time limits that must be respect if an application will be rejected.

In practice, because of the extensive delays in processing application, most of them are analysed in an extended procedure, since "the IND will process the application for a temporary asylum residence permit in the extended asylum procedure if the IND has exceeded the terms of the general asylum procedure."[47] Placing an asylum seeker in an extended procedure is not the same as extending the time limits of a general procedure. Since an analysis under Track 4 is designed as a "short asylum procedure," meaning it lasts 8 working days, with a possible extension by 6, 8 or 14 working days. However, the IND "is reluctant to make use of the option" to extend. Statements made by public officials with working experience in assessing claims to asylum have also indicated Tracks 3 and 5 are not often used in practice.[48]

While discouraging extension to the general procedure, the amendments in WBV 2016/4 are also clear about the cases where an extension can be applied, if requested by the applicant: when an interpreter falls unexpectedly ill and cannot be replaced, when the applicant must attend a doctor's appointment or has been subjected to a custodial measure, or in cases where the applicant has not received a medical clearance during the R&P period. Further reasons to extend the general procedure, which do not require the applicant to make a request, include discrepancies in the nationality claimed by the applicant during R&P and general procedure, when doubts regarding the age of an applicant emerge, or that further investigation of documents submitted should take place.

Another topic that often emerges when discussing the implementation guidelines for asylum policies is that of the border procedure. The European framework does allow more ambiguous interpretation of border procedures, and therefore offers the possibility for larger discretionary powers to public officials working in this environment. The Implementation Guidelines address this.

46 Art. 3.114, Aliens Decree 2000.
47 WBV 2016.4. (n 32).
48 Interviews conducted with IND officials, for the purposes of this research, in March 2020.

> During the processing of the application for a temporary asylum residence permit, the IND continuously checks whether the application can be processed within the border procedure [...] This may be derived from the availability of necessary information either earlier or later in the asylum procedure.

While the use of a *may* clause grants some discretion when assessing the availability of information, non-discretionary situations are also described that immediately translate into a decision of no longer processing said application within the border procedure. The following guidelines all start with the assumption that, after the first interview, the identity, nationality, and country of origin of the asylum seeker are "established with sufficient certainty" and, the applicant does not fall within the scope of exclusion as defined by the Geneva Convention:

- The foreign national falls under the scope of *non-refoulment.*
- The foreign national is from a country of origin where the relevant country-specific policy states that there is an exceptional situation as defined in Article 15(c) of the Qualifications Directive.
- The first interview conclusively determines that reasons for protection are valid.

If it is evident that a decision cannot be made in a border procedure, the asylum seeker will be given access to either the general or extended application on the territory. On the other hand, permission is also given to refuse allowing an asylum seeker access to the general procedure, even if the processing cannot be completed within the established time limit. This permission is conditioned by the suspicion of the IND that another Member State is responsible for processing the application,[49] that the application will be categorized as inadmissible based on an option for protection existing in another Member State or third country, if another country has granted a residence permit to the applicant, if the applicant submits a subsequent application with no new elements,[50] or that the application is manifestly unfounded as a result of the applicant's provision of irrelevant, inconsistent or false information, destroying relevant documents, coming from a safe country of origin, refusal to comply with requirements of fingerprinting, or categorisation as a threat to public order or national security.[51] Furthermore, Article 3(6) of the Aliens Act must

49 Art. 30, Aliens Act 2000.

50 Art. 30(a), Aliens Act 2000.

51 Art. 30(b), Aliens Act 2000. Another indicator for declaring an application manifestly unfounded is given: the foreign national has been entered the territory unlawfully, or has

still be observed, which states that if within four weeks of notifying the applicant of the postponement of the decision to refuse entry to the Netherlands a decision has not yet been taken on whether the application will be processed, the applicant will be granted access to the territory.

Legal basis for granting refugee status lies in Article 28 of the Aliens Act, which gives the Ministry of Security and Justice the authority to "grant, reject, refuse to process, declare inadmissible or set aside an application." Article 29, meanwhile, clarifies that a residence permit in this sense can be granted to a foreign national who is a refugee according to the Convention, or who has made it plausible that has reasonable grounds to believe that he runs a real risk of serious damage if deported, consisting of (1) death penalty, (2) torture, inhuman, or degrading treatment or punishment, or (3) serious and individual threat to the life or person of a civilian as a result of arbitrary violence.

Article 31 of the Act further develops what elements should be considered when making a decision:

- all relevant facts related to the country of origin at the time a decision is made, including laws, regulations, and administrative provision, *and how they are applied.*
- Documents and statements submitted.
- Individual situation and circumstances, *including* background, sex, and age, and to see if these add to risk of persecution or serious harm.
- If the actions of the applicant were merely done to create the conditions necessary for submitting an application for international protection.
- Whether it can be reasonably expected that the foreign national can avail him or herself of the protection of another country.

Former exposure to risk is an indicator that the applicant has a well-founded fear of persecution or serious harm. Furthermore, there is clear guidance of when *the benefit of doubt* should be given to an applicant who cannot substantiate the application with documents. This should be the case when

- the foreign national has made a sincere effort to substantiate his application.
- all relevant elements at the disposal of the foreign national have been submitted, and a satisfactory explanation has been given regarding the lack of other relevant elements.

---

unlawfully extended his or her stay, and did not report as soon as possible the intention to seek international protection. This provision is irrelevant for a border procedure, as the location of the assessment makes it clear that the request for protection is made *while* entering the territory.

- the statements of the foreign national have been found to be coherent and plausible and do not conflict with available general and specific information that is relevant to his application.
- the foreign national has submitted his application as soon as possible, unless he can provide good reasons why he failed to do so; and
- It has been established that the foreign national can be considered as credible in general terms.

In order to meet the requirements for information to be analysed set forth in the Aliens Act, Article 3.105ba calls for a list of safe countries of origin to be established, which "should be based on information including other MS, EASO, UNHCR, Council of Europe, and other relevant international organisations." Furthermore, under Art. 3.123b, in case of an increase in the number of asylum applications and if there are indications that a certain group of applicants is foreseeable to be eligible for granting protection status, the regular procedure is altered: no rest and preparation period takes place, and a decision is made based only on the first interview, which in this case also gives the applicant the opportunity to explain motives for asylum.

3.2 *Conditions of Work: Implementing Provisions at the Street-Level*

Many insights into how bureaucrats are expected to carry out their jobs are evident from the legislative framework given. However, this provides only half of the picture of how implementation of asylum policies takes place. Important to this study, there are several mechanisms by which ambiguities are identified and addressed, but few provide as much insight as the documents relating to the oversight role that the States General has over the Ministry of Security and Justice, and therefore asylum policies. In the explanations provided by high-ranking officials from the Ministry, several pieces of information may be identified: how the interpretation of certain terms has changed to meet changing contexts, how and why policy adjustments are made, how crisis situations are handled, how resources are allocated, and most importantly what problems arise in implementing the provisions of legal acts, both from a practical but also ethical point of view. Furthermore, the internal Working Instructions of the IND, official reports of the Inspectorate for Security and Justice, and further statements made by officials of the IND are used to contextualise and add to the information emergent in the relationship between the Ministry and the States General. Below is an analysis of the themes emerging form this analysis.

Because of the active oversight role of the States General, several important insights emerge into how the bureaucratic machinery is instructed to interpret certain terms and European standards. In a letter from the State Secretary for Security and Justice to the States General, the interpretation at the time of the terms "particularly serious offense," "serious offense," and "danger to the community" is described, since these "are not further standardised in the Qualifications Directive."[52]

- Particularly Serious Offense: if the foreign national has been sentenced by an irrevocable court decision to imprisonment or a custodial measure, the unconditional part of which is at least 24 months in total;
- Serious Offense: if there is an irrevocable court judgment with a conviction to a prison sentence or a custodial measure where the unconditional part is at least 18 months in total and in any case one of the crimes is by nature a danger to the community
- Danger to the community: this is assumed in any case when it comes to drug, sexual and violent crimes, arson, trafficking in human beings, illegal trade in weapons / ammunition / explosives, illegal trade in human organs and tissues.

These terms are then further contextualised based on the different situations with which a decision-maker might be presented when reaching a decision. In cases of family members of asylum seekers, who have received residence permits based on family reunification schemes, "the same conditions to withdrawing that permit apply" as the principal recipient of international protection. Still, even if a revocation of a residence permit takes place based on these considerations, the principle of non-refoulment still stands: even if Article 1F of the Geneva Convention is invoked, authorities will not remove someone who runs the risk of harm when returned.[53]

Nonetheless, the very lack of any European guidance on how these terms should be interpreted also shows how understandings may change to reflect current priorities. The very same explanation of the current standards for serious and particularly serious offenses also makes a case for adjusting the national use of the European law standards 'serious crime' and 'particularly serious crime'. The following actions are given as examples under a reform proposal that would tighten the rules for revoking a residence permit:

52 Parliamentary Paper 19637–2078 of Nov. 25, 2015.

53 According to Parliamentary Paper 19637–2152 of Feb. 25, 2016, 950 applications were excluded from consideration based on Art. 1F from 1992–2016.

Serious Offense	– Assault resulting in serious bodily harm. – Deliberately inflicting serious physical injury. – Bag robbery with frequent recidivism. – Home invasion, with frequent recidivism. – Selling, delivering, or otherwise providing user quantities of hard drugs for more than a month, but less than 3 months, with some regularity.
Particularly Serious Offense	– Distributing, producing, or profiting from child pornography. – Deliberately inflicting serious bodily harm using a weapon. – Selling, delivering, or otherwise providing user quantities of hard drugs with some regularity for six to twelve months.

Importantly to notice, however, is that the proposal lowers the standard for severity of crimes, as it lowers the threshold for prison time required for each offense. Under this proposal, serious offenses are considered those punished by at least 6 months imprisonment, and particularly serious ones are those punished with an irrevocable prison sentence of at least 10 months.

Interpretations of terms are also spelled out in some of the Working Instructions aimed at case workers assessing asylum applications. WI 2019/18, which instructs caseworkers on how to assess applications where the main motive involved is religious conversion, relies on the definitions of religion, as well as its subdivisions, from the Qualifications Directive. It also makes certain interpretations of those definitions that the legislation does not. For instance, a non-practicing believer is not to be considered the same as an atheist or agnostic, while any reference to religion is to be taken to refer only to theistic and non-theistic religions. Where 'faith' or 'belief' is invoked, however, religions, as well as atheism or agnosticism, are all referenced. Apostasy, meanwhile, is the term given to someone who has turned away from their religion, either by converting to another, or becoming atheist or agnostic. Crucially, apostasy does not have to be accepted by the applicant, but it is sufficient for his or her community to consider that such is the case.[54]

3.3 *European Framework and Safe Countries of Origin*

The clarifications brought to the interpretation of criminal offenses leads one to wonder how far the European framework allows this to go. As the State Secretary from the Ministry of Security and Justice wrote in 2015,

> the European framework determines the margins within which a policy change can be implemented. It is not possible to deport asylum seekers who are guilty of any crime (such as bicycle theft) unconditionally, but there is room to tighten current policy in certain areas. [This includes] maximum use of the statutory decision period and a substantial lowering of the standard under which the residence permit can be refused or withdrawn.[55]

In other words, the IND should extend as much as possible the time to take an asylum decision, "if and as long as there are ongoing criminal proceedings that may affect the admissibility of the application, unless there are other grounds on which the application can be rejected earlier."

The call to a wider framework of European guidance is nothing new when discussing Dutch asylum policy. The need to harmonise land-based asylum policies in the EU is referenced on several occasions, especially since this was one of the projects undertaken by the Dutch EU Presidency in 2014.[56] It is also argued that an European framework is needed to resolve the problems of the Mediterranean, especially when it comes to solving the dilemma of when people smuggling stops and when rescuing migrants at sea begins, as State Secretary Broekers-Knol argued during a hearing in front of the lower house of parliament.[57] Despite these calls for deeper European involvement in dealing with certain issues, officials of the IND reported no major changes in their working relationship with EASO since 2015.[58]

Another frequent topic that is present in communications is that of safe countries of origin, how these should be designated, and what changes are made to the designated list such countries. Indeed, interviews with the IND

54 IND. 'Werkinstructies WI 2019/18 Bekeerlingen' [*Converts*]. December 30, 2019.
55 Parliamentary Paper 19637–2078, of Nov. 26, 2016.
56 See Parliamentary Paper 19637–2416, of July 11, 2018.
57 Parliamentary Paper 19637–2529 of Sept. 18, 2019.
58 Interviews conducted with IND officials, for the purposes of this research, in March 2020.

show that this list is frequently consulted by employees of the institution. It is sometimes lamented that there isn't a more common European-wide arrangement on the establishment of such list, leading to substantial differences among EU Member States.[59] For this reason, the Netherlands also welcomes EU level country guidance reports, as they "are relevant to create an EU-wide level playing field in the assessment of asylum applications."[60] While the criteria for when a country is considered safe country of origin have been established in EU legislation, no method of assessment for this has been decided. In the view of the Ministry of Security and Justice, four main factors need to be assessed:

- Relevant legal framework in the country in question.
- Compliance with the rights and freedoms spelled out in the ECHR or other human rights conventions, in particular with regard to the right to life, the prohibition of torture, the prohibition of slavery and forced labour and the prohibition to arbitrarily impose punishment.
- Compliance with the principle of *non-refoulement*.
- The availability of a system of effective remedies against violations of human rights.

Information to assess these criteria is gathered preferably from primary sources (such as persons or authorities related to the events or with first-hand information about them). This means that extensive use is made of reports issued by the United States Department of State, EU Progress Reports, and other reports developed by agencies of the UN, Human Rights Watch, Amnesty International, and EASO/EUAA. Most importantly, dynamics by which safe countries of origin are determined render acceptance rates of asylum seekers unusable as a criterion for designating a country as safe. Nonetheless, as the State Secretary argues, "after an assessment has been made of the situation in the country itself, based on the criteria and sources mentioned above, the acceptance rate can be part of the overall assessment of whether with regard to the country concerned safe countries of origin policy will be applied." This is very much in line with the arguments presented earlier in this book, where it is shown why general asylum rates may represent part, but not the entirety, of a picture of asylum policy implementation in the EU.

---

59 In Parliamentary Paper 19637–2566 of Dec. 16, 2019, the State Secretary for Security and Justice argues in favour of the need for a harmonised list of safe countries of origin at the EU level, even for the purposes of combating secondary migration. See also Parliamentary Paper 19637–2413 of June 26, 2018, for the same argument.

60 Parliamentary Paper 19637–2644, of July 31, 2020.

In theory, the description provided here does not offer much more insight into the dynamics behind the designation of safe countries of origin. However, practical examples are also available. Based on these considerations, we notice that even countries that fit the criteria on paper do not always carry this designation without some caveats. While Ghana is said to *may* be regarded as a safe country of origin, increased attention should be paid to cases of LGBTI people, journalists, and other persons who may be victims of social discrimination. Special attention given to otherwise "safe countries of origin" is also apparent when it comes to Jamaica, Morocco, and Senegal. India also received the safe-country designation in 2016, if special attention is given to cases involving religious minorities or people with criminal records.[61]

In September 2017, an even more detailed explanation was given of how reassessment of a safe country of origin designation may be triggered. If a significance deterioration is observed in terms of democratic governance, protection of the right to liberty and security, and freedom of speech, a reassessment is immediately triggered, and the current designation is suspended. Furthermore, if other rights, such as freedom of religion and association, protection against discrimination and persecution by third parties, access to independent research, access to an independent judiciary, and access to legal remedies, are also under threat, a similar reassessment is prompted.[62] EU Member States, the same communication argues, cannot be legally classified as safe countries of origin in this framework, since the Asylum Procedures Directive "only pertains to applications for international protection submitted by third-country nationals or stateless persons."

Such reassessments, however, do not always concern the designation of safe countries of origin. Often, they lead to categorising groups based on their exposure to persecution. In October 2017, it is explained that despite the IND's thematic country report for Pakistan indicating a deteriorating situation for Ahmadi Muslims, there are no indications that every person belonging to this group has a well-founded fear of persecution. An individual assessment is still thoroughly required, although the classification of Ahmadi Muslims for Pakistan remains as "risk group." On the other hand, based on similar reports, apostates of the Islamic faith, i.e., converts from Islam to other faiths, face increasing pressure, discrimination, and persecution, despite there being no law (outside religious dogma) that forbids apostasy. As such, this group is now labelled as a "high-risk group," meaning that they can demonstrate fear of

61 Parliamentary Paper 19637–2123 of Feb. 09, 2016.

62 Parliamentary Paper 19637–2349 of Sept. 26, 2017.

persecution with a lowered standard of proof, and a domestic alternative to protection cannot be invoked against such applicants.[63] A similar calculation is made in July 2018 regarding the classification of Palestinians from Iraq as a "vulnerable minority group," with the exception of those coming from the Kurdish Autonomous Region.[64] This decision was also based on a report by the UNHCR which showed that Palestinians in Iraq faced routine detentions, kidnapping, murders, disappearances, threats, and physical violence.

Official information, it is evident, plays an important role in assessing the situation of specific populations in specific regions. An example of how this information is gathered and processed can be seen in the communications regarding the thematic country report for Afghanistan, carried in July 2018. This assessment, which covers the condition in the country over a year and a half from November 2016 until May 2018, describes the security situation as continuing to be "worrisome," especially since control over an area can change quickly and fighting between many warring factions, including the government, the Islamic State and the Taliban, is persisting across the country. Interestingly, when discussing large scale attacks on civilians resulting from this fighting, it is noted that many "received a lot of attention in the Dutch media," a slight indication that public perception also plays a role in the elaboration of these reports. Furthermore, the Ministry of Security and Justice points to the importance of using the EU level Country Guidance on Afghanistan, since agencies base their "assessment of the security situation on more recent information than the Ministry of Foreign Affairs in the thematic country report."[65] It is important to note that, following the takeover of Taliban rule in Afghanistan in 2021, the Netherlands did update its policy toward afghani asylum seekers, expanding its categorisation of risk groups to include interpreters and their families, journalists, representatives of the judicial branch, police, or defence ministry, women who have been working, particularly, in non-profit sector, education, or health, citizens who have supported the previous administration,

---

63 Parliamentary Paper 19637–2350 of Oct. 31, 2017.

64 Parliamentary Paper 19637–2417 of July 11, 2018. In another communication form the same day, namely Parliamentary Paper 19637–2416, it is explained that "The foreign national who belongs to a population group that has been designated as a vulnerable minority group in the country-specific policy, can, if credible and individualizable explanations exist, demonstrate that he fears serious harm with limited proof [...] A population group can be designated as a risk group if it appears that prosecution of foreign nationals belonging to this population group occurs in the country of origin. If there are credible and individualizable statements, the foreign national who belongs to a high-risk group can, with limited indications, demonstrate a well-founded fear of prosecution."

65 Parliamentary Paper 19637–2416 of July 11, 2018.

TABLE 11 Sliding scale model for assessing risk due to indiscriminate violence

Category	Description
0	Areas where the mere presence presents serious risk.
1	Areas where the level of indiscriminate violence is such that minimal individual elements are sufficient to demonstrate a serious risk.
2	Area where the risk of serious harm can be assumed when the applicant is particularly concerned for reasons related to personal circumstances.
3	Area where the level of indiscriminate violence is so low that there is no risk of serious harm.
4	Area where there is no armed conflict as referred to Article 15(c) of the Qualifications Directive.

foreign nationals who have criticized the Taliban, non-practicing Muslims or convers, among others.[66]

The Dutch interpretation of the EASO country guidance in 2018 is insightful because it highlights deviation from European guidance in interpreting reasons for persecution. First, it starts by emphasising that both the thematic country report and the EASO report reach the same conclusion: the situation in Afghanistan is not such that civilians cannot generally return to the country. The difference, however, is that EASO uses the sliding scale model to assess Article 15(c) of the Qualifications Directive (i.e., serious risk due to indiscriminate violence), a fundamentally different methodological structure of assessment than the one used by the Dutch authorities. Specifically, EASO's method distinguishes between 5 categories (see Table 11).

The Netherlands, on the other hand, only uses categories 0 and 4 for the purposes of assessing Article 15(c), while all other considerations are part of the regular assessment of an asylum application. Interviews with officials of the IND confirm that the sliding scale model is not used when assessing the level of indiscriminate violence to which an applicant may be subjected.[67] This

66 Decree of the State Secretary for Justice and Security of 13 July 2022, number WBV 2022/19, amending the Circular on Foreign Nationals 2000.

67 Interviews conducted with IND officials, for the purposes of this research, in March 2020. See also Werkinstructies WI 2020/12 *De toepassing van de glijdende schaal.*

is not because indiscriminate violence does not play a role in assessing applications, but rather that the security situation is part of individual assessments. "The worse the security situation, […] a risk must be assumed of a violation of Article 3 ECHR. In addition, the general situation, and in particular the bad situation in which certain groups may find themselves, has given rise to designating risk groups and vulnerable minority groups in the Dutch country-specific asylum policy."[68] Nonetheless, it was indicated at that time that the designation of Kabul as an area of possible domestic protection will remain as such, even if this changed in 2021.[69] Furthermore, ethnic and religious minorities, LGBTI people, converts and apostates, women in public employment, and persons working in politics, journalism, non-governmental sector, or the judiciary were then also categorised as either a risk or vulnerable minority group, even before the Taliban's return to power. This means also that invoking Kabul as a possible area of domestic protection for these groups is not possible. Furthermore, as of this communication, families with minor children were also included in the groups for which this protection alternative cannot be used.[70]

3.4 *Institutional Capacity*

Interviews with IND officials highlight the importance of operating with proper institutional capacity. Several elements affect the number of cases that can be handled, such as the number of immigration staff, legal aid workers, interpreters, and even suitable interview locations. When the influx of applications is rising, an effort is made to maximise the number of applicants that can be dealt with at a time, but the limits listed still exist. Nonetheless, there are constant efforts to adapt to changing situations, and to improve procedures. For example, in 2015, when the main nationalities applying for protection in the Netherlands were from Syria and Eritrea, those cases were seen as advantageous from an efficiency perspective: the war in Syria and the situation in Eritrea made it quite likely that the applications were seen as well founded, and specific country policy allowed for a quicker assessment in these cases.

68 IND. 'Werkinstructies WI 2020/12' [*The Application of the Sliding Scale*]. August 11, 2020.

69 In Parliamentary Paper 19637–2105 of Dec. 9, 2015, a similar assessment is also made for Baghdad, whereby information of the existence "to some extent" of a security structure, combined with a ruling of the British Upper Tribunal which declared that there is no exceptional security situation in the Iraqi capital were used as justification for designating the city a domestic protection alternative.

70 According to Parliamentary Paper 19637–2644 of July 2, 2020, in 2018 there were applications from over 70 nationalities for which there is no official country report, meaning that information must be sought elsewhere.

Furthermore, IND officials also report that the 5 Track system, which was implemented partly as a response to the crisis, did help manage the influx of applicants. Even though tracks 3 and 5 are not often in practice, the fact that Tracks 1 and 2 exist still helps shorten the times that it takes to examine Track 4 applications. Furthermore, since Tracks 1 and 2 are dealt with by case workers focusing specifically on those issues, this separation also helps deal with Dublin cases much faster as well.[71]

The backlog in analysing cases, and the resulting delays and associated costs, is a constant concern for the way the IND can conduct its work. In April 2019, increased processing times and lack of sufficient staff were reported, resulting from an unexpected number of arrivals, a switch in the composition of asylum seekers, with more unsuccessful applications which take longer to process, and an increase in the number of subsequent applications.[72] In other instances, the backlog was also blamed for the inability to enforce revocation decisions, as these take too long to process.[73] In 2019 the IND pledged that it would be able to once again assess Track 4 cases within the legal term only by 2021. In the same year, the institution clarified that many hires were being made to handle to backlog, but the pledge to meet the 2021 deadline would be difficult given the long times it takes to train new hires: 8 weeks training in asylum law, and up to 9 months total time to for the official to become an independent decision maker.[74] As of 2023, the backlog of applications was still a problem. Further reports from the inspectorate of the Ministry for Security and Justice also indicate that staff in reception centres do not have the practical nor the legal tools to handle 'problematic' residents,[75] and the Ministry does not possess the information necessary to make timely adjustments.[76] This includes policies aimed at creating bonds with the residents, documenting incidents for nuisance and imposing sanctions, and measuring the satisfaction of residents.

71 Information acquired during Interviews conducted with IND officials, for the purposes of this research, in March 2020.

72 Parliamentary Paper 19637–2492, Apr. 17, 2019. These reasons are also supported by the Inspectorate for Security and Justice in its plan of action for assessing the general asylum procedure from May 28, 2020.

73 See Parliamentary Paper 19637–2529 of Sept. 18, 2019.

74 "0–100% deployability within 9 months" is the official wording used by the Secretary of State from the Ministry of Security and Justice in Parliamentary Paper 19637–2543 of Nov. 18, 2019.

75 Inspectorate for Security and Justice, 'Inspection: EBTL personnel are insufficiently equipped for the task' (News Release: January 22, 2019).

76 Inspectorate for Security and Justice, 'Insufficient insight into the social safety of residents in asylum seekers' centres' (News Release: October 19, 2018).

The combination creates a problematic mix of long waiting periods, coupled with improper exchange of information between governance authorities and clients of the asylum system.

In March 2020, the Ministry of Justice reported on the results of a progress report that found "that having sufficient decision-making capacity is an undeniable condition to be able to cope with the backlog."[77] The measures proposed by the Ministry of Justice, however, seem to have done little to address the sufficiency of decision-making capacity. These were: (1) adding a new managerial position to oversee implementation of measures to deal with the backlog, (2) treating delayed cases on a project-based approach and separating them from the work those analysing new applications, (3) improving operational management by establishing clear managerial goals and ensuring that employees are aware of the expectations of results, quality, and workloads, and (4) introducing a management process for the completeness of applications, by appointing a separate group of employees to look into the completeness and correctness of documents prior to the asylum procedure.[78] Indeed,

> the IND is making use of the power laid down in Article 42(4)(b) of the Aliens Act to extend the term by 6 months in individual cases. This means that of all applications for a temporary asylum residence permit for which the statutory decision period has not yet expired on the date of entry into force of the WBV 2020/12, the statutory decision period will be extended by 6 months. According to the Asylum and Migration Guidelines of the European Commission published on 16 April 2020, such an extension is justified.[79]

Interviews conducted in March 2020 with officials of the IND confirm that the backlog of cases at the IND still affected the ability of decisions to be issued within the desirable time limits.[80]

Of particular concern regarding the backlog is not only the IND's ability to deal with the number of applications, but also the effect this has on the capacity of reception centres to house applicants. In Parliamentary Paper 19637–2582, the members of the lower house of the States General are informed that because of the backlog, arrangements are being made with municipalities to

77 Parliamentary Paper 19637–2585, of Mar. 03, 2020.
78 Ibid.
79 Aliens Act Implementation Guidelines 2000(C).
80 Interviews conducted with IND officials, for the purposes of this research, in March 2020.

find additional housing facilities for asylum seekers, even if "the use of such reception locations is obviously not preferred." This is nothing new. As early as February 2006, it was noted that solutions must be found for the correct implementation of unambiguous agreements struck between the central government and municipalities in the field of asylum management, and similar actions are mentioned in 2015 as well, with the mention that multilevel cooperation is needed to deal with the crisis.[81] In concrete terms, there are several actions taken to help deal with backlog of applications, especially at the height of the 2015/2016 refugee crisis and as a result of a rise in new arrivals. For example, mandatory tuberculosis screenings for all incoming asylum seekers were suspended due to the low incidence among Syrian asylum seekers, who made up large portion of new applicants in 2015.[82] Other efforts to streamline the IND's ability to handle applications in 2015 and 2016 included prioritisation of those applications that would fall in the Dublin procedure and that come from safe countries of origin and invoking Art. 42 of the Aliens Act to extend decision times by 9 months.[83]

3.5 *Work Guidance*

There are several ways of seeing the specific guidance given to street-level bureaucrats analysing requests for international protection, as well as the relationship that these workers have with their managers. It is in the working procedures of the IND, as well as in other policy or legislative documents that we see how bureaucrats are expected and instructed to do their jobs and based on which criteria their performance is measured.

We can first see a direct reference in how a decision from the CJEU impacts procedures for frontline workers of the IND.

> It follows from a judgment of the European Court of Justice on 7 November 2018 that, if an application is submitted outside the application period, Member States must assess whether there are "special circumstances that are objectively excusable". On this basis, [the IND] will include some form of an excusability test in policy or regulations.[84]

81 Parliamentary Paper 19637–2050, of Sept. 28, 2015.
82 Parliamentary Paper 19637–2049, of Sept. 21, 2015.
83 Parliamentary Paper 19637–2124, of Feb 10, 2016.
84 Parliamentary Paper 19637–2492, of April 17, 2019.

A proposal for an "Asylum Chain Flexibilization Program," first cited in the same letter mentioned above and dated April 17, 2019, is mentioned as the answer to properly responding to fluctuations in the asylum chain, and thus optimising the processes at the IND.

In these settings we also see direct references to attempts at addressing the "vulnerabilities in the work processes of the IND," as these was the goal of a report conducted by outside consultancy agency PricewaterhouseCoopers (PWC) in the summer of 2018, at the request of the Ministry of Security and Justice.[85] The full text of the report is not available for public consultation, as disclosure of the vulnerabilities in the work processes of the IND is argued to create an "unacceptable risk that admissions procedures will be misused by malicious parties," but vulnerabilities were identified in both the organisation and personnel management.[86] Specific measures proposed to address these vulnerabilities were improvement in the screening methods for employees, increased integrity and awareness training, and enhanced separation of duties among workers.

Specifics of the way bureaucrats are expected to do their jobs – and the metrics that matter in assessing these – come up in the process of oversight that the States General has. In another letter of the State Secretary for Security and Justice, dated November 18, 2019, it is made clear that recent analyses have been done to see how work can be done "faster and smarter."[87] Specific measures adopted in this regard, measures which directly influence the work processes of asylum case workers, are:

- Introduction of a target group-oriented approach in which complex but similar matters are dealt with within one team, allowing for the build-up of expertise at the street-level.
- Abolishment of the necessity to conduct a further interview for repeat asylum applications without prospects, as of July 2019. This, the State Secretary claimed, has accelerated the processing of such applications.
- The start of an improvement process for the (internal) information, with the goal of ensuring that the IND has a better picture of the status of the processing times and stocks.

Further measures are also proposed, such as the possibility of prioritizing promising cases, specifically as it concerns "applications from asylum seekers with nationalities who are already residing in the reception centre and where

85 Parliamentary Paper 28844–164, of January 09, 2019.
86 Ibid.
87 Parliamentary Paper 19637–2543, of Nov. 18, 2019.

the chance of being granted refugee status is very high from a historical perspective, and on the basis of the applicable country policy." While specific country policy is necessary in decision making, this does allow for the faster processing of asylum applicants that will likely receive a positive decision, and for whom the long waiting period is referred to as "unfair." Fairness, it this case, is not judged by the correct assessment of the veracity of a claim, but rather by the ease with which a case can be assessed.

Case workers in the IND are also guided to pay particular attention to LGBTI applicants. A specific change in the way decisions are supposed to be made is evident in the removal of "self-awareness" or "self-acceptance" as required criteria for analysing from LGBTI applicants. Nonetheless, the mere exclusion from the official work guidance does not mean that these criteria will not play a role in the decision-making process. As it is explained in March 2020, workshops, trainings, and written instructions tell the case workers that

> the focus in general [should be] on the answers to questions about the foreign national's own experiences and personal perception regarding his sexual orientation and what this has meant for him and his environment. The foreign national is asked to explain how he realized that he was 'different'/LGBTI, how he personally experienced this, and how (and if) the environment reacted. This does not mean that the IND considers in all cases that an internal struggle must have taken place before the foreign national has accepted his LGBTI orientation. However, it may be expected that in the case of a foreign national who comes from a country where people do not accept LGBTI orientation and where this may have been made punishable, there will be a (thought) process in which the foreign national will, among other things, be able to answer questions about what it means to be different from what society (and the law) expects, and how he lives up to this.[88]

This should not be taken to mean that a policy change has taken place, it is extensively argued. Instead, this change simply represents an improvement in the way asylum applications are assessed. A similar decision was made in November 2018, where work instructions where updated to clarify that religious conversion can come about in various ways, and there is no longer a need to expect that the applicant has studied religious texts or participated in any religious movements prior to conversion, but rather that 'knowledge'

88 Parliamentary Paper 19637–2593, of March 24, 2020.

of religious practices should be assessed in general terms.[89] Also important is the fact that LGBTI claims are not assessed using medical tests, by requesting sexually explicit documentary evidence, or by asking for explicit description of acts, in line with the privacy consideration made by the Court of Justice of the European Union.

It should be noted that a pilot project was administered where applications from LGBTI asylum seekers were sent only to those workers with experience (but not specific training) in handling LGBTI cases. However, this was framed as unsuccessful because it was hard to tell in advance exactly what reasons might exist behind an application, making it impractical to schedule and plan the work structure of those specific employees. That being said, the State Secretary of the Ministry of Security and Justice admits in a parliamentary paper that employees of the IND assessed the pilot program as positive, while coordinators reported to have benefited from the increased transfer of knowledge resulting from its implementation.[90] The shortcoming of the pilot program are echoed by the responses given by IND officials regarding the work structure of their jobs. Most notably, because the complexity of a case cannot be predicted, even when at first glance it may be deemed simple, other elements might emerge that change its complexity.[91]

It is also important to point out that communications between the Ministry of Security and Justice and the States General are spurred by outside reports or requests. The clarifications made in March 2020 regarding the cases of LGBTI applicants, for example, came as a result of a letter written by outside actors asking, among other things, to clarify how the work instructions of the IND have been updated. It was in the same letter that a request for introducing the four-eyes principle on all LGBTI cases was made. The wording to the response given on behalf of the ministry is interesting in this case: formalisation of the four eyes principle for LGBTI cases takes too much capacity and is superfluous considering the established practices. The four eyes principle already exists, the State Secretary from the Ministry argues, because informal consultations among colleagues are already the norm, especially in cases where there are doubts about the decision to be made. In fact, internal discussions about how to handle the specifics of more complex cases is highlighted as one of the important aspects of best practice sharing among workers of the IND.

Each step of the procedure may be handled by different employees, meaning that each time a new action is taken a review of previous actions is also

89 Parliamentary Paper 19637–2440, of Nov. 13, 2018.
90 Parliamentary Paper 19637–2593, of March 24, 2020.
91 Interviews conducted with IND officials, for the purposes of this research, in March 2020.

conducted, in theory. If several interviews are conducted, case workers may therefore also check if the stories are consistent from one interview to another. Furthermore, in cases where an appeal to a decision is lodged, representatives of the IND's legal department may decide to recommend that case workers review certain decisions, if these do not conform to the standards of the institution. In other words, they can choose not to defend a decision in court, but rather tell the case workers that it must be reassessed.[92]

Further clarifications on how decisions should be made is given regarding the assessment of medical availability in the country of origin. Here, a difference is made between the availability of a treatment, and the accessibility to said treatment based on financial, geographical, racial, religious, social, or political considerations. Unlike other European countries, where different thresholds are used for when medical considerations should matter, ranging from "late-stage disease" to "significant deterioration in health," the Netherlands automatically considers medical care as part of the asylum procedure. Availability is taken into consideration, as is whether there is any short-term emergency without the treatment, however only political and geographic accessibility criteria are analysed, as other criteria are considered to also be a part of the general asylum assessment, "thus making the matter less ambiguous."[93] Furthermore, no economic accessibility criteria is used because it is not considered practical to assess from the Netherlands access to funds or support networks. Other problems in the process of assessing claims are also pointed out by the Inspectorate for Security and Justice. In 2016, for instance, it reported that the identification process of asylum seekers had been greatly improved, but collecting signals about human trafficking, smuggling, and terrorism was still a shortcoming in the entire process.[94]

As already indicated, issues of conversion and apostasy are very relevant for asylum assessments. The working instructions currently in force (WI 2022/3), which are meant for "hearing and decision officials of the IND who are involved in their work with 'conversion' as an asylum motif," offer workers insight into what conversion is, how it can come about, and how it develops. A framework for assessment is provided, and tools for analysis are offered, while admitting there is no standard answer to the question of how conversion happens

92 Interviews conducted with IND officials, for the purposes of this research, in March 2020. This process should not hide the fact that formal quality assessment is also regularly conducted by employees specifically tasked with this.

93 Parliamentary Paper 19637–2066, of Oct. 06, 2015.

94 Inspectorate for Security and Justice, 'Identification of asylum seekers further improved; detection of human trafficking/smuggling and terrorism in is not realistic' (News Release: December 21, 2016).

and if it is credible.[95] Some general points of analysis, nonetheless, are given. Specifically, the credibility of a conversion claim should focus on three elements: (1) motives and process for conversion, (2) knowledge of the new faith, and (3) activities taken, and changes observed as a result of belonging to a new religious community. While the first point is talked about below, it is important to note that the requirement of knowledge should be interpreted in general terms, in that the applicant knows the essence of his or her new religious conviction, as well as whether there are possible religious rituals with which the applicant might be familiar.

The WI document is very detailed in how the process of conversion should be reviewed. The starting point for analysis must be the life of the applicant before conversion: not only the circumstances pertaining to religious adherence and expression, but also the way religion might have affected the applicant's social context. This line of inquiry must then lead into the moment of first contact with the new religion, how he or she feels in the new belief system, and the reasons why the old religion no longer felt adequate. The process of conversion can unfold in diverse ways, the WI explains, influenced by elements such as time, emotional engagement, and rational considerations. The statements of the individual should be viewed cohesively, considering their life before conversion and the context in which the old religion was practiced. Whether the conversion is passive or active, the focus should be on understanding how the individual's spiritual journey developed, especially after the conversion event. Additionally, attention should be given to the positive and negative impacts of the conversion on the person's life, as well as their ability to articulate the reasons for leaving the old religion. Case officers are instructed to maintain an open-minded approach, taking into account the individual's personal circumstances and avoiding bias from their own context. The assessment should consider the overall narrative, including information from third parties and previous proceedings, ensuring a comprehensive understanding of the individual's experience.

Other specific instructions are given for very specific cases that may arise. In January 2019 it was clarified that a westernised lifestyle for women is not reason enough to invoke in a claim to asylum, as the legislation on this matter is not meant to resolve differences in gender rights, and a western lifestyle cannot be regarded as a political, religious, or social group. Such a conclusion comes from the interpretation that "grounds for political and religious

95 IND. 'Werkinstructies WI 2022/3 Bekeerlingen en afvalligen' [*Converts and apostasy*]. November 22, 2022.

persecution concern characteristics so fundamental to a stranger's identity or moral integrity that she should not be asked to give up." For this reason, exception from the interpretation above may be made in cases where westernisation happened as a result of the applicant being turned away by her religion, or in cases where the applicant can nonetheless prove that the 'western' characteristics are unchangeable.[96]

3.6 *Credibility Assessment*

What could arguably be considered the most important Work Instructions document is 2014/10, as it instructs decision makers, especially those working on first instance decisions, on how to conduct a "integral credibility assessment" of the applicant. While the duty to provide information and to substantiate the burden of proof lies with the asylum seeker, "the limits of the burden of proof stretch as far as what can reasonably be expected."[97] The IND, then, can help meet the requirements of burden of proof by conducting its own research, through interviews, language analysis, age assessment, or requesting official reports on the country of origin of the asylum seeker. "The government must supplement relevant elements (ex officio) and general information where necessary." This points to a general trend observed of deference to expertise when it comes to gathering information. This, as we will observe, is not only the case between case workers and asylum seekers, but also among different actors with the chain of asylum policy management.

The application must undergo a 'integral credibility assessment' which weighs and searches for the connection between all the relevant elements. The sequence that this assessment must undergo is as follows:

Step 1. Determining the relevant elements, where a relevant element is defined as a fact or circumstance that relates to at least one of subject or storyline as is related to refugee status. These can refer to facts pertaining to the person of the foreign national in question, or to facts

96 IND. 'Werkinstructies WI 2019/1 Het beoordelen van asielaanvragen van verwesterde vrouwen' [*Assessing asylum applications from westernized women*], July 1, 2019. In other words, the requirement to wear a burqa in a country, coupled with a personal desire to not be subjected to such a requirement, is not enough to invoke refugee status, as such aspects are not considered fundamentally unchangeable.

97 IND. 'Werkinstructies WI 2014/10 Inhoudelijke beoordeling (asiel)' [*Substantive Assessment (asylum)*]. January 1, 2015. The applicant is expected to provide statements, during interview or in writing, and all documentation in their possession which may point toward age, background, identity, nationality, previous residence, previous asylum applications, travel itineraries, and reasons for requesting international protection (for applicant and relevant family members).

and circumstances that have occurred in the country of origin. They may come from the direct observation of the applicant, but also from what they may have heard from third parties. In this case, particular attention should be given to the association of certain events to each other, and the applicant's understanding of the cause/effect relationship between these.

Step 2. Once the main elements have been identified, the second step focuses on the credibility of said elements.

> It must be assessed whether there are relevant elements that are sufficiently substantiated and therefore credible beyond doubt. These are elements substantiated with objective evidence, such as authentic documents that confirm what the foreign national has declared and/or objective public sources that confirm statements made by the foreign national.

Each of the elements identified must be examined within its own context. For example, a lack of credibility regarding elements relating to travel to the Netherlands should not negatively impact the credibility of other elements pertaining to the application.

It is important from a managerial point of view for the decision maker to understand that there is a need for giving the applicant the benefit of the doubt, as "there will almost never be certainty," of an applicant's statements. Importantly, however, is that applicants are not required to prove that specific events happened to them, but only that their fear of persecution or serious harm is justified. Nonetheless, as there is almost no guarantee of certainty when confirming a statement, there are also cases where the evidence provided is not sufficient to make a positive credibility assessment. In these cases, the credibility indicators described in Table 12 below should be used "as an aid for an objective, structured, and transparent assessment of the credibility of the relevant elements." These are divided in two categories: internal, or credibility arising from the elements presented by the applicants, and external, or credibility arising from testing the applicants' statements against other sources.

While Table 12[98] does paint a very detailed instruction for assessing credibility, room for interpretation clearly exists. 'Adequate' explanations, for example, are very much subjective to the personal threshold of what 'adequate' might be. In fact, as Step 3 below shows, WI 2014/10 takes this into account by asking

98 IND. Werkinstructies WI 2014/10 (n 97).

for a correct consideration of the facts to be conducted to assess how circumstances diminish or enhance the credibility of an element. Nonetheless, even if interpretive terms are left to the latitude of the street-level bureaucrat, the experiences of those working directly with asylum cases show that the way they apply these interpretations is not left unchecked.

Step 3. After assessing the credibility of elements, a weighing of these assessments must take place. "There are statements, documents and information sources that give credibility to a relevant element and [others] that weaken the credibility of a relevant element. Ultimately a balance must be drawn up. The result of this weighting results in deciding if a relevant element is plausible or not." The credibility of each element must be assessed against the personal circumstances of the applicant, and whether such circumstances could explain any inconsistencies in the application. Finally, the aggregation of these assessments is taken as a whole, both to separate plausible elements from implausible ones, but also to assess the mutual coherence of the applicant's storyline. This assessment of the overall coherence of the applicant's story represents the final two steps in the procedure that bureaucrats are told to follow during a credibility assessment.

Step 4. In the second to last step, bureaucrats are told to indicate which relevant elements should be tested further, and which are implausible and will not be subjected to further scrutiny. This means not only to assess the reasons for which a fear of persecution or harm exist, but also to evaluate the plausibility of the applicants' suspicions of what will happen if they are returned.

> This review should include considerations for both refugee status and subsidiary protection. This is because the country-specific policies designate specific groups as facing certain risks of violations. The fact that the foreign national belongs to a risk group (refugee status) or a vulnerable minority (Art. 3 ECHR) is more indicative that the suspicion about what will happen upon return are real.

In other words, the burden of proof for the suspicion of being subjected to serious harm if returned to a country of origin must be lowered in cases where the applicant is categorized as a risk group or vulnerable minority.

Step 5. The final step is to use the relevant elements to assess whether the assumptions derived about what an applicant might be subjected to upon return are plausible. This is done by assessing whether the suspicions of the applicant are plausible considering the credibility assessment and

TABLE 12 Internal and external credibility indicators

Internal credibility indicators	External credibility indicators
Extent of detail and specificity – No vagueness and sufficient detail to consider the statements as coming from personal experience.	Consistency with information from other witnesses and consistency with available information – Official country reports from the Government are the main objective source, as these are 'expert reports.' If no such official report exists, information should be based on reports from other countries or international organisations.
Internal Consistency – No contradictions or inconsistencies in the information provided by the applicant. – Contradictions between the first and follow-up interviews cannot be taken at face value, as the first interview is not intended to establish reasons for seeking asylum. – If contradictions exist, then the applicants must 'adequately' explain these. In some cases, "the information provided is so contradictory that it affects the credibility of the entire story."	Consistency of statements from third parties – In cases where the applicant invokes information learned from third parties, is important to assess how such information fits with other credible statements, how the information was obtained (who the third party is), and if this information matches the facts known of the country of origin.
	Authenticity of Documents – The following questions should be asked when assessing the authenticity of any document submitted as evidence: – Is it genuine? – Who is the issuer, and is this consistent with the general information available? – How was the document obtained, and is this consistent with the general information available? – Does general information suggest that such documents can easily be obtained illegally?

> the known situation in the country of origin. "This connection between the credible relevant elements and the resulting risks upon return must be made according to a reasonable degree of probability."

After the assessment of the risk upon return, a clear conclusion regarding the plausibility of the application's elements is drawn. The bureaucrats' analysis must thus incorporate not only justifications for persecution or risk of harm, but also the plausibility of suspicions of what might follow because of such acts. If the credible relevant elements and plausible suspicions can be traced back to the Refugee Convention, then a well-founded fear for persecution exists and the applicant is granted refugee status. Alternatively, when elements and suspicions cannot be traced to the Convention, an assessment for subsidiary protection must be made, based on the any potential risk violations as spelled out in Article 3 ECHR. If the latter is the case, the IND is obliged to assess whether a protection alternative exists, and whether the applicant can invoke such an alternative. If official reports or sources indicate that protection alternatives exist, the burden of proof lies on the applicants to justify the inability to avail themselves of such protection.

In practice, when assessing the asylum claim, the case worker first allows the applicant to tell their "free narrative," during which they explain their reasons for applying for asylum. After the narrative, the IND official asks follow up questions about specific parts of the story, to verify whether the applicant can provide a reasonable degree of consistency and detail. The officer can check external sources if such sources are available. Whether such sources are available depends on the nature of the claim, but generally the consistency of the story is a main indicator of credibility. Nonetheless, if someone claims for example, a certain nationality, yet they are in possession of a passport indicating a different nationality, the external source (in this case the passport) can be a leading factor in assessing credibility. Such assessments depend on the nature of the external source and on the nature of the claim, showing what the weighing of elements is meant to help the bureaucrat put in balance. Interview reports contain very detailed transcripts of the interview, are stored in the internal system of the IND, and shared with the applicant and lawyer. Besides that, an internal source of information exists, which caseworkers can consult and use to register and describe other observations made during the interview. IND officials with experience in handling asylum claims report that they do not view their tasks as proving applicants right or wrong, but rather only to probe the credibility and plausibility of their stories.[99]

99 Interviews conducted with IND officials, for the purposes of this research, in March 2020.

Workers of the IND also shed light on why most changes brought to procedures seem to be focused on the assessment of LGBTI applications, or those from religious converts. In the past 10 years there has been an increase in such applications across the EU, and these two topics have specifically been mentioned as particularly difficult to assess. Other common reasons invoked for asylum, at least in the perception of those interviewed, are belonging to a persecuted religious group, war, political activities, indiscriminate violence (e.g., applicants from Taliban controlled areas), gender violence (e.g., female genital mutilation in certain African countries). Easily accessible and translatable documents are usually indicative of a case that will be somewhat easy to assess, but such assumptions cannot be taken at face value: what was originally perceived as an easy case may often turn complex, reinforcing the claim made by the State Secretary and presented earlier in this chapter, that it is difficult to assign specific experts to specific cases due to the unpredictable nature of applications. Lastly, while an individual assessment is always carried out, IND officials have indicated that there usually is an expectation of outcome of an application based on nationality – at least when the expectation is that the applicant will be granted asylum. It is worth noting that interviewees also reported that they have had no experience dealing with any applications that invoked 'climate change' as a reason for protection, likely because for applicants to portray themselves as such could be detrimental to their application. In a specific case of applicants coming from an island country and requesting international protection because of a natural disaster, the case workers' recollection was that there was a certain degree of certainty that protection would not be granted because the reasons invoked were purely based on natural disasters, and not persecution or threat of serious harm.[100]

The work of bureaucrats tasked with making first instance asylum decision is one characterised by a complex and extremely detailed system, that nonetheless still leads to a perception of flexibility among workers of the IND. Leaving from a starting point of decentralisation, a deference to expertise is often seen as the norm, rather than a deference to hierarchy. This is seen even in the process of effective remedy, where courts cannot make a full review of the credibility of an applicant during appeal, because the "IND has the expertise, not the courts."[101] This expertise, however, is reportedly nourished: discussions and analyses are conducted about implications of rulings of the CJEU, and decisions are made collectively about necessary changes to policy. Since case

---

100 Interviews conducted with IND officials, for the purposes of this research, in March 2020.
101 Angelina van Kampen (n 18), 26.

officers themselves participate in such scenarios, the guidelines for implementation are perceived as encompassing most asylum scenarios. In cases where there is a lack of clarity on how legislation should be interpreted, recourse is usually made to the legal department of the IND.[102]

4 Conclusion

The Dutch system of governance allows for several ways in which international law or practice can influence national policy, without always saying so in as many (legislative) words. Bureaucratic procedures, however, paint a different story. This is evident in the case of asylum, as we see reliance on such instruments for designating safe countries of origin, but also in that street-level bureaucrats are directed toward these sources when deciding cases of applicants from countries for which the Dutch government does not have an official policy. In fact, possible reasons for which we observe more directly the influence of international mechanisms on bureaucratic practice and not legislative norms is because the Netherlands has spent very little of the previous decades making legislative amendments necessary to align it law with the EU acquis. Indeed, as this chapter shows, the previous years saw a great deal of changes made to bureaucratic procedures, and these because of the need to manage an unsustainable backlog.

We are then confronted with delineating, based on the information contained in this chapter, if there is any observable difference between bureaucratic practice and policy rule. Surely, legal scholars might argue, it is the latter that creates the former. There is no denying that policy rules have the most influence on how employees conduct their jobs: from recruitment to career advancement, to the standards by which work quality is assessed, the ways in which these are carried out is directly derived from formally established rules. But as the results presented here suggest, discretion, from an asylum policy perspective, is handled in a way that responds the needs of a bureaucratic process defined by emergencies: it gives the bureaucrats the necessary space – albeit regulated – to conduct their day-to-day jobs without undue influence. Interviews at the IND confirm this trend, at least from a bureaucratic perspective: despite the work of the institution frequently receiving public attention – either from the media or politicians – this does not influence the way applications are assessed. Even when presented with a hypothetical scenario of a

102 Interviews conducted with IND officials, for the purposes of this research, in March 2020.

governing coalition that wishes to restrict the right to asylum, employees of the IND foresee this as having a minimal impact on their jobs: EU legislation, regardless of politics, must still be followed.[103]

From a strictly policy architecture perspective, the conclusions that Dörrenbächer[104] and other have reached in their work, namely that the work of Dutch immigration officials is characterised by a lack of discretionary space, holds. The guidelines based on which bureaucrats must make decisions are extremely detailed, and by the Government's own account the management of public service in the Netherlands skews power toward the managers. Nonetheless, interviews conducted with IND officials show that their involvement in the process by which these detailed procedures are decided, and the diverse and horizontal nature of quality assessment, gives them the power to contribute to their own working conditions. In other words, while indeed it seems that their discretionary space is highly restricted, street-level bureaucrats consider their participation in its restriction as a fair counterbalance to a highly regulated working environment. In fact, those interviews at the IND do not mention any influence outside of that from their peers as being relevant in their decision making. If a request to re-assess a case is made, this usually originates from another department within the IND, such as the legal department, and not from a hierarchical superior.[105] This is further enforced by a working environment in which, by the very nature of its architecture, bureaucrats build upon each other's work, and informally implement a 4-eye principle, although such mechanism is not officially called for in legislative or policy documents.

The balance between a lack of formal discretion and the ability of bureaucrats to shape their restricted discretionary space is exemplified by Art. 4.82 of the General Administrative Law Act. For a public official "to explain the reasons for an order, it shall only be sufficient to refer to a fixed practice insofar as this practice is contained in a policy rule." As the argument went earlier in this chapter, we are told here that interpretative ambiguities can be settled through usual work practices, with the only condition being that these practices be contained in a policy rule. Bureaucrats have to make certain decisions on their own, such as assessing which Track an application must be placed in,

103 Interviews conducted with IND officials, for the purposes of this research, in March 2020.

104 Nora Dörrenbächer, 'Frontline Uses of European Union (EU) Law: a Parallel Legal Order? How Structural Discretion Conditions Uses of EU Law in Dutch and German Migration Offices' (2017) 38 *Journal of Public* 455.

105 This should not be taken to indicate that no such oversight exists. It was not however one of the oversight factors brought up by employees of the IND during the interviews conducted in March 2020.

if a medical examination may be required during the R&P period, or if 'any relevant circumstances' that are not foreseen in the work instructions should contribute to the conclusions of an age assessment. It is also up to these bureaucrats to make their own decision for the best available information on countries for which the Dutch government does not have an official report. On the other hand, arbitrary decisions made by superiors at the Ministry of Security and Justice, or by senior managers of the IND, have to do with controlling the 'triage' of clients: suspending certain medical tests during registration, the hiring and training practices, and the changes made in the information sought during the first interview of the procedures, and the implementation of the 5 Track system, are all decision made that take away the power of bureaucrats to choose or handle their own work-flow, but not that directly impact the way an assessment of application must be made. In the few cases where such amendments are brought to bureaucratic policy, such as when the interview process for LGBTI applicants was altered, this is as a response to rulings of the CJEU or other changes brought at the European level. However, given that asylum case workers are often involved in the drafting of positions of the Netherlands before the CJEU, alongside other workers from the IND's legal department or the Ministry of Security and Justice, allows these workers to take an active role in the shaping of their discretionary space. A similar perception was reported regarding the sharing of best practices among EU member states, as well as with EASO: the involvement of caseworkers in these processes gives them the power to shape their own discretionary space based on their expertise.[106]

If a general trend must be concluded based on the information contained in this chapter is that the Dutch asylum system tries to position itself as one categorised by a deference to expertise, not hierarchy. Interviewees for this research have repeatedly claimed that asylum case workers see a variety of complex cases, and it is with experience that a worker in this environment starts having a 'feel' for when a story is genuine or not. There is no standard asylum story, but as case workers do further research, it becomes easier to understand what information is needed: depending on documents, on the travel itinerary, behaviour on social media, etc. It is their own expertise that allows them to make these assessments, and it is the expertise of their peers, as well as the institutional trainings and guidance, that allows them to trust any quality assessment of their work.

Unfortunately, this does little to address the larger question of what the Dutch case says about how countries with long-standing relationship with the

106 Interviews conducted with IND officials, for the purposes of this research, in March 2020.

EU implement asylum policy. The architecture of the Dutch asylum system – with the 5-Tracks – deviates from the 'usual' architecture that the CEAS constructs. This does not mean that it is non-compliant, but rather that conclusions based on comparisons between this, and other asylum systems become fragile. While it could be argued that the familiarity of street-level bureaucrats with the rulings of the CJEU shows more willingness to engage with the EU level of governance, there was not any indication that the state legacy has any part to play in such willingness. Indeed, many other factors – such as the general deference to expertise – found in Dutch public administration are just as likely to be responsible for this willingness. As it was shown during the research, the EU institutions also reach out to Dutch experts for advice on policy creation, showing that expertise is what contributes to the creation of a two-way street flow of information. To clarify these aspects, research should look specifically at how street-level bureaucrats interact with the EU level on specific issues, rather than with a birds-eye lens applied in the current work.

CHAPTER 7

Beyond Black on White: A Nuanced View of Discretion

Traditional approaches to street-level bureaucracy focus on the conditions of work and the conflictual nature of jobs to explain the behaviour of those tasked with working on the frontlines of policy delivery.[1] Insights from the role conflict theory point to additional factors that might affect service delivery outside of the restrictions imposed by the organisational environment in which these workers are embedded. Between the two approaches, an image emerges that informs a more comprehensive understanding of how bureaucrats carry out a job that is not only defined by institutional rules and formal norms, but also by intangible factors unrelated to the role of 'bureaucrat.'

In his work, Lipsky showed that street-level bureaucrats hold significant discretion in how they execute their job, especially when it is up to them to manage their workflow as well as the relations with those they interact with. It means that there must be some leeway allowing for this flexibility to take place. But little is said about what discretion looks like beyond a strict black-on-white understanding. For those working in the field of asylum, does discretion manifest itself in different standards of proof used when assessing applications? Or is it exercised to fill information gaps in institutional provisions regulating systematic asylum application assessments? As the opening chapters of this book argued, formal discretion is a specific type of ambiguity – an intentional one – which is meant to give implementers the power to interpret provisions in a way that best reflects the needs of the specific work they are tasked to conduct. Given the complexity of the entire regime of asylum in the EU, the construction of discretionary space is of paramount importance, and first instance decisions are only one part of this system. It is important then to spend a few sentences on visualising the range policy areas that converge to implement asylum policy in its entirety.

For the purposes of this explanation, the 'institution' of asylum must be differentiated from the institutions in which bureaucrats work. The work of caseworkers making first instance decisions in the Netherlands doesn't only

1 Michael Lipsky, *Street-Level Bureaucracy: Dilemmas of the Individual in Public Service* (Russel Sage Foundation 2010).

 | DOI:10.1163/9789004700826_008

add up to the institutional behaviour of the IND or the Ministry of Security and Justice, but also adds to the institutional behaviour of asylum governance system in general. Those making first instance decisions implement CEAS provisions alongside others who analyse the applicability of Dublin provisions or ensure access to housing and healthcare, legal representatives, and many more other workers that interact directly with asylum seekers. Therefore, the work processes used for the implementation of policy must be included in considerations aimed at assessing the extent to which the goal of uniform implementation of the CEAS is being achieved.

This book has adopted a perspective which emphasises the way institutions are affected by sequences of political events, as well as cross-temporal transformations. The varied institutional legacies under which administrative structures operate make black letter approaches insufficient, especially in cases where the street-level of bureaucracy is the final step of the policy process. Based on such considerations, a proper analysis of the success or failure of the implementation of certain policies which emanate from the EU, the street-level must be given equal analytical weight as black letter approaches.

We should not expect a model of public administration research to consider all national and historical contexts as constants, even in the case of the Common European Asylum System, where the 'rules of the game' are spelled out in a common set of directives and regulations. The organisational features specific to asylum do not happen in a vacuum; they are dependent on the historic development of the state's institutions. While legacies of the past may have been forgotten to history, they very much play a role in the way institutions are designed today. In the Netherlands, for example, the rules and standards of the CEAS have been entrenched in national procedures, particularly by the country's direct involvement in shaping Europe's asylum system since its inception. This, it should be noted, in spite the fact that there is no constitutional weight given to the effect of international law in national policy development. In Romania, on the other hand, international law is constitutionally recognised as a source of authority. Yet, as one of the last members to join the EU, Romania simply adopted the rules of CEAS as they had already been established and negotiated.

An analysis of how these different contexts affect policy implementation needs to focus not only on the legal texts adopted – i.e., transposed, – but also on the strategies used for implementation. This book has argued that one way to assess such strategies is by investigating the bureaucratic mechanisms used to settle ambiguities in documents. In doing so, it is important to consider both the mechanisms that are intentionally built in, meaning formal discretion, and those unintentional ambiguities that result from a lack of necessary information or conflicting goals and objectives. As such, ambiguity is generally defined in this work as any provision that contributes, intentionally or not, to the building of the implementer's discretionary space. While assessing an application for refugee status at first instance, street-level bureaucrats who interact with applicants are expected to answer certain questions for which information is not always obvious. How, for instance, should armed conflict be assessed to understand if it falls within the scope of the Qualifications Directive or the Asylum Procedures Directive, or what elements from an applicant's past represent grounds for exclusion?

Understanding how the rules of game were developed, and at which point in time each of the countries had to adopt them is thus a crucial consideration. As mentioned, the path followed by the Netherlands to get to the CEAS of today is vastly different than that followed by Romania, because the starting point of rule perpetuation and reinforcement in their respective national systems is different. This is why I began the analysis with the early development of asylum provisions, the motivations behind these, as well as the emergence and interpretation of ambiguities over time. I was able to show that the objectives of the Union are a moving target, shifting from deterrence to protection. Because some EU Member States participated in the construction of this system, while latecomers merely adopted an already existing set of rules, processes through which ambiguities are addressed is crucial in knowing how the goal of harmonised implementation is sought.

Taking the work of bureaucrats as a presupposed residual of policy implementation leads to ignoring important considerations such as ambiguity and conflict.[2] Bureaucrats are workers whose behaviour is relevant to, congruent with, and accepted by a bureaucratic apparatus. Relevance indicates that bureaucrats are subjected to a certain set of expectations associated with their role, while congruency and acceptance point to compliance to those expectations and a formal connection to the institution that sets them. Several important insights emerge from this. First, behaviour is system depended, meaning that expectations outside of those set by the institutions with which a formal connection exists bear little to no relevance. Secondly, ambiguities must be settled for bureaucrats to meet the criteria listed above.

Ignoring the added value of understanding the full institutional context in which these dynamics take place would prove fatal to attempts of understanding the implementation of asylum policy. Thinking of Europe's approach to

2 Peter Hupe and Michael Hill, '"And the Rest Is Implementation.' Comparing Approaches to What Happens in Policy Processes beyond Great Expectations' (2015) 31 *Public Policy and Administration* 103.

asylum management, the way expectations are set bears just as much importance as what those expectations are. Given the complexity of the CEAS, there are many points at which ambiguities may arise and noncompliance occur. This confers heightened importance to the process by which gaps of information necessary for performing specific tasks are settled, therefore fulfilling the delivery of services to the clients of bureaucracy. This book began by identifying how the cornerstone of asylum policy around the world, the 1951 Convention Relating to the Status of Refugees, exemplifies the ambiguous nature of developing policies meant to offer international protection to those in need. From then on, the process of upholding the values of the Convention, and of translating these values in actionable policies, became an exercise of either interpreting ambiguities or delegating their interpretation. The way the Common European Asylum System was built represents this, since its creation is "based on the full and inclusive application of the Geneva Convention."[3] Figuring or delegating interpretation of ambiguities has implications that cannot be overlooked when discussing policy integration in the European Union. If times of crisis indeed lead to further integration because they help identify and address policy shortcomings,[4] the process by which gaps of information are filled represents the process through which integration occurs.

Institutionally, the differences are not hard to observe. From 2005 until 2018, 8 countries, including Romania, had sent no preliminary reference relating to migration, while the Netherlands and Germany alone accounted for a third of all such requests sent to the Court of Justice.[5] On the other hand, the example of the Romanian Constitution, which does not allow for any international provisions on human rights to take effect if the national legislation offers higher standards, shows that safeguards against a race to the bottom in case of incomplete ambiguities do exist. But since this book argues vehemently for the need to include street-level processes in any policy analysis, the question of what influence street-level bureaucrats have on the implementation of the Common European Asylum System remains. This question guided the line of inquiry present throughout the entirety of this book.

3 Council of the European Union 'Presidency Conclusions, Tampere European Council' 15–16 October 1999.

4 Sandra Lavenex, "Failing Forward' Towards Which Europe? Organized Hypocrisy in the Common European Asylum System' (2018) 56 *Journal of Common Market Studies* 1195.

5 Daniel Thym, 'A Bird's Eye View on ECJ Judgments on Immigration, Asylum and Border Control Cases' (2019) 21 *European Journal of Migration and Law* 166.

1 European Ambiguity

While the conclusions reached by the Council at Tampere in 1999 had placed focus and emphasis on the rights of asylum seekers, the original goals based upon which Europe's system of asylum was built stemmed more from exclusion for the sake of protecting a border-free union, and not out of an understanding of the need to offer proper protection to those in need. Yet as the mechanisms of the Common European Asylum System were developed, the need to identify and address ambiguities became clear. Dublin II clarified some of the vagueness of the original Dublin Convention, as it is evidenced by the introduction of the need to offer special protections to unaccompanied minors, or by clearly defining who is a 'family member' of an applicant. Furthermore, for interpreting other ambiguities as they arise, EASO was also created to serve as a formal hub for expertise to which national administrations can turn, followed in 2021 by its successor, the EUAA. The very existence of these agencies shows once more the importance of this book's argument: their influence ends at the point where domestic administrative discretion begins, illustrating the organic boundaries between different levels of governance.

Before delving into the guidelines for interpreting ambiguities based on the work of the CJEU, a look at those intentional ambiguities written into the Asylum Procedures Directive and Qualifications Directive is appropriate. This will allow, as the discussion progresses, to keep in mind the frames that are considered ambiguous and worthy of interpretation at the EU level, and how these compare to what is observed nationally. From a purely literal analysis, the Qualifications Directive is straight-forward, with only 12 provisions relevant to first-instance decisions granting discretionary powers, two of which have to do with the permission to adopt more favourable conditions. On the other hand, the Asylum Procedures Directive includes 122 such provisions. Most of the relevant first instance provisions that grant discretionary powers come out of 17 frames, out of 25 total frames identified. These include protection against *refoulment*, border procedures, security, or obligations of applicants, among many others. There are no verbal discretionary provisions when it comes to access to effective remedy. Yet, this is one of the topics that is most widely subjected to the preliminary procedure at the CJEU. On the other hand, when making decisions based on national security or public order, Member States, have, theoretically, discretion in making decisions.

The preliminary ruling procedure of the Court of Justice of the European Union adds to this first step in the analysis by showing that, aside from discretion granted through language, interpretative ambiguity abounds. Much of the Court's work deals with provisions pertaining to who the actors of protection are, the content of protection offered, particularly vulnerable applicants, non-refoulment, and other frames which, in a literal reading, all convey non-discretionary calls to action. In its rulings on the matter, the CJEU draws inspiration from three formal sources of human rights law: the European Convention of Human Rights (ECHR), the EU Charter of Fundamental Rights, and the "general principle of EU law," or principles derived from national constitutions or other treaties to which Member States are parties, again illustrating the organic boundary between levels of governance.[6]

Non-refoulment and family protection are two of the areas that are treated with little formal discretion in legal documents yet receive a surprising number of requests for interpretation from the Court. From a formal reading of documents, non-refoulment and protection of family unity are so paramount in any considerations that there seemed to be little room left for interpretation. *Non-refoulement* is one of the cornerstones of today's global approach to asylum as framed by the 1951 Geneva Convention. "The Common European Asylum System," the Court claims, "is based on the full and inclusive application of the Geneva Convention and the guarantee that nobody will be sent back to a place where they again risk being persecuted."[7] To clarify this, the Court points to the difference that the Qualifications Directive establishes between 'refugee' and 'refugee status.' Simply revoking refugee status does not mean that a person ceases to be a refugee, and Member States would still be bound by requirements of the Charter of Fundamental Rights. Furthermore, given the emphasis that each new CEAS iteration placed on removing vagueness from who is a family member of an applicant, the CJEU clarified that a Member State is permitted to provide for an extension of the scope of protection from an applicant to other family members, as this is consistent with the rationale of family unity enclosed in the system of international protection. Furthermore, an individual assessment of an applicant's request for international protection must also include an assessment of "of the threat of persecution and of serious harm in respect of a family member."[8] This goes even further in the proposed reforms in the Pact, where the definition of family is extended to also include marriages concluded after the applicant fled their country of origin.

6 Paul P. Craig and Grainne De Burca, *EU Law: Text, Cases and Materials* (Oxford University Press 2015), 380.

7 Joined Cases C-411/10 and C-493/10 *N. S. v Secretary of State for the Home Department and M. E. and Others v Refugee Applications Commissioner and Minister for Justice, Equality and Law Reform* (2011) I-13905.

8 Case C-652/16 *Nigyar Rauf Kaza Ahmedbekova and Rauf Emin Ogla Ahmedbekov v Zamestnik-predsedatel na Darzhavna agentsia za bezhantsite* [2018].

By far most requests for interpretation can largely be categorised in two frames: burden of proof and the procedure by which a claim is assessed. Through this, the court makes clear what the general approach to the implementation of the CEAS must be. Provisions regarding assessment procedures must be used by national authorities as guiding rules to determine if an applicant has satisfied the material conditions for qualification as a refugee.[9] For these conditions to be met, an applicant is required to submit proof in the form of statements or documents of all the components of the concept of the reason for persecution, in this case religion.[10] There are, however, several clarifications that the Court was compelled to make, specifically when it comes to assessing the reasons invoked for persecution.

Applicants invoking religious reasons, for example, should not be expected to produce proof of every component of 'religion' descried in the Qualifications Directive.[11] Moreover, it has also been clarified that actions that don't target one religion, but any religion contrary to the one of the applicant's country, are also to be considered acts that put the asylum seeker at risk.[12] The CJEU has not defined exactly what 'real risk' means. What it has made clear, however, is that general situation in a country cannot, in it of itself, be taken as indication of substantial proof of 'real risk,' and the sliding-scale concept should be applied.[13] The Court thus made clear that the existence of armed conflict alone is not sufficient to assume that it poses a risk to the individual applying for protection.

In terms of who is a civilian or a participant in armed conflicts, the Court employed a different approach then what had been seen at national levels. National courts relied on international humanitarian law to define civilians as those who take no active part in hostilities, including former members of armed forces. The CJEU, however, employed a contextual perspective, leading to an interpretation where even a member of certain armed forces who has not taken pro-active steps toward disengagement could qualify for subsidiary protection. The Court needed to clarify this definition not because of a lack of information, but because the information available did not reflect the scope of subsidiary protection provisions from the CEAS.

---

9 Case C-277/11 *M. M. v Minister for Justice, Equality and Law Reform and Others* [2012].

10 *Ahmedbekova and Ahmedbekov* (n 8) para 76.

11 C-56/17, *Bahtiyar Fathi v Predsedatel na Darzhavna agentsia za bezhantsite* [2018] para 102.

12 Case C-150/15, *Der Bundesbeauftragte für Asylangelegenheiten beim Bundesamt für Migration und Flüchtlinge v N* [2016].

13 Case C-465/07, *Meki Elgafaji and Noor Elgafaji v Staatssecretaris van Justitie* [2009] Opinion AG Maduro, para 37.

This interpretation also has consequences for who can be excluded from receiving protection. Membership to an armed group does not automatically point to non-civilian status. Even more interesting in this case, however, is the approach to the provisions which requires that applicants be excluded from refugee status if they are receiving assistance from other actors of protection. The Court makes it clear that such protection does not automatically lead to non-assessment of a claim. Even in these cases, an individual assessment is needed as to whether said actor can provide effective protection.

Lastly the Court makes several clarifications that can be categorised under a frame of good administration, in keeping with a strict adherence to the Charter of Fundamental Rights as a source of inspiration. Not only does the Charter guarantee the rights of individuals, but it also enshrines the principle of good administration for the purpose of delivering said rights. The Court equates good administration to the proper following the EU procedures, by pointing out that single procedure for assessing refugee or subsidiary protection must be followed as determined at the EU level, regardless if national legislation says otherwise.[14] Furthermore, administratively speaking, categories of asylum applications can be drawn up based on nationality or country of origin information, and these can inform accelerated procedures, but an individual assessment of facts is still required for each applicant.[15] Administrative effects are supposed to take effect based on these decisions. The outcome of a procedure, for example, may be challenged, but not the motivation for entering the specific type of procedure (i.e., accelerated). Furthermore, the Court also makes clear national courts or tribunals can dismiss an appeal altogether without hearing the applicant, if there is no doubt that the appeal is unfounded.[16]

2 Building the Discretionary Space

The principle of good administration forces us to ask what role international provisions play in national legislation and administration. The Court made it clear that compliance to international obligations is a key component of good governance. Romania's constitution specifically addresses these issues, by guaranteeing the obligation of the state to abide by all international human rights

---

14 Case C-604/12, *H.N. v Minister for Justice, Equality and Law Reform and Others* [2014] para 50.

15 Case C-175/11 *H.I.D. and B.A. v Refugee Applications Commissioner and Others* [2013].

16 Case C-348/16, *Moussa Sacko v Commissione Territoriale per il riconoscimento della Protezione internazionale di Milano* [2017].

treaties to which the state is a signatory. Even more important, if there are any inconsistencies between said agreement and national legislation, international regulations have priority. There is, however, a caveat. The Constitution or internal laws take precedence if they include more favourable provisions, providing thus a safeguard against a race to the bottom that might occur on the international stage. Despite the Constitutional provisions, the efficacy of this safeguard has been questioned in practice, especially from the inability of Romania to adequately adapt to the process of Europeanisation.[17]

Of specific importance is also how the behaviour of those representing the state is regulated, since issues of supervision and working conditions are paramount to considerations of street-level bureaucracy. Administrative capacity is defined in national legislation as the ensemble of financial, material, institutional, and human resources that an administrative-territorial unit has at its disposal, the legal framework under which it operates, and the way these resources are valued in its activities. This makes clear the fact that public authorities work within an ensemble of prerogatives and restrictions found in law regarding the exercise of attributes by public authorities and institutions, and that it is the competency of these authorities that confers onto them the role associated to their specific activity. There is also a trend of de-concentration of competencies. Because of a strong deference to hierarchy, the existence of a strong central authority exists even in policy fields such as asylum, where decision making is delegated to geographically diverse institutions.

De-concentration moves away only physically from the central authority, while maintaining strong bonds of supervision. Deference to hierarchy is ever present in Romania's administrative structure, even more so for government employees whose job is regulated by a special statue. There are however hints of the importance for flexibility in reaching objective decisions, by invoking a public official's 'capacity for judgement.' Romanian legislation acknowledges that any exercise of the capacity for judgement which leads to a violation of rights is to be considered abuse of power, meaning that indeed flexibility must exist in interpreting facts, but only if these are not abused.[18]

---

17 Paul Blokker, 'Romanian Constitutionalism: Form without Content?' [2012] *SSRN Electronic Journal* 1; Venelin I. Ganev, 'Post-Accession Hooliganism: Democratic Governance in Bulgaria and Romania after 2007' (2013) 27 *East European Politics and Societies: and Cultures* 26; Svetlozar A. Andreev, 'The Unbearable Lightness of Membership: Bulgaria and Romania after the 2007 EU' (2009) 42 *Communist and Post-Communist Studies* 375.

18 High Court for Cassation and Justice of Romania. Decision on denying the appeal of G.C. against civil sentence nr. 942 from April 07, 2007, of the Bucharest Appeal Court, section VIII Administrative and Fiscal Conflicts. February 5, 2008.

Flexibility in administrative decision making is also present in the case of the Netherlands. All administrative orders must be issued based on adequate information matching the purpose of the issuing authority and based on 'proper reasons.' Furthermore, legislative guidelines clarify that interpretative ambiguities can be settled through usual work practices if these practices are contained in a policy rule. A better understanding of the discretionary space in the Dutch context is through the 'mandate,' or the power of a public official to make orders in the name of administrative authority, within limits. The limits placed on – and inversely the enhancement of – the powers conferred by statutory regulations are crucial in understanding the factors that influence how decisions are reached, not only what those specific decisions should be.

This reliance on statutory regulations is understandable in this scenario. Unlike the Romanian Constitution, its Dutch counterpart is limited in the amount of direct relevance it gives international law. This is not to say that international law is restricted on the effect it has – quite the contrary. Despite there being no direct reference to EU law or European integration in the document, Dutch administration operates in a system so open to influence from international law that the EU is often referred to as the "fourth tier of government."[19] Governance and bureaucratic procedures must then be set forth through other statutory acts. The constitution serves to enumerate the principles upon which the Dutch system should rest, but it is in specific legal documents that more specific mechanisms should be sought out.

Because of this reliance on statutory regulations, which are updated to match the current needs of society, Dutch civil service is one best categorised as fluid, reacting to trends such as increased globalisation, changing economic conditions, or the diminishing need for certain institutions or professions.[20] These trends have created two shifts: one from government to governance, with less overseeing by central government authorities, but one that still acknowledges the realities of multilevel governance, including a strong relationships of cooperation and interdependence within the European sphere. Unlike Romania, this decentralised unified approach does raise questions within the Dutch public administration sphere "about the extent to which [the activity of public officials] can still be steered and monitored just as effectively by their Ministers and State Secretaries in The Hague [since] the complexity of the

19 Ministry of the Interior and Kingdom Relations (BZK), 'The Dutch Public Service: Organisation and functioning of the government in the Netherlands, the position of civil servants and the main developments' (2016), 60.

20 Ibid 66.

decision-making in international organisations can be expected to increase the discretionary freedom of civil servants."[21]

Hierarchical consideration also matters here, since the construction by which public officials enter government service, and the way their work is assessed, reflects the inequality between the government and those who work for it. Yet the administrative legislation shows the need for ambiguity when it comes to maintaining a 'decentralised unified state.' The guideless that regulate the job of public officials generally are devoid much substance, as the main rules are established elsewhere. It is on this vagueness that the mutually conflictual relationship between managers and street-level bureaucrats is based, as it forms the basis for more concrete requirements that civil servants and their employers can impose on each other.

How do these general administrative structures translate into the applicable guidelines for implementing asylum legislation? In Romania, where IGI-DAI is the main authority charged with the implementation, the proper codes of behaviour are found either in the Norms of Implementation for the legal act that transposes the CEAS requirements, or in a varying number of orders meant to address specific scenarios. Order nr. 82/2018 regarding the rules for wearing police uniforms, for example, showed an instance where ambiguity rose due to conflicting information: the order required that most officers of the Ministry of Internal Affairs that undergo activities with the public to wear the institutional uniform, while the Norms of Implementation developed for the law regulating asylum state that no uniforms can be worn by public officials conducting interviews.[22]

Specific asylum legislation and implementing guidelines still adhere to a strong sense of hierarchy. Furthermore, it is the same institution that implements this legislation, the IGI-DAI, which is also charged with evaluating its own policy implementation. This consists of a sample of interviews and decision made in the regional centres, and reports are drafted with the observations and recommendations of the evaluators meant "to ensure a unitary practice and to improve the way in which asylum applications are analysed."[23] But influence and evaluation of the improper implementation of international standards also comes from the structural safeguards emergent from the

21 Ibid.

22 Art. 23. Methodological Norms for implementing Law nr. 122/2006 regarding asylum in Romania.

23 Information obtained from the Ministry of Interior's Office of Information and Public Relations, September 2020, through information requested according to Law 544/2001 regarding the freedom to access information for the public interest.

constitutional provisions of upholding international standards. Parliament, for instance, has used its powers of legislation to ensure that proper amendments are implemented in the scope of completing harmonisation of Romanian legislation to the community acquis. This was not only the case in the context of accession, but also to ensure that developments at the EU level were accounted for, especially by amending definitions as necessary to comply with the new Directives and Regulations of the CEAS.

There are still gaps that appear in Romanian legislation that, theoretically, should be filled by the time implementation happens. The definition for "application for international protection," for instance, is "a request made by a foreign national or a stateless person for international protection from the Romanian state." The European acquis, nonetheless, refers to such requests as those that "can be understood" to be for refugee or subsidiary protection status. This wording, not present in the Romanian version, allows for an application for international protection to be made implicitly, and for the need for protection to be deduced by public officials without an explicit request being made. In this case, and at least partly because of this legislative omission, there are no guidelines formally developed at any level of governance for identifying implicit requests.

Nonetheless, public officials are expected to play an active role in investigating all applications in law and fact, even if any matter emerges that was not present in the initial claim.[24] Guidelines are very specific in how to assess matters of race, religion, nationality, social groups, and political opinions, while also making it clear that other matters may also emerge and need to be accounted for – likely by relying on their 'capacity for judgment'. A similar non-exhaustive list is also given for what actions should be considered deceitful, in this case with the purpose of determining if an application should be categorised as unfounded. On the other hand, very explicit instructions are given on the obligation of these officials to provide the necessary information to applicants throughout the asylum procedure, in line with the non-discretionary approach observed in the European sphere. Other specific instructions on what an "active role" involves lead to problematic implementation results. The

24 Elements that must be taken into account are: documents that the asylum seeker possess that can elucidate his or her identity, age, or nationality, information given by the asylum seekers regarding his or her personal situation, but also regarding the country or region where they or their relatives held previous residence, previous lodged asylum applications, travel itinerary and documents, as well as justifications invoked in the application for asylum. This is a non-exhaustive list, indicated by the fact that any assessment must 'at least' include these elements.

need for a direct link to exist between motives invoked and the acts of persecution, for instance, limit the applicability of the sliding-scale model of assessing the risk an applicant is exposed to because of indiscriminate violence.

In any case, there are clear actions taken with the aim of harmonising national legislation and practice to EU standards. Family reunification takes noteworthy precedence in the asylum procedure, including a request for *ex-officio* family reunification procedure in the case of unaccompanied minors. A point in law was also amended, which originally categorised as unfounded applications from asylum seekers that could have benefitted from internal refuge as recognised by the UNHCR. This is in line with the ruling from the CJEU which clarified that even in cases were an actor of protection is present, an individual assessment must still be made. Lastly, legislation passed in 2013 ensured that national procedures reflect the practice that rejecting an application for international protection does not automatically lead to an obligation to leave the country.

Relations with the EU sphere are less clear once the street-level is looked at in isolation. While the law calls for all public officials in the field of asylum to be adequately trained, including through interactions with institutions at the European level, knowledge of developments at the CJEU or ECtHR are not part of the required training of asylum public officials. The compliance to the requirements for proper training is verified through annual evaluations and spot inspections. Nonetheless, there is a belief that further European cooperation on developing a common list of safe-third countries would facilitate national bureaucratic implementation of the CEAS.[25] This points to a lack of resource necessary for conducting the proper assessment of countries of origin, something that is also hinted at in the Dutch case. Other such resource gaps that affect proper implementation of asylum procedure are a lack of adequately trained interpreters, which leads to inefficient and dubious practices of double translation. This is even though access to adequate interpretation is guaranteed in legislation at all levels of governance – from the EU all the way down to the norms of implementation.[26]

What the Romanian example shows is that architecturally and institutionally, there are actions taken to align national legislation to European standards. These is one of the streams of actions that dictates the policy direction, in the

25 Information obtained from the Ministry of Interior's Office of Information and Public Relations, September 2020, through information requested according to Law 544/2001 regarding the freedom to access information for the public interest.

26 See Decisions 2201/2018 and 3595/2018 of the Rădăuţi Regional Court, and Decision 5170/2018 of the Giurgiu Regional Court.

specific Romanian administrative context. In the case of the Netherlands, different dynamics are observed. Less focus is placed on harmonisation to EU legislation, most likely as a nod to the fact that the Netherlands had played an active role in developing this system from its very inception. The focus away from such a harmonisation is observed from the very beginning: the system created does not identically match the architecture envisioned by the asylum process as spelled out in the Common European Asylum System.[27] The strategy by which asylum is bureaucratically administered can be categorised as being driven by two considerations: managing a shortage of resources and ensuring a smooth (and fair) assessment of application under migratory pressures.

While the Netherlands is not a country that lies directly on a migratory route, the pressures felt in Europe beginning in 2015 are clearly more of a driving force in current strategy formulation for asylum governance. It is not hard to understand why, given the lack of capacity that the IND, the implementing institution of asylum policy, has faced in recent years.[28] The number of immigration staff, legal aid providers, interpreters, and physical space to conduct interviews are all crucial in the ability of public officials to conduct their jobs, and any rise in the number of applications puts pressure on the ability to ration these resources effectively, particularly if, as in recent years, there is an unexpected number of arrivals or a switch in the composition of asylum seekers.[29]

As a result of these pressures the managerial strategy has been to focus on 'smarter and faster' work, with measures meant to introduce a group-oriented approach to complex matters to build expertise, or ensuring that a better internal information process is in place for monitoring the status of the backlog.[30] But most interesting about an approach that attempts to build expertise is that it also creates a system of horizontal cooperation and co-production of bureaucratic norms. This dynamic is recognised not only within the IND, but also in relationships with other state institutions, such as the judiciary.[31] Internally however, developments in case law and best practices are discussed informally and based on such assessment policy changes are brought about. There is a sense among workers of the IND that their input is included in the

27 This is because the 5-track system was a policy innovation of the Dutch system that still adheres to procedural requirements of the CEAS. Also, as Chapter 6 points out, the general procedure by which bureaucratic orders should be issued is very similar to the one required for implementing asylum.

28 Parliamentary Paper 19637–2431 of Nov. 7, 2018.

29 Parliamentary Paper 19637–2492, Apr. 17, 2019.

30 Parliamentary Paper 19637–2543, of Nov. 18, 2019.

31 Angelina van Kampen, 'Country Report: Netherlands' (2019) *Asylum Information Database* (*AIDA*), 26.

way bureaucratic norms are built, and therefore their discretion is not seen as restricted. Rather, they view themselves as co-creators of their own working rules.

This dynamic exists also for supervision and quality assessment. This is evidenced by the guidelines on age assessments, or by the relationship between the legal department of the IND and the case officers making decisions. Workers of the IND do not mention any effect for outside factors others than those originating from their peers as being relevant in their decision making. If a request to re-assess a case is made, this usually comes from within the IND, from peers working in the legal department, and not from a hierarchical superior. This is further enforced by a working environment in which bureaucrats build upon each other's work, and informally implement a 4-eye principle, although such mechanism is not officially called for in legislative or policy documents. Furthermore, the case workers are also involved in drafting any positions of the Netherlands before ethe CJEU.

While the working guidelines are detailed, the lack of a strong hierarchical pressure takes away from the conflictual nature of the working environment. Research shows that the decisions made by senior management have more to do with controlling the 'triage' of asylum seekers, while street-level bureaucrats are relied upon for the expertise they build on the job. At the street-level, few decisions are made based on individual judgments without strong guidance, such as an own understanding of what "unforeseen relevant circumstances" may be, if a medical examination may be required, if an extended procedure is needed to assess credibility, or what the best available information regarding a country may be if the Dutch government does not have an official report.

Other than these few instances, instructions abound in how to handle cases in a variety of scenarios. The factors that should be taken in mind when assessing if an application can be made in border procedure, how availability of medical treatment in country of origin should be assessed, not to mention a detailed step-by-step guidance for credibility assessments are only some of the examples for which formal norms exist, aside from the general rules for assessing persecution based on straight-forward reasons which can be traced back to the 1951 Geneva Convention or European standards. Ensuring that said standards are clear, then, must be guaranteed.

To achieve this, bureaucratic guidelines offer a guide to assessing applications specifically based on the motive involved, while also adding important definitions that are not always found elsewhere in legislative documents (e.g., apostate, agnostic or non-practicing believer). Furthermore, while lists of safe countries of origins exist, there are several notices given for specific minorities within those countries, such as journalists coming from Ghana or religious minorities coming from India or Pakistan. The other side to that coin comes from cases where, in countries that are otherwise deemed to be dangerous, specific areas of protection can still exist, such as the case of Kabul in Afghanistan before 2021.[32] Perhaps the best example of how detailed working instructions are comes in cases concerning LGBTI applicants, where recent changes in how a case should be assessed removed "self-awareness" or "self-acceptance" as required criteria for analysing from LGBTI applicants. Nonetheless, there is an understanding that the mere exclusion from the official work guidance does not mean that these criteria will not play a role in the decision-making process.

Yet, despite the details given in guidance, there is a strong indication that a more detailed and unambiguous guidance from the European sphere on certain mattes would be welcomed and beneficial. As Romanian authorities, there is a belief that a common European-wide arrangement on the establishment of list of safe third countries would lead better implementation of the asylum acquis, as well as combating the phenomenon of secondary migration. It is for the same reasons that country guidance reports drafted by EASO or the EUAA are highly welcomed, as they "are relevant to create an EU-wide level playing field in the assessment of asylum applications."[33] Despite these calls for deeper European involvement in dealing with certain issues, officials of the IND reported no major changes in their working relationship with EASO between 2015 and 2021.

3 Final Thoughts on Discretionary Implementation

What do the previous pages say about the amount of influence that street-level bureaucrats can exert over the implementation of the Common European Asylum System? In the two cases analysed, the differences in administrative structure show that a simple comparison between the legal provisions of Romania and the Netherlands does not yield any straightforward conclusions. Proper implementation is best seen as a strategy for avoiding the bottoming out of the system and done so within the scope and with the mechanisms determined by the legal administrative context. While this book did not attempt to showcase instances of bureaucrats influencing the output of asylum policies, it did find where such opportunities lie, albeit not if and how advantage is taken of these opportunities.

32 See Chapter 6 for an assessment of how the lack of the sliding-scale model impacts these designations.

33 Parliamentary Paper 19637–2644, of July 31, 2020.

Nonetheless, I was able to highlight the importance of discretionary implementation as the set of safeguards that prevent a race to the bottom in terms of asylum standards. The analysis of the European sphere pointed to several ambiguities, some intentional some not. Analysis of the way EU institutions have approached the issue of asylum in recent years shows a clear switch in focus from the need for a strong push from the European level toward the responsibility of individual Member States to correctly implement the CEAS. The work of street-level bureaucrats is crucial not only because of potential non-compliance. In line with the findings in other studies, street-level bureaucrats serve as a safeguard for improper policy implementation, particularly where they have a chance to play an active role in the development of the rulebook which they are also meant to implement (e.g., in the Dutch system), and doing so while keeping in mind developments such as the case law of the CJEU.

The amount of influence that street-level bureaucrats have the opportunity to yield is then more dependent on national administrative structures than on the specific legislative measures at the EU. The 'capacity for judgement' given to Romanian bureaucrats, or the co-creation of norms in which Dutch public officials partake are signs that the opportunities to influence policy lie beyond straightforward discretionary clauses found in legislation. Because Romania's mechanisms for protecting human rights are found in legislative documents, from the Constitution all the way down to Ministerial Orders, hierarchy plays an important consideration in the day-to-day practices, even more so because of policy de-concentration. The work of street-level bureaucrats tasked with making first instance decisions is defined largely by the black-on white guidelines. However, given the lack of any real migratory pressure, these safeguards, whose effectiveness is based on a hierarchical implementation of procedures, have not been truly tested. It cannot be overlooked, nonetheless, that the method for evaluating bureaucratic processes, based on annual randomised evaluations of a sample of cases, do little to respond to changing conditions on the ground, and even less to ensure the quality of a decision at a time when its annulment could still make a difference.

In turn, because the Netherlands leaves such protections to be drafted and implemented by legislation specific to the policy field in which they are meant to take effect, day-to-day bureaucratic practices are developed with input from street-level bureaucrats themselves.[34] Even in cases that deviate from the European model, such as not using the sliding-scale model to assess the

34 Legally, Romania also allows for co-creation of norms between managers and subordinates, but only for the purpose of ensuring a better working environment.

impact that indiscriminate violence has on an applicant, the detailed guidelines ensure that vulnerability assessments are still part of the procedure. Such guidelines are how case officers of the IND can influence their own discretionary space: through best practice sharing and horizontal quality assessment among peers, norms for adequate behaviour are developed at the street-level about how an application should be handled, while managers usually deal with issues of client triage and ensuring access to proper resources. It is for this reasons that in the case of the Netherlands the IND does not automatically defend any cases that are brought up on appeal, but it rather first undergoes its own internal assessment of the quality of the decision being challenged. These findings are in line with the arguments by Rebecca Hamlin: administrations that are insulated are better at responding to changing global conditions and adapting internal procedures accordingly.[35]

On paper, both Romania and the Netherlands seem to give little influence to bureaucrats over the implementation of the CEAS. And naturally, any kind of deviation from clear policy objectives established at the European level is not possible, as the role of oversight in local systems has shown to be effective. In practice, the way asylum institutions fit into a larger system of governance and administration shows that these workers are not as devoid of influence as a strict black-letter assessment might let on. And yet, there is a possibility for this influence to grow, in a way that may benefit the goal of harmonisation in the EU. Since EU institutions should ensure the proper cooperation and sharing of good practices, the development of a European list of safe-third countries, for example, is measure that is welcomed by both the Romanian and Dutch governments and would also consider the expertise of street-level bureaucrats. Dutch case workers already experience such influence because of their involvement in drafting the country's positions before CJEU, therefore contributing to the development of case law in the EU. But in the case of Romania, because of a lack of preliminary reference requests in the field of asylum, the use of such expertise remains untapped.

---

35 Rebecca Hamlin, 'International Law and Administrative Insulation: A Comparison of Refugee Status Determination Regimes in the United States, Canada, and Australia' (2012) 37 *Law & Social Inquiry* 933.

Bibliography

Acosta Arcaranzo D, 'The Good, The Bad and The Ugly in EU Migration Law: Is the European Parliament Becoming Bad and Ugly?' in Elspeth Guild and P. E. Minderhoud (eds) *The First Decade of EU Migration and Asylum Law*, (Martinus Nijhoff 2012).

Acosta Arcarazo D, and Geddes A, 'The Development, Application and Implications of an EU Rule of Law in the Area of Migration Policy' (2013) 51 *Journal of Common Market Studies* 179.

Adler-Nissen R, 'Symbolic Power in European Diplomacy: the Struggle between National Foreign Services and the EU's External Action Service' (2013) 40 *Review of International Studies* 657.

Affolter L, 'Shaping Administrative Practice: The Institutional Habitus' (2020) in Laura Affolter, *Asylum Matters* (Palgrave Macmillan 2020).

Alpes MJ, and Spire A, 'Dealing with Law in Migration Control' (2013) 23 *Social & Legal Studies* 261.

Andreev SA, 'The Unbearable Lightness of Membership: Bulgaria and Romania after the 2007 EU' (2009) 42 *Communist and Post-Communist Studies* 375.

Angenendt S, and Parkes R, 'A New Impulse for EU Asylum Policy? The Potential of the European Asylum Support Office' [2010] *Stifung Wissenschaft Und Politik Comments no. 21.*

Asgeirsson H, *The Nature and Value of Vagueness in the Law* (*Law and Practical Reason*) (Hart Publishing 2020).

Baez B, and Abolafia MY, 'Bureaucratic Entrepreneurship and Institutional Change: A Sense- Making Approach' (2002) 12 *Journal of Public Administration Research and Theory* 525.

Baier VE, March JG, and Saetren H, 'Implementation and ambiguity' (1986) 2 *Scandinavian Journal of Management Studies* 197.

Ballin EH, and Senden LA, *Co-Actorship in the Development of European Law -Making* (TMC Asser Press 2005).

Bastien J, 'Goal Ambiguity and Informal Discretion in the Implementation of Public Policies: the Case of Spanish Immigration Policy' (2009) 75 *International Review of Administrative Sciences* 665.

Battjes H, 'Subsidiary Protection and Other Alternative Forms of Protection' in Vincent Chetail and Céline Bauloz (eds) *Research Handbook on International Law and Migration* (Edward Elgar 2014).

Belabas W, and Gerrits L, 'Going the Extra Mile? How Street-Level Bureaucrats Deal with the Integration of Immigrants' (2015) 51 *Social Policy & Administration* 133.

Beyers J, and Trondal J, 'How Nation States 'Hit' Europe: Ambiguity and Representation in the European Union' (2004) 27 *West European Politics* 919.

Blokker P, 'Romanian Constitutionalism: Form without Content?' [2012] *SSRN Electronic Journal* 1.

Brekke JP, and Brochmann G, 'Stuck in Transit: Secondary Migration of Asylum Seekers in Europe, National Differences, and the Dublin Regulation' (2015) 28 *Journal of Refugee Studies* 145.

Brower RS, Abolafia MY, and Carr JB, 'On Improving Qualitative Methods in Public Administration Research' (2000) 32 *Administration & Society* 363.

Buchanan A, and Keohane RO, 'The Legitimacy of Global Governance Institutions' (2006) 20 *Ethics and International Affairs* 405.

Caplan G, *An Approach to Community Mental Health* (Routledge 2011).

Case C-56/17 *Bahtiyar Fathi v Predsedatel na Darzhavna agentsia za bezhantsite* [2018].

Case C-113/17 *QJ v Ministerstvo vnútra SR Migračný úrad* [2018].

Case C-150/15 *Der Bundesbeauftragte für Asylangelegenheiten beim Bundesamt für Migration und Flüchtlinge v N* [2016].

Case C-175/11 *H.I.D. and B.A. v Refugee Applications Commissioner and Others* [2013].

Case C-175/17 *X v Belastingdienst/Toeslagen* [2018].

Case C-238/19 *EZ v Bundesrepublik Deutschland* [2020].

Case C-277/11 *M. M. v Minister for Justice, Equality and Law Reform and Others* [2012].

Case C-285/12 *Aboubacar Diakité v Commissaire général aux réfugiés et aux apatrides* [2014].

Case C-31/09, *Nawras Bolbol v Bevándorlási és Állampolgársági Hivatal* [2010] I-05539.

Case C-322/17 *Eugen Bogatu v Minister for Social Protection* [2019].

Case C-348/16 *Moussa Sacko v Commissione Territoriale per il riconoscimento della Protezione internazionale di Milano* [2017].

Case C-364/11, *Mostafa Abed El Karem El Kott and Others v Bevándorlási és Állampolgársági Hivatal* [2012].

Case C-369/17 *Ahmed v. Bevándorlási és Menekültügyi Hivatal* [2018].

Case C-373/13 *H. T. v Land Baden-Württemberg* [2015].

Case C-4/11 *Bundesrepublik Deutschland v Kaveh Puid* [2013].

Case C-465/07 *Meki Elgafaji and Noor Elgafaji v Staatssecretaris van Justitie* [2009], Opinion of AG Maduro.

Case C-472/13 *Andre Lawrence Shepherd v Bundesrepublik Deutschland* [2015].

Case C-473/16 *F v. Bevándorlási és Állampolgársági Hivatal* [2018].

Case C-481/13 *Criminal proceedings against Mohammad Ferooz Qurbani* [2014].

Case C-542/13 *Mohamed M'Bodj v État belge* [2014].

Case C-556/17 *Alekszij Torubarov v Bevándorlási és Menekültügyi Hivatal* [2019].

Case C-56/17 *Bahtiyar Fathi v Predsedatel na Darzhavna agentsia za bezhantsite* [2018].

Case C-562/13 *Centre public d'action sociale d'Ottignies-Louvain-la-Neuve v Moussa Abdida* [2014].

Case C-563/22 *Zamestnik-predsedatel na Darzhavna agentsia za bezhantsite* [2024], Opinion of AG Emiliou.

Case C-573/14 *Commissaire général aux réfugiés et aux apatrides v Mostafa Lounani* [2017].

Case C-585/16 *Serin Alheto v Zamestnik-predsedatel na Darzhavna agentsia za bezhantsite* [2018].

Case C-586/17 *Staatssecretaris van Veiligheid en Justitie and I. v D* [2019].

Case C-604/12 *H.N. v Minister for Justice, Equality and Law Reform and Others* [2014].

Case C-638/16 PPU, *X and X v État belge* [2017].

Case C-652/16 *Nigyar Rauf Kaza Ahmedbekova and Rauf Emin Ogla Ahmedbekov v Zamestnik- predsedatel na Darzhavna agentsia za bezhantsite* [2018].

Case C-69/10 *Brahim Samba Diouf v Ministre du Travail, de l'Emploi et de l'Immigration* [2011] I-07151.

Case C-713/17 *Ahmad Shah Ayubi v Bezirkshauptmannschaft Linz-Land* [2018].

Case C-720/17 *Mohamed Bilali v. Bundesamt Für Fremdenwesen und Asyl* [2019].

Case C-74/13 *GSV Kft. v Nemzeti Adó- és Vámhivatal Észak-Alföldi Regionális Vám- és Pénzügyőri Főigazgatósága* [2014].

Chowdhury N, and Wessel RA, 'Conceptualising Multilevel Regulation in the EU: A Legal Translation of Multilevel Governance?' (2012) 18 *European Law Journal* 335.

Cialdini RB, and Goldstein NJ, 'Social influence: compliance and conformity' (2004) 55 *Annual Review of Psychology* 591.

Commission, 'A Common European Asylum System' (2014).

Commission, 'Communication from the Commission to the European Parliament and the Council: Towards a Reform of the Common European Asylum System and Enhancing Legal Avenues to Europe' COM(2016) 197 final.

Commission, 'Communication from the Commission to the European Parliament, the Council, the European Economic and Social Committee and The Committee of the Regions on A New Pact on Migration and Asylum' COM 2020(609) final.

Commission, 'Proposal for a Regulation of the European Parliament and of the Council on the European Union Agency for Asylum' COM(2016) 271 final.

Commission, 'Report from the Commission to the European Parliament and the Council on Progress in Romania under the Cooperation and Verifications Mechanism' (2017).

Commission, 'Report from the Commission to the European Parliament and the Council on Progress in Romania under the Cooperation and Verifications Mechanism' (2018).

Comte F, 'A New Agency Is Born in the European Union: The European Asylum Support Office' (2010) 12 *European Journal of Migration and Law* 373.

Costello C, 'The Asylum Procedures Directive and the Proliferation of Safe Country Practices: Deterrence, Deflection and the Dismantling of International Protection?' (2005) 7 *European Journal of Migration and Law* 35.

Costello C, and Hancox E, 'The Recast Asylum Procedures Directive 2013/32/EU: Caught between the Stereotypes of the Abusive Asylum-Seeker and the Vulnerable Refugee' in Vincent Chetail, Philippe de Bruycker, and Francesco Maiani (eds), *Reforming the Common European Asylum System: the New European Refugee Law* (Brill Nijhoff 2016).

Costello C, and Mouzourakis M, 'EU Law and the Detainability of Asylum-Seekers' (2016) 35 *Refugee Survey Quarterly* 47.

Costello C, and Mouzourakis M, 'The Common European Asylum System: Where Did It All Go Wrong?' in Maria Fletcher, Ester Herlin-Karnell, and Claudio Matera (eds), *The European Union as an Area of Freedom, Security and Justice* (Routledge 2017).

Council of the European Union 'Presidency Conclusions, Brussels European Council' December 10–11, 1993.

Council of the European Union 'Presidency Conclusions, London European Council' December 6, 1986.

Council of the European Union 'Presidency Conclusions, Strasbourg European Council' December 8–9, 1989.

Council of the European Union 'Presidency Conclusions, Tampere European Council' 15–16 October 1999.

Council of the European Union 'Presidency Conclusions, Vienna European Council' December 11–12, 1998.

Craig, PP and De Burca G, *EU Law: Text, Cases and Materials* (Oxford University Press 2015).

De Dreu CK, Gross J, Meder Z, Giffin M, Prochazkova E, Krikeb J, and Columbus S, 'In- Group Defense, out-Group Aggression, and Coordination Failures in Intergroup Conflict' (2016) 113 *Proceedings of the National Academy of Sciences* 10524.

De Witte B, and Tsourdi E, 'Confrontation on Relocation – The Court of Justice Endorses the Emergency Scheme for Compulsory Relocation of Asylum Seekers within the European Union: Slovak Republic and Hungary v. Council.' (2018) 55 *Common Market Law Review* 1457.

Dekker R, 'Frame Ambiguity in Policy Controversies: Critical Frame Analysis of Migrant Integration Policies in Antwerp and Rotterdam' (2016) 11 *Critical Policy Studies* 127.

Demetriou O, 'Complementary Protection and the Recognition Rate as Tools of Governance: Ordering Europe, Fragmenting Rights' (2022) 48 *Journal of Ethnic and Migration Studies* 1264.

Dlewati, H. 'Asylum Seekers Stranded in Swedish Bureaucracy' *National Geographic* (22 June 2016) https://blog.nationalgeographic.org/2016/06/22/asylum-seekers-stranded-in- swedish-bureaucracy/.

Dörrenbächer N, 'Europe at the Frontline: Analysing Street-Level Motivations for the Use of European Union Migration Law' (2017) 24 *Journal of European Public Policy* 1328.

Dörrenbächer N, 'Frontline Uses of European Union (EU) Law: a Parallel Legal Order? How Structural Discretion Conditions Uses of EU Law in Dutch and German Migration Offices' (2017) 38 *Journal of Public Policy* 455.

Dörrenbächer N, and Mastenbroek E, 'Passing the Buck? Analyzing the Delegation of Discretion after Transposition of European Union Law' (2017) 13 *Regulation & Governance* 70.

Eckes C, 'International Law as Law of the EU: The Role of the ECJ' in Enzo Cannizzaro, Paolo Palchetti and Ramses A. Wessel (eds), *International Law as Law of the European Union* (Martinus Nijhoff 2011).

Edlins M, and Larrison J, 'Street-level bureaucrats and the governance of unaccompanied migrant children' (2018) 35 *Public Policy and Administration* 403.

Eule TG, Borrelli LM, Lindberg A, and Wyss A, *Migrants before the Law: Contested Migration Control in Europe* (Palgrave Macmillan, 2019).

European Asylum Support Office (EASO), *Asylum Procedures and the principle of non-refoulment – Judicial Analysis* (2018).

European Asylum Support Office (EASO). *Article 15(c) Qualification Directive (2011/95/ EU) – A judicial analysis* (2014).

European Migration Network, *Annual Report on Migration and Asylum 2018* (2019).

European Migration Network, *Annual Report on Migration and Asylum 2016* (2017).

Ferraro F, and De Capitani E, 'The New European Border and Coast Guard: Yet Another 'Half Way' EU Reform?' (2016) 17 *ERA Forum* 385.

Finkel SE, Humphries S, and Opp K-D, 'Socialist Values and the Development of Democratic Support in the Former East Germany' (2001) 22 *International Political Science Review* 339.

Fuglerud O, 'Constructing Exclusion. The Micro-Sociology of an Immigration Department' (2004) 12 *Social Anthropology* 25.

Ganev VI, 'Post-Accession Hooliganism: Democratic Governance in Bulgaria and Romania after 2007' (2013) 27 *East European Politics and Societies: and Cultures* 26.

Geddes A, and Scholten P, 'Policy Analysis and Europeanization: An Analysis of EU Migrant Integration Policymaking' (2013) 17 *Journal of Comparative Policy Analysis: Research and Practice* 41.

Geddes A, and Scholten P, *The Politics of Migration & Immigration in Europe* (Sage 2016).

Genschel P, and Jachtenfuchs M, 'From Market Integration to Core State Powers: The Eurozone Crisis, the Refugee Crisis and Integration Theory' (2017) 56 *Journal of Common Market Studies* 178.

Gill N, 'Presentational State Power: Temporal and Spatial Influences over Asylum Sector Decisionmakers' (2009) 215 *Transactions of the Institute of British Geographers* 215.

Givens T, and Luedtke A, 'The Politics of European Union Immigration Policy: Institutions, Salience, and Harmonization' (2004) 32 *Policy Studies Journal* 145.

Greve HR, and Rao H, 'History and the present: institutional legacies in communities of organizations' (2014) 34 *Research in Organizational Behavior* 27.

Grigonis S, 'EU in the Face of Migrant Crisis: Reasons for Ineffective Human Rights Protection' [2017] *International Comparative Jurisprudence.*

Guild E, Costello C, Garlick M, and Moreno-Lax V, 'Enhancing the Common European Asylum System and Alternatives to Dublin' [2015] *CEPS Papers in Liberty and Security in* Europe no. 83.

Gundhus H, 'Shaping migrants as threats: multilayered discretion, criminalization, and risk assessment tools' (2021) 10 *International Journal for Crime, Justice and Social Democracy* 56.

Hamlin R, 'International Law and Administrative Insulation: A Comparison of Refugee Status Determination Regimes in the United States, Canada, and Australia' (2012) 37 *Law & Social Inquiry* 933.

Hamlin R, *Let me be a refugee.* (Oxford University Press 2010).

Heidbreder EG, 'Strategies in Multilevel Policy Implementation: Moving beyond the Limited Focus on Compliance' (2017) 24 *Journal of European Public Policy* 1367.

Heyer K, 'Keeping migrants at the margins. Governing through ambiguity and the poiltics of discretion in the post-2015 European migration and broder regime' (2022) 97 *Political Geography* 102643.

Hill M, and Hupe P, *Implementing public policy* (2nd edn., Sage 2009).

Holzer M and Yang K, 'Administrative Discretion in a Turbulent Time: An Introduction' (2005) 29 *Public Administration Quarterly* 128.

Holzer T, Schneider G, and Widmer T, 'The Impact of Legislative Deterrence Measures on the Number of Asylum Applications in Switzerland (1986–1995)' (2000) 34 *International Migration Review* 1182.

Honig MI, 'Street-Level Bureaucracy Revisited: Frontline District Central-Office Administrators as Boundary Spanners in Education Policy Implementation' (2006) 28 *Educational Evaluation and Policy Analysis* 357.

Hooghe M, and Quintelier E, 'Political Participation in European Countries: The Effect of Authoritarian Rule, Corruption, Lack of Good Governance and Economic Downturn' (2013) 12 *Comparative European Politics* 209.

Horvat P, and Evans G, 'Age, Inequality, and Reactions to Marketization in Post-Communist Central and Eastern Europe' (2011) 27 *European Sociological Review* 708.

Hupe P, and Hill MJ, "And the Rest Is Implementation.' Comparing Approaches to What Happens in Policy Processes beyond Great Expectations' (2015) 31 *Public Policy and Administration* 103.

Hupe P, 'What Happens on the Ground: Persistent Issues in Implementation Research' (2014) 29 *Public Policy and Administration* 164.

Hurwitz A, 'The 1990 Dublin Convention: A Comprehensive Assessment' (1999) 11 *International Journal of Refugee Law* 646.

IND. 'Werkinstructies WI 2014/10 Inhoudelijke beoordeling (asiel)' [*Substantive Assessment (asylum)*].

IND. 'Werkinstructies WI 2019/1 Het beoordelen van asielaanvragen van verwesterde vrouwen' [*Assessing asylum applications from westernized women*], July 1, 2019.

IND. 'Werkinstructies WI 2019/18 Bekeerlingen' [*Converts*]. December 30, 2019.

IND. 'Werkinstructies WI 2020/12' [*The Application of the Sliding Scale*]. August 11, 2020.

IND. 'Werkinstructies WI 2022/3 Bekeerlingen en afvalligen' [*Converts and apostasy*]. November 22, 2022.

Inspectorate for Security and Justice, 'Identification of asylum seekers further improved; detection of human trafficking/smuggling and terrorism in is not realistic' (News Release: December 21, 2016).

Inspectorate for Security and Justice, 'Inspection: EBTL personnel are insufficiently equipped for the task' (News Release: January 22, 2019).

Inspectorate for Security and Justice, 'Insufficient insight into the social safety of residents in asylum seekers' centres' (News Release: October 19, 2018).

Jędrzejowska-Schiffauer I, and Schiffauer P, 'New Constraints on Mobility in Europe: Policy Response to European Crises or Constitutional Ambiguity?' (2017) 10 *Journal of International Studies* 9.

Joined Cases C-148/13, C-149/13 and C-150/13 *A, B and C v Staatssecretaris van Veiligheid en Justitie* [2014].

Joined Cases C-175/08, C-176/08, C-178/08 and C-179/08, *Aydin Salahadin Abdulla, Kamil Hasan, Ahmed Adem, Hamrin Mosa Rashi and Dler Jamal v Bundesrepublik Deutschland* [2010] I-01493.

Joined Cases C-297/17, C-318/17 and C-319/17 *Bashar Ibrahim, Mahmud Ibrahim and Others, Nisreen Sharqawi, Yazan Fattayrji, Hosam Fattayrji v Bundesrepublik Deutschland and Bundesrepublik Deutschland v Taus Magamadov* [2019].

Joined Cases C-331/16 and C-366/16 *K. v Staatssecretaris van Veiligheid en Justitie and H.F. v Belgische Staat* [2018].

Joined Cases C-391/16, C-77/17, C-78/17, *M and Others v Commissaire général aux réfugiés et aux apatrides* [2019].

Joined Cases C-402/05 P and C-415/05 P, *Kadi and Al Barakaat International Foundation v Council and Commission* [2008] I-06351.

Joined Cases C-404/15 and C-659/15 PPU *Pál Aranyosi and Robert Căldăraru v Generalstaatsanwaltschaft Bremen* [2016].

Joined Cases C-411/10 and C-493/10 *N. S. v Secretary of State for the Home Department and M. E. and Others v Refugee Applications Commissioner and Minister for Justice, Equality and Law Reform* (2011) I-13905.

Joined Cases C-443/14 and C-444/14 *Kreis Warendorf v Ibrahim Alo & Amira Osso v Region Hannover* [2014].

Joined Cases C-540/17 and C-541/17 *Bundesrepublik Deutschland v Adel Hamed and Amar Omar* [2019], and Case C-517/17, *Milkiyas Addis v Bundesrepublik Deutschland* [2020].

Joined Cases C-57/09 and C-101/09, *Bundesrepublik Deutschland v B & D* [2010] I-10979.

Jørgensen TB and Sørensen D-L, 'Codes of Good Governance. National or Global Public Values?' (2012) 15 *Public Integrity* 71.

Jung K, Song M, and Park HW, 'Filling the Gap between Bureaucratic and Adaptive Approaches to Crisis Management: Lessons from the Sewol Ferry Sinking in South Korea' (2017) 52 *Quality & Quantity* 277.

Kahn RL, Wolfe DM, Quinn RP, Snoek DJ, Rosenthal RA, *Organizational Stress: Studies in Role Conflict and Ambiguity* (Wiley 1964).

Karré PM, van der Steen M, van der Wal Z, and Schillemans T, 'Public Administration in the Netherlands: State of the Field' in Geert Bouckaert and Werner Jann (eds), *European Perspectives for Public Administration* (Leuven Univeristy Press 2020).

Lavenex S, "Failing Forward' Towards Which Europe? Organized Hypocrisy in the Common European Asylum System' (2018) 56 *Journal of Common Market Studies* 1195.

Łazowski A, and Wessel RA, 'When Caveats Turn into Locks: Opinion 2/13on Accession of the European Union to the ECHR' (2015) 16 *German Law Journal* 179.

Leebron D, 'Lying down with Procrustes: An Analysis of Harmonisation Claims' in Jagdish Bhagwati and Robert Hudec (eds) *Fair Trade and Harmonisation* (MIT Press, 1996).

Leong C, and Qian N, 'Ambiguity, bureaucracy and certainty: The ABCs of enabling water self-sufficiency' (2016) 35 *Policy and Society* 165.

Letki N, and Evans G, 'Endogenizing Social Trust: Democratization in East-Central Europe' (2005) 35 *British Journal of Political Science* 515.

Lindblom CE, and Woodhouse EJ, *The Policy-Making Process* (Prentice Hall 1993).

Lipsky M, *Street-Level Bureaucracy: Dilemmas of the Individual in Public Service* (rev edn, Russel Sage Foundation 2010).

Lord C, and Magnette P, 'E Pluribus Unum? Creative Disagreement about Legitimacy in the EU' (2004) 42 *Journal of Common Market Studies* 183.

Lussier DN, 'Contacting and Complaining: Political Participation and the Failure of Democracy in Russia' (2011) 27 *Post-Soviet Affairs* 289.

Majone G, 'Policy Harmonization: Limits and Alternatives' (2014) 16 *Journal of Comparative Policy Analysis: Research and Practice* 4.

Maynard-Moody S, and Musheno M, 'Social Equities and Inequities in Practice: Street-Level Workers as Agents and Pragmatists' (2012) 72 *Public Administration Review* S16.

McAdam J, 'The European Union Qualification Directive: The Creation of a Subsidiary Protection Regime' (2005) 17 *International Journal of Refugee Law* 461.

Memisoglu F, and Ilgit A, 'Syrian Refugees in Turkey: Multifaceted Challenges, Diverse Players and Ambiguous Policies' (2016) 22 *Mediterranean Politics* 317.

Meyer-Sahling J-H, and Yesilkagit K, 'Differential Legacy Effects: Three Propositions on the Impact of Administrative Traditions on Public Administration Reform in Europe East and West' (2011) 18 *Journal of European Public Policy* 311.

Milward B, Jensen L, Roberts A, Dussauge-Laguna MI, Junjan V, Torenvlied R, Boin A, Colebatch HK, Kettl D, and Durant R, 'Is Public Management Neglecting the State?' (2016) 29 *Governance* 311.

Ministry of the Interior and Kingdom Relations (BZK), 'The Dutch Public Service: Organisation and functioning of the government in the Netherlands, the position of civil servants and the main developments' (2016).

Miranda CP, 'Checks, Balances, and Resistance: The Impact of an Anti-Immigrant Federal Administration on a School for Immigrant Teenagers' (2017) 48 *Anthropology & Education Quarterly* 376.

Moreno-Lax V, 'Dismantling the Dublin System: M.S.S. v. Belgium and Greece' (2012) 14 *European Journal of Migration and Law* 1.

Moreno-Lax V, 'Must EU Borders Have Doors for Refugees? On the Compatibility of Schengen Visas and Carriers' Sanctions with EU Member States' Obligations to Provide International Protection to Refugees' (2008) 10 *European Journal of Migration and Law* 315.

Moreno-Lax V, 'Seeking Asylum in the Mediterranean: Against a Fragmentary Reading of EU Member States' Obligations Accruing at Sea' (2011) 23 *International Journal of Refugee Law* 174.

Morgades-Gil S, 'The Discretion of States in the Dublin III System for Determining Responsibility for Examining Applications for Asylum' (2015) 27 *International Journal of Refugee Law* 433.

Nancheva N, 'The Common European Asylum System and the Failure to Protect: Bulgaria's Syrian Refugee Crisis' (2015) 15 *Southeast European and Black Sea Studies* 439.

Netherlands Institute for Multiparty Democracy & Instuut voor Publiek en Politiek. 'The Dutch Political System in a Nutshell' (2008).

Nica F, 'Country Report: Romania' [2018] *Asylum Information Database* (AIDA).

Niemann A, and Zaun N, 'EU refugee policies and politics in times of crisis: theoretical and empirical perspectives' (2017) 56 *Journal of Common Market Studies* 3.

Noll G, 'Asylum Claims and the Translation of Culture into Politics' (2006) 41 *Texas International Law Journal* 491, 497.

Noll G, 'Formalism v. Empiricism: Some Reflections on the Dublin Convention on the Occasion of Recent European Case Law' (2001) 70 *Nordic Journal of International Law* 161.

Noll G, *Proof, Evidentiary Assessment and Credibility in Asylum Procedures* (Brill Nijhoff 2005).

Nugent N, *The Government and Politics of the European Union* (Palgrave Macmillan 2017).
O'Sullivan C, and Ferri D, 'The Recast Reception Conditions Directive and the Rights of Asylum Seekers with Disabilities: Opportunities, Challenges and the Quest for Reform' (2020) 22 *European Journal of Migration and Law* 272.
Oomen B, Baumgärtel M, Miellet S, Durmus E, and Sabchev T, 'Strategies of divergence: local authorities, law, and discretionary spaces in migration governance' (2021) 34 *Journal of Refugee Studies* 3608.
Pearson CM, and Mitroff II, 'From Crisis Prone to Crisis Prepared: a Framework for Crisis Management' (1993) *Academy of Management Perspectives* 48.
Peers S, *EU Justice And Home Affairs Law* (Oxford University Press 2016).
Peters J, 'The Dutch Constitution and Dutch Constitutional Values' in Alfred Kellermann (ed.) *EU Enlargement* (TMC Asser Press 2001).
Plender R, 'EU Immigration and Asylum Policy – The Hague Programme and the Way Forward' (2008) 9 *ERA Forum* 301.
Pott A, Rass C, and Wolff F, *Was Ist Ein Migrationsregime?* (Springer VS, 2018).
Raad van State. "Jaarverslag 2017," (April 2018).
Roberts A, 'Administrative Discretion and the Access to Information Act: An 'Internal Law' on Open Government?' (2002) 45 *Canadian Public Administration* 175.
Room G, 'Policy Benchmarking in the European Union' (2005) 26 *Policy Studies* 117.
Roots L, 'The New EURODAC Regulation: Fingerprints as a Source of Informal Discrimination' (2015) 5 *Baltic Journal of European Studies* 108.
Rosenthal U, Hart P, and Kouzmin A, 'The Bureau-Politics of Crisis Management' (1991) 69 *Public Administration* 211.
Schammann H, Gluns D, Heimann C, Müller S, Wittchen T, Younso C, and Ziegler F, 'Defining and transforming local migration policies: a conceptual approach backed by evidence from Germany' (2021) 47 *Journal of Ethnic and Migration Studies* 2897.
Schittenhelm K, 'Implementing and Rethinking the European Union's Asylum Legislation: The Asylum Procedures Directive' (2019) 57 *International Migration* 229.
Schneider S, and Nieswandt C, 'EASO – Support Office or Asylum Authority? Boundary Disputes in the European Field of Asylum Administration' (2018) 43 *Österreichische Zeitschrift Für Soziologie* 13.
Scholten P, and Penninx R, 'The Multilevel Governance of Migration and Integration' in Blanca Garcés-Mascareñas and Rinus Penninx (eds) *Integration Processes and Policies In Europe: Contexts, Levels and Actors* (Springer Open 2016).
Spencer S, and Delvino N, 'Municipal activism on irregular migrants: the framing of inclusive approaches at the local level' (2019) 17 *Journal of Immigrant & Refugee Studies* 27.
Spriggs JF, 'Explaining Federal Bureaucratic Compliance with Supreme Court Opinions' (1997) 50 *Political Research Quarterly* 567.

Stark A, 'Bureaucratic Values and Resilience: an Exploration of Crisis Management Adaptation' (2014) 92 *Public Administration* 692.

Stevens D, 'Asylum, Refugee Protection and the European Response to Syrian Migration' (2017) 9 *Journal of Human Rights Practice* 184.

Tavits M, 'Representation, Corruption, and Subjective Well-Being' (2008) 41 *Comparative Political Studies* 1607.

Taylor T, Zarb S and Jeschke N, 'Ambiguity, Uncertainty and Implementation' (2021) 3 *International Review of Public Policy* 100.

Teske P, and Laumann J, 'Principals, Agents, and the Impact of Regulatory Federalism on the Savings-and-Loans Crisis of the 1980s' (2003) 3 *State Politics & Policy Quarterly* 139.

Thielemann E, 'Why Asylum Policy Harmonisation Undermines Refugee Burden-Sharing' (2004) 6 *European Journal of Migration and Law* 47.

Thielemann E, and Armstrong C, 'Understanding European Asylum Cooperation under the Schengen/Dublin System: a Public Goods Framework' (2013) 22 *European Security* 148.

Thomann E, and Sager F, 'Toward a Better Understanding of Implementation Performance in the EU Multilevel System' (2017) 24 *Journal of European Public Policy* 1385.

Thomson R, Torenvlied R, and Arregui J, 'The Paradox of Compliance: Infringements and Delays in Transposing European Union Directives' (2007) 37 *British Journal of Political Science* 685.

Thym D, 'A Bird's Eye View on ECJ Judgments on Immigration, Asylum and Border Control Cases' (2019) 21 *European Journal of Migration and Law* 166.

Tiong TN, 'Crisis Theory and SARS' (2004) 14 *Asia Pacific Journal of Social Work and Development* 7.

Toshkov D, 'The Dynamic Relationship between Asylum Applications and Recognition Rates in Europe (1987–2010)' (2013) 15 *European Union Politics* 192.

Toshkov D, and de Haan L, 'The Europeanization of Asylum Policy: an Assessment of the EU Impact on Asylum Applications and Recognitions Rates' (2013) 20 *Journal of European Public Policy* 661.

Trauner F, 'Asylum Policy: the EU's 'Crises' and the Looming Policy Regime Failure,' (2016) 38 *Journal of European Integration* 311.

Tsianos VS and Kuster B, 'Eurodac in Times of Bigness: The Power of Big Data within the Emerging European IT Agency' (2016) 31 *Journal of Borderlands Studies* 235.

Tsitselikis K, 'Refugees in Greece: Facing a Multifaceted Labyrinth' (2018) 57 *International Migration* 158.

Tsourdi E, 'Bottom-Up Salvation? From Practical Cooperation towards Joint Implementation through the European Asylum Support Office' (2016) 1 *European Papers* 997.

UN High Commissioner for Refugees (UNHCR), 'UNHCR Statement on the 'Ceased Circumstances' Clause of the EC Qualification Directive' (2008).

Valenta M, and Berg B, 'User Involvement and Empowerment among Asylum Seekers in Norwegian Reception Centres' (2010) 13 *European Journal of Social Work* 483.

van Kampen A, 'Country Report: Netherlands' *Asylum Information Database* (AIDA), (2019).

van Wolleghem PG, and Sicakkan HG, 'Asylum seekers in the machinery of the state: administrative capacity vs. Preferences. Recognition rates in EU member states' (2023) 24 *European Union Politics* 348.

Velluti S, *Reforming the Common European Asylum System – Legislative Developments and Judicial Activism of the European Courts* (Springer 2014).

Virtanen T, 'Context in the context – missing the missing links in the field of public administration', in Christopher Pollitt (ed.) *Context in public policy and management: The missing link?* (Edward Elgar 2013).

Wendehorst S, 'Religious Rights between International Law and Constitutional Law: A System of Communicating Vessels – From Premodern Historical Evidence to a Reassessment of Doctrine' in Robert Uerpmann-Wittzack Evelyne Lagrange, and Stefan Oeter (eds.) *Religion and International Law: Living Together*, (Brill Nijhoff, 2018).

West WF, 'Structuring Administrative Discretion: The Pursuit of Rationality and Responsiveness,' (1984) 28 *American Journal of Political Science* 340.

Whittington D and Wu X, 'Water resource development on the Ganges: moving beyond ambiguity' (2013) 15 *Water Policy* 1.

Wilson W, 'The Study of Administration,' (1887) 2 *Political Science Quarterly* 197.

Wouters J, and Wessel RA, 'The Phenomenon of Multilevel Regulation: Interactions between Global, EU and National Regulatory Spheres' (2008) 4 *International Organizations Law Review* 259.

Zacka B, *When the state meets the street: public service and moral agency* (Harvard University Press 2017).

Zahariadis N, 'Ambiguity and Choice in European Public Policy' (2008) 15 *Journal of European Public Policy* 514.

Zbiral R, Princen S, and Smekal H, 'Differentiations through flexibility in implementation: Strategic and substantive use of discretion in EU directives' (2022) 24 *European Union Politics* 102.

Zielonka J, 'Ambiguity as a Remedy for the EU's Eastward Enlargement?' (1998) 12 *Cambridge Review of International Affairs* 14.

Zouridis S, and Leijtens V, 'Bringing the law back in: the law-government nexus in an era of network governance' (2020) 4 *Perspectives on Public Management and Governance* 118.

Index

Admissibility 119
Age assessment 108, 183–184
Ambiguity 3, 4, 6, 21, 33–36, 218, 220–223
  Ambiguous clauses 56–60
  Intentional ambiguity 35
  Unintentional ambiguity 35–36
Amsterdam Treaty 45
Asylum Procedures Directive 60–68, 71, 104–124
  Lodging an application 106–109
  Personal interview 111–114
  Procedural guarantees 109–111

Border procedures 163, 165–166, 186–188

Capacity for judgement 2, 135–136
Carrier sanctions 12–13
Cessation of protection
  Refugee status 90, 94
  Subsidiary protection 99–100
Co-creation of norms 2
Compliance 3
  See also non-compliance
Council Conclusions 42–45
Court of Justice of the European Union
  Case Law 75–80
  Preliminary reference procedure 4
  Rulings on Asylum Procedures Directive 104–124
  Rulings on Qualifications Directive 80–104
Credibility assessment 24, 206–212

Decentralisation 133, 174–175
De-concentration 133–134, 141, 224
Discretion 5, 6, 21–24, 223–231
  In Romania 133
  In the Netherlands 173, 179–180
  Discretionary space 3, 5, 14, 27, 36–38
  Discretionary implementation 1–2, 3, 17, 21, 28
Dublin Regulation 12, 46–48, 148
  In case law 77–79
  Right to intervention 75

EASO 48–52
Effective remedy 120, 122–124, 163
EUAA 48–52
EURODAC 52–53
European Convention on Human Rights 76
Exclusion from protection
  Refugee status 93–94, 95
  Subsidiary protection 99–100

Geneva Convention 10, 12–13, 57, 77

Hamlin, Rebecca 25
Harmonisation 9, 20
Humanitarian protection 72, 149

Inadmissible applications 119, 120–121, 188

Legal migration 69
Lipsky, Michael 27–32, 216
Lisbon Treaty 24

Maastricht Treaty 24, 42–44
Medical examinations
  For age assessment 108
  In Romania's asylum procedure 138, 157, 161
  To identify serious harm 114
Multilevel
  Governance 22–23
  Implementation 4, 9, 14

New Pact on Migration and Asylum 1, 73–75
Non-compliance 26
Non-refoulment 11–12, 63, 77, 96, 103, 109, 152

Persecution 88, 194–195, 159
  LGBTI 201–203, 211
  Apostasy 204–205
  Religious conversion 205–207, 211
  Westernisation 205–206
Personal interview 185
Procedural guarantees
  In Romania 150–153

Qualifications Directive 12, 55, 80–104

Receptions Conditions
Directive 53–55
Refugee status 158, 210
Granting of 94–96
Revocation of refugee status 97
Role conflict theory 1, 36–39
Role behaviour 37
Role conflict 37–38
Role ambiguity 38

Safe country of origin 119–120, 192–195
Safe third country 119, 189, 162, 165
Single European Act 42
Sliding scale 97, 99, 159, 196
Solidarity 75

Street-level bureaucracy 1, 2, 5, 27–32
Resources 29–30
In Romania 134, 138–139, 142–144, 153–159, 166–167
In the Netherlands 174–177, 200–212
Subsequent applications 121–122
Subsidiary protection 57–58, 96–100, 158, 210
Granting status 100–101

Unaccompanied minors 116–117
Unfounded applications 119, 187

Vulnerable groups 115–116
In Romania 152, 153

Withdrawal of protection 122